Jungian Psychology in Perspective

Mary Ann Mattoon

THE FREE PRESS
A Division of Macmillan, Inc.
NEW YORK
Collier Macmillan Publishers
LONDON

The Free Press
A Division of Macmillan, Inc.
866 Third Avenue, New York, N.Y. 10022

Collier Macmillan Canada, Inc.

First Free Press Paperback Edition 1985

Printed in the United States of America

printing number

1   2   3   4   5   6   7   8   9   10

Library of Congress Cataloging-in-Publication Data

Mattoon, Mary Ann.
  Jungian psychology in perspective.

  1. Psychoanalysis. 2. Jung, C. G. (Carl Gustav), 1875–1961. I. Title.
BR173.J85M27   1985   150.19′54   85–10287
ISBN 0–02–920650–2 (pbk.)

To my students

Contents

Acknowledgments

Like any teacher and practicing analyst, I am indebted to my students, analysands, and colleagues, for their explicit and implicit enrichment of my understanding of the wide range of subject matter included in this book and, especially, for their challenges to my unexamined assumptions. Further debts are acknowledged to:

Sylvia W. Rosen, for skilful editing of the manuscript; Elizabeth Mueller and Shirley Dahlen, for typing the manuscript; Ruth Goodwin, Melinda Davis, and the University of Minnesota Libraries, for research assistance; Charles Braden, Helen Johnson, Lydia Neideffer, Molly Hurley, and Bonnie Marsh, for checking references and helping with the final preparation of the manuscript; Jennette Jones and Emily White, for sharing their specialized knowledge; and Mary Lynn Kittelson and Lynda S. Cowan, for proofreading.

Preface to the Paperback Edition

Since the initial publication of this book in the hardcover edition (1981), the literature on Jung and Jungian psychology has grown rapidly. At least seventy new books are in print, and about an equal number of doctoral dissertations that relate directly to Jungian psychology have been completed. All the periodicals listed in the hardcover bibliography have continued publication, and at least one new journal (*Chiron*) has appeared. A supplementary volume to Jung's *Collected Works* has been published (Vol. A, *The Zofingia Lectures*) as well as *Dream Analysis*, the first of several planned volumes of his previously unpublished seminars.

The burgeoning of literature and research on Jungian psychology reflects a growing interest in the nonrational aspects of the psyche, which first became widespread during the 1960s. Many people who share that interest have found a major resource in Jungian psychology. They find that it makes a unique contribution to the understanding of the psyche, especially through its description of normal personality and its concept of the collective unconscious.

Psychological theory, including Jungian, is never static. The major modifications made in Jungian theory in recent years have become apparent primarily in relation to therapeutic practice. Practitioners continue to apply Jungian theory creatively and empirically to the range of situations that their clients bring into the consulting room. Most striking are the deepening concerns with the phenomena of transference and countertransference and with specific pathologies such as narcissism and borderline personality.

The world of academic psychology has changed also, becoming more receptive to the study of cognitive content. No longer do American psychologists limit their research and teaching to consideration of overt behavior. Consequently, general courses in personality theory in the United States include more sympathetic attention to Jungian theories. (Europe has long provided a hospitable climate for the study of Jungian psychology.)

This book, which combines a survey of Jungian theory with a presentation of empirical research, is unique. It is appropriate for independent study, informal groups, and courses (credit and noncredit) in Jungian psychology, general personality theory, and such related fields as the humanities and religion.

In this edition of the book, typographical and textual errors have been corrected and the bibliography has been updated and modified. It now includes only works that focus on the psychological aspects of Jungian thought; works that primarily apply Jungian theories to other fields (e.g., literature) are omitted. Moreover, I omit a few works that have been out of print for many years. Within these limits, the bibliography is as inclusive as the available information makes possible. All technical terms are defined in the text, following their first use, and are carefully indexed. A glossary thus would be redundant. In the bibliography, some titles are indicated by double asterisks (**). These works are suggested for further reading because they represent Jungian psychology as a whole, are of high quality, and/or reflect specific points of view.

After many years of teaching Jungian psychology, I find that the content sustains its appeal to people who are disenchanted with mainstream academic psychology. It also adds a dimension of understanding of the subjective aspects of the psyche for people who come to the study via other courses in psychology. I continue to be impressed with the insights that Jungian theory brings, even in an academic setting, to persons of varying backgrounds and temperaments.

Preface

If you have wrestled with Jung,
you are never the same again.
—William Douglas, *Contemporary Psychology*

A psychotherapist who uses the terms *complex, persona, extraversion,* or *introversion,* administers a word association test, or encourages a troubled child to draw pictures is knowingly or unknowingly using concepts that were developed by Carl Gustav Jung. Despite some popular opinion to the contrary, Jung's theories are not idiosyncratic derivatives of psychoanalysis; they are, rather, elements of an original system of psychology which are based on views of human nature and interpretations of clinical data that are different from Freud's. Yet Jung's ideas did not receive wide acceptance in the United States until relatively recently. Interest in his theories is increasing because the nonrational facets of human experiences he explored have been accepted as valid.

Jung produced a great body of writing during his lifetime. Unfortunately, much of it is difficult for many people to read. Several students of Jung's thought have provided excellent introductions to Jungian psychology (For example, F. Fordham, 1966; Hall and Nordby, 1973; and Jacobi, 1962); others have sampled Jung's writings in useful anthologies (Campbell, 1971;

de Laszlo, 1958, 1959; and Jacobi and Hull, 1970); however, no one has produced a comprehensive, systematic work that is suitable both for the beginning student of the science of psychology and the general reader interested in an introduction to and perspective on Jung's psychological theories. Consequently, for my classes at the University of Minnesota, I wrote and duplicated my lectures to use as the textbook. Those lectures became the basis of this book. It is suitable for independent study and for use as a textbok in credit and informal courses. It introduces the reader to all the major concepts of Jung's Analytical Psychology and evaluates these concepts. In addition, the book gathers for the first time the results of empirical studies in which Jungian hypotheses have been tested.

My point of view combines the Jungian clinical approach and the empirical approach of academic psychology: those of a Jungian analyst, trained at the C. G. Jung Institute of Zurich (the Mecca of Jungian psychology) and an academic psychologist, schooled at the University of Minnesota, which has been called the center of "dust-bowl empiricism." The combination of these two approaches has strengthened my appreciation of the capacity of Jungian psychology to lead to a profound understanding of the human psyche. In addition, it has given me the background to show in this book the empirical base that undergirds the theories of Analytical Psychology and to identify the place of Jung's formulations in the field of psychology.

My concern with Jung's place in psychology does not diminish my appreciation for the fact that Jung's theory, especially that portion dealing with archetypes and the collective unconscious, has had greater impact on scholarly and scientific fields other than psychology: the arts, particularly literature; the humanities, especially history; and anthropology. Examples of Jung's influence are found in the literary works of Joseph Campbell, the historical works of Arnold Toynbee, and the anthropological works of Jacquetta Hawkes.

Jung never attempted to organize his system of thought, although many of his students and other admirers tried to persuade him to do so. He told one person that to complete such a task "would take more than a lifetime" (Harms, 1962, p. 732). The best clue to what Jung might have written is his essay, "Approaching the Unconscious," in Man and His Symbols. (He completed this essay only a few weeks before his death.) In this work he focused on the understanding of symbols, their emergence from the unconscious and appearance in dreams, personality differences as reflected in Jung's theory of types, and the role of dreams and their interpretation in healing the split between consciousness and the unconscious. This essay reflected what Jung may have considered the major thrust of his work but it by no means touched on all his important theories. In this book I have attempted to present Jung's main theories and their empirical bases.

Academic psychologists have had little interest in Jung because he was as much poet as scholar and as much intuitive thinker as empiricist. His writing style has obscured his many creative contributions to our understanding of psychology and he has acquired the erroneous reputation of a mystic—in the sense of a person who deals with mysteries beyond ordinary human knowledge. Nevertheless, some of Jung's original ideas are incorporated in the current psychological repertory, often with no acknowledgment of their origins in Jung's thought. For example, in the eight developmental stages described by Erikson (1963), Ellenberger (1970) attributed the first five to Freud's stages of libidinal development and the remaining three to Jung's concept of individuation.

Despite the philosophical and methodological barriers, academic psychologists are beginning to move away from a strictly laboratory approach to their discipline and are admitting observable data that cannot be subjected to experimental controls (e.g., Levinson, 1978). They have been influenced, perhaps, by the limitations of statistical studies and the burgeoning public interest in oriental philosophies, humanistic psychologies, and parapsychological experiences that do not lend themselves to experimentation. These influences have contributed, no doubt, to the acceptance by the psychology faculty at the University of Minnesota of a credit course in Jungian psychology, the course I have been teaching for nine years.

A basic knowledge of Freudian principles is a prerequisite for admission to my course because many of Jung's statements, especially those that were often repeated, reflected his disagreements with Freud. In this book I make occasional comparisons between Jungian and Freudian theory, but presentations of the similarities and differences have been made more completely by others (e.g., Frey-Rohn, 1974).

The backgrounds of the students in my classes ranged from no previous knowledge of Jungian psychology to many years of study. Indeed, several students had attended courses at the C. G. Jung Institute in Zurich. The classes were organized to take into account the students' different levels of preparation. Work groups were formed so that students could assist one another in understanding the material and identifying questions on which they required elucidation. Since the lectures were duplicated and distributed in advance, class time could be devoted largely to the group meetings and to class discussions.

The lectures were revised many times: to add newly available theoretical and empirical material, to incorporate the answers to students' questions, and to provide the first draft of this book.

Plan of This Book

In organizing and ordering the topics of Analytical Psychology, a certain arbitrariness is unavoidable. Many of the topics are interrelated; hence an understanding of each is aided by exposure to one or more of the others. Other instructors and readers may want to take up the topics in an order different from the one I have followed. My presentation of the topics of Analytical Psychology begins with the common structure of the psyche: the various conscious and unconscious components, and the underlying collective unconscious. This structure is varied by differences in the attitudes of introversion and extraversion; in the functions of sensation, intuition, thinking, and feeling; and between females and males. Interrelating the parts of the psychic structure are the dynamic factors of psychic energy and self-regulation, complexes and projection. Out of the interplay of these factors arise the phenomena of symbol and synchronicity and the malfunctioning of the psyche known as psychopathology. The psychic components, varieties, and dynamics all contribute to the process of development from birth to old age, a process that may lead into the wholeness and differentiation of individuation. Genuine religion is the expression of such psychic integration. The understandings accumulated through all of these concepts can be applied to specific issues of relationships and sexuality, psychotherapy, dream interpretation, and social and political problems.

These topics are complemented by Chapters 1 and 19. The first, the introduction, presents the context of the development of Analytical Psychology in terms of Jung's life and the times in which he lived. The half century from about 1890 to World War II was an intensive period of discoveries and the development of new theories in what Ellenberger (1970) termed "dynamic psychiatry." These theories reflect the social, political, and cultural ferment of that period in Europe. Chapter 19, "Research," deals with a frontier area of Analytical Psychology that is little discussed among Jungians but is of major concern in the application and evaluation of Jung's system of thought and to psychologists of other schools.

In addition to Jung's theories I present some of my ideas and those of other Jungians; these views are clearly identified. In this way, a more complete but still Jungian personality theory is made available, controversial issues are raised, and alternative points of view are presented.

Jung was a prolific writer; the volumes of his *Collected Works* number eighteen (nineteen, if the two parts of volume nine are counted as separate volumes), plus a one-volume *General Bibliography* and a one-volume *General Index*. Not included in the *Collected Works* are the three volumes of letters (one volume of Jung's correspondence with Freud and two of his other letters), his memoirs (*Memories, Dreams, Reflections*), a book of interviews (*C. G. Jung Speaking*), and more than twenty volumes of privately printed seminar notes; some of the latter are in the process of being edited for publication. Despite the quantity of Jung's work I believe that the beginning student and general reader will find the major aspects of Jung's theory presented in this book.

A comprehensive bibliography of Jungian psychology, organized by major topics, follows Chapter 19. Some of the works listed appear also in the list of references. In the textual citations, the volumes in Jung's *Collected Works* are denoted as *CW1, CW2*, etc., and his autobiographial work, *Memories, Dreams, Reflections* as *MDR; MHS* refers to *Man and His Symbols; Let 1 and 2* to Jung's *Letters, DA* to the *Dream Analysis* seminars, *FJ* to the *Freud/Jung Letters*, and *SE* to the *Standard*

Edition of Freud's works. *MAM notes* refers to notes of Mary Ann Mattoon. A reader seeking a complete listing of references (articles as well as books) on any particular topic can consult Vincie and Rathbauer-Vincie (1977) and *CW20*, which is a general index to those works.

It is often said that Jung contradicted himself on many points, and he did so in expounding the fine points of his thoughts. In the major concepts, however, he was remarkably consistent. In an earlier work (Mattoon, 1978[a]), I dealt with such points in one major area of Jung's theory, interpretation of dreams. Because the present work focuses on major concepts, it has not been deemed necessary to mention minor contradictions.

1

Introduction:
The Development of
Analytical Psychology

Jungian psychology, also known as Analytical Psychology, was first outlined in Jung's dissertation for the degree of Doctor of Medicine (M.D.) in which he grappled with the concepts—in embryonic form—of complexes and individuation. These concepts, along with that of the unconscious, were to become central to his personality theory. The early work centered on clinical observation, especially on Jung's study of a young woman's mediumistic experiences, which provided the data for his dissertation. Subsequently, as a hospital psychiatrist, he continued his empirical research, using a word association test. His interpretation of the findings furthered his understanding of complexes and their unconscious roots. Because he considered complexes to be crucial to understanding the unconscious, he wanted to call his body of theory *Complex Psychology*. Some of his associates argued for the broader term *Analytical Psychology* and it prevailed.

Despite Jung's medical-psychiatric background, his theories evolved into a description of normal personality more than of psychopathology. Perhaps because of this fact, his theories are of interest and of use to many different disciplines, especially literature and the humanities.

Analytical Psychology and Freudian theory share some common ground (e.g., recognition of the unconscious and the use of dream interpretation in psychotherapy) but the two theoretical systems also contain some fundamental differences. For example, Jung never accepted Freud's principle of the universality of the sexual etiology of neurosis. Whereas Freud held that all the contents of the unconscious are derived entirely from personal experience, Jung held that some of the contents are collective, that is, part of humanity's heritage. And, finally, Freud based his theory of dream interpretation on the latent (underlying) content of dream images, while Jung based his theory on the manifest content (images remembered by the dreamer) of the dreams.

The idea of unconscious mental contents was not the unique discovery of Freud and Jung. It had been in existence for a long time, although often under other labels. Indeed, the idea has a history as long, in a sense, as human history, in such millenia-old beliefs as the meaningfulness of dreams (see De Becker, 1968). As a specific concept, "the idea of unconscious mental processes was, in many of its aspects, conceivable around 1700, topical around 1800, and became effective around 1900, thanks to the imaginative efforts of a large number of individuals of varied interests in many lands" (Whyte, 1960, p. 63; author's italics). Most of the "discoverers" before 1730 were philosophers and literary figures, with a sprinkling of physicians, physicists, mystics, and theologians. From 1730 to 1800 philosophers and poets continued to be the most frequent hypothesizers of the unconscious but scientists and identifiable psychologists exerted increasing influence (see Ellenberger, 1970). During this period F. A. Mesmer (1733–1815) developed the concept of hypnotism, which aroused the interest of the French psychiatrists who influenced Freud and Jung. Primary among those psychiatrists were Jean Martin Charcot and Pierre Janet.

From 1800 to 1850 philosophers and poets, in about the same proportion as earlier, continued to advance the concept of the unconscious, but relatively more medically trained scientists began to make contributions to the study. Between 1850 and 1880 the number of investigators was so great that it is not feasible to classify their professional fields. Because many of these contributors were German, it is not surprising that the pioneer psychologists of the unconscious—Freud and Jung—were inhabitants of German-speaking countries.

The nineteenth century in Europe was a period of intense interest in psychological phenomena. Philosophers, theologians, physiologists, and neurologists, as well as psychiatrists, all speculated on the determinants of human behavior and the etiology of mental illness; some advanced organic theories, others, emotional. Despite lack of agreement on the causes of mental illness, major advances were made in the care of mentally ill persons. Sexuality and psychopathology were discussed rather widely in literature and in scientific treatises. The psychology of children began to be explored, and investigations were undertaken in the significance of occult experiences and dreams.

Jung was influenced profoundly by the prevailing intellectual climate and interests of his time. Not only was he familiar with the classical Greek and Latin philosophers and the Protestant theological tradition but, also, the works of anthropologists, historians, and philosophers. He was influenced, especially, by the eighteenth- and nineteenth-century philosophers Immanuel Kant and Friedrich Nietzsche. Undergirding all of Jung's theories, however, was his work with psychotic, borderline, and neurotic patients, and, most of all, his own inner life and self-analysis.

Jung's Life and Work

Switzerland is a country of high mountains, secluded valleys, and many lakes. It is a federation of cantons, each with its own language, customs, and traditions. The culture and language are predominantly German in the northern part of the country (sixteen cantons out of a total of twenty-two), where it has a common border with Germany. In the northeast the boundary is Lake Constance, the second largest body of water in the Alpine region. It was on the southern shore of this lake, in the small town of Keswil, that Carl Gustav Jung was born on July 26, 1875. He was named for his paternal grandfather, a German-born physician, who had fled Prussia to escape the political oppression of university students advocating a united Germany. In Switzerland, the elder Jung became a professor of surgery at the

University of Basel. His son, Johann, was a parson in the Swiss Reformed Church by vocation and a student of the classics and Oriental religions by avocation. When the younger Carl was four years old, Johann became pastor of a new church and the family moved to Klein-Hüningen, a suburb of Basel. It was there that Carl's schooling began and his sister Gertrud was born (1884).

At age six Carl began to receive instruction in Latin from his father. An apt pupil, he continued the study of the language until he became proficient in reading little-known old texts with ease. At an even earlier age he was introduced to comparative religions, through an illustrated book from which his mother, Emilie Preiswerk Jung, read to him often. He never tired of studying the pictures of exotic Hindu gods.

As a student in a gymnasium (roughly equivalent to an American high school and junior college) and later at the University of Basel, Jung was attracted to a career in archaeology. When he realized that he could not afford to attend a university offering such a course of study, he sought an alternative, one in which he could pursue his interest in science while making an adequate living. The study of medicine met both conditions. In the spring of 1895 Jung matriculated at the University of Basel with the financial assistance of his father and a University stipend. When his father died the following year, Jung was forced to take on various jobs to continue his medical course.

The medical curriculum required studies in psychiatry, but the subject did not interest Jung until his last year when he was introduced to Richard von Krafft-Ebing's *Lehrbuch der Psychiatrie* (*Textbook of Psychiatry;* first published in 1879). At once he saw the specialty as a way of combining his philosophical interests with his commitment to the natural sciences.

During Jung's last year in medical school two experiences brought to the fore what was to be a lifelong fascination with parapsychology (the study of phenomena that cannot be explained by natural laws). The first occurred while he was studying at home one day. He heard a loud noise, like a pistol shot, from the dining room, which was next to his room. The noise had issued from a seventy-year-old, solid walnut, round table, which had split from the rim to beyond the center. No explanation could be found for the occurrence.

The second experience came two weeks later. Upon his return home one evening, Jung found the household in great distress. His mother, sister, and the maid had heard another loud report in the dining room but they could find nothing broken. Jung searched the room. Finally, in a cupboard, he discovered the bread knife broken into four pieces, each piece lying in a different corner of the breadbasket. The improbability of a natural explanation for the explosive break and the distribution of the pieces impressed him deeply; he kept the remains of the knife all his life as evidence of the event.

Jung's concern with parapsychology intensified a few weeks after the knife incident, when he observed a fifteen-year-old girl of little education who, while in trances, saw visions and received mediumistic communications. The trances, according to Jung's description, were spontaneous. While in such states she spoke stilted High German instead of her accustomed Swiss dialect. Jung's notes on the girl and the séances in which she participated formed an important part of his doctoral thesis. The paper was published in 1902 under the title, "Zur Psychologie und Pathologie sogennanter occulter Phänomene" ("On the Psychology and Pathology of So-Called Occult Phenomena"; CW1).

Upon the award of his medical degree in 1900, Jung was appointed assistant physician (equivalent to a psychiatric resident in the United States) at the respected Burghölzli Hospital, a public psychiatric institution in Zurich in which Eugen Bleuler was the chief psychiatrist. Two years later Jung was promoted to senior physician (equivalent to a staff physician in the United States) and appointed lecturer in psychiatry at the University of Zurich.

During the winter of 1902–3 Jung studied in Paris with Pierre Janet, who "was the first to found a new system of dynamic psychiatry aimed at replacing those of the nineteenth century" (Ellenberger, 1970, p. 331). Janet's influence on Jung was profound. Indeed, years later, Jung stated that he had had "only two teachers"—Bleuler and Janet (Campbell, 1971, p. xi. In MDR, Jung mentioned Freud also.).

At the Burghölzli, before and after Jung's sojourn in Paris, Bleuler took considerable interest in Jung's career. Jung was always grateful, especially for the example Bleuler set of "total respect for his vocation as a psychiatrist. Above all, Jung felt indebted to the exacting methods of observation of all forms of hallucination and derangement he acquired from [Bleuler]" (van der Post, 1975, p. 108). Bleuler helped Jung set up a laboratory in the hospital for his work in parapsychology and encouraged the investigations by accompanying Jung to séances.

It was at Bleuler's suggestion, also, that Jung began, in 1904, to lead some colleagues in experiments with a word association test (see Chapter 7). Bleuler's encouragement of Jung's investigations is especially interesting because most Swiss psychiatrists of the period considered mental illness to be organic in etiology. Indeed, Jung spent considerable time examining brain tissue to test the hypothesis. Unfortunately, the study of brain chemistry was not yet a known science.

Jung's work on the Word Association Test led to his friendship and association with Freud. The account of that association and its erosion comprise a later section of this chapter.

Jung had married Emma Rauschenbach in 1903 and they had four daughters and a son. Carl and Emma built a house in Küsnacht, a suburb of Zurich, where they lived throughout their lives. Until her death in 1955, Emma collaborated closely with Carl in his work.

Like his early hospital and university colleagues, Jung carried on a private practice. It became sufficiently time-consuming and remunerative to enable him to resign from his hospital post in 1909 and from the university in 1913.

After the break with Freud, Jung was able to pursue more freely his own theory of the contents of the unconscious mind. His work rapidly lost whatever Freudian cast it had had and revealed increasingly his interest in archetypal symbolism. For the next six years (1913–19) he went through a period of what he termed "inner uncertainty" or "disorientation" (MDR, p. 170). (Ellenberger, 1970, called the experience a "creative illness.") During this time, Jung spent considerable time working on his dreams and fantasies and seeking to understand them, as far as possible, in terms of his daily life (see MDR, Chapter VI). The investigation of these contents led Jung to develop many of his psychological theories. From 1919 until he was halted by a severe illness in 1944, he wrote most of his major works, many in the form of individual essays which were collected later into the Collected Works.

In addition to his prodigious writing, Jung spent considerable time traveling, often to lecture but frequently to gather information regarding dreams and other aspects of his theory. He journeyed to Africa and India, made numerous trips to

England, and several to the United States. Also, he held weekly seminars in Zurich, some in German and some in English. The students, his analysands and those of his close associates, came from England and the United States, as well as from Europe. Some of them became the first Jungian analysts. The didactic study and case supervisions were informal, but Jung initiated and held to the principle that all prospective analysts must undergo personal analysis. The principle has been adopted, also, by all Freudian analytic institutes and many schools of psychiatry.

Jung's seminars and supervision of prospective analysts were the basis for the founding, in 1948, of the C. G. Jung Institute in Zurich. Jung was its first president. Students came to it, and continue to do so, from many countries. Some of the Institute's courses are open to students who are not in training to be analysts; other courses are available only to trainees.

Institutes for the training of Jungian analysts have been established in many places (see Chapter 16). Jungian psychology is disseminated, also, by an increasing number of journals. The first of these, the *Journal of Analytical Psychology*, began publication in London in 1955.

Jung's capacity for stirring his analysands and students to their depths produced reports that make him sound godlike, but the general agreement is that he was an intensely human person. In physical appearance he was tall, broad-shouldered, strong, and healthy-looking, with a "cheerful open face" (Bennet, 1962, p. 5). A mountain climber and expert sailor, he always lived next to a river or a lake. He was a good listener and conversationalist, although he did not waste time in trivialities. He had a keen sense of humor, which was equaled, perhaps, by his quick temper.

His family was important to Jung, yet he had a great need for solitude; he spent weeks at a time away from home, many of them in his "tower" at Bollingen (up the Lake of Zurich from Küsnacht), much of which he built himself. His power of concentration was prodigious, as evidenced by his encyclopedic knowledge and the quantity of his writings.

Jung's openness to new ideas reflected the nondogmatism that is expressed in his oft-quoted statement, "I am not a Jungian." His fascination with his own inner life, so apparent in *Memories, Dreams, Reflections*, resembled that of a scientist with a specimen; observations of his inner life profoundly affected all aspects of his psychological theories. The fascination was especially evident in the large proportion of time and effort he spent studying archetypal materials.

Beginning with his doctoral thesis, Jung investigated many aspects of human life which, generally, have been considered to be outside the purview of science. His investigations reflected his view that all human phenomena are products of the psyche and, hence, subject to psychological investigation (see Chapter 19).

For a time after the Second World War, Jung's views were discounted by many people who believed the accusations that Jung was anti-Semitic and, indeed, a Nazi sympathizer. These accusations seemed to stem from the fact that he assumed the presidency of the General Medical Society for Psychotherapy, which was based in Germany, and the editorship of the society's journal. He accepted the presidency in order to make the society international and to enable German-Jewish psychiatrists to continue to be members. He succeeded in both objectives. Moreover, the journal became the organ of the internationalized society, whose headquarters were in Zurich. One can fault Jung's strategy but not his motives.

Jung's editorship of the journal resulted in a disastrously embarrassing situation for him. Aniela Jaffé (1971) described the event as follows:

> It had earlier been planned that Professor Göring would bring out a . . . special German supplement to the [journal], for exclusive circulation in Germany. It was to contain a signed declaration by Professor Göring obliging the members of the German Society to adopt Hitler's political and ideological principles. Whether through negligence or by mistake (or, one asks retrospectively, by design), Göring's manifesto appeared not only in the supplement . . . but, in slightly different form, also in the current December 1933 issue of the [journal]—without Jung's having been apprised of this fact. An issue appearing under his name as editor and carrying the Nazi manifesto was a grave embarrassment to him. (p. 80)

The controversy over Jung's views on Nazism and anti-Semitism began with the episode of the journal and still continues, despite the availability of the facts. Perhaps even more convincing evidence that Jung was not anti-Semitic or pro-Nazi is the fact that many Jewish people from Hitler-dominated countries have testified to the help, both personal and financial, they received from him, help that saved their lives. Also, as the English novelist J. B. Priestley (1954) pointed out, "[Jung] may in passing have overrated Mussolini, but then so did a great many other people, including [G. B.] Shaw and [H. G.] Wells. . . . And on Germany Dr. Jung had no illusions. He declared in the twenties . . . that these strange people would explode in fury and madness" (p. 541).

When he reached the age of seventy, in 1945, Jung saw a decreasing number of patients and concentrated on writing and teaching. He died in Küsnacht on June 6, 1961, a few weeks short of his eighty-sixth birthday.

Jung and Freud

Just as Jung's intellectual development reflected the social climate of Basel at the turn of the century, so Freud's reflected that of Vienna. Vienna was the cultural, philosophical, and medical center of Europe, whereas Basel provided a staid and conservative environment. It is not so remarkable that Freud was a product of Vienna as it is that Basel could produce a creative intellect of the caliber of Jung's.

In order to understand Jung's theories it is essential to look at his association with Freud. Nineteen years younger than Freud, Jung began his work as a psychiatrist and psychological theorist independently of the older man. Nevertheless, the six or seven years during which their interests converged were crucial to Jung's intellectual and professional development. He never ceased to acknowledge his debt to Freud.

When Freud's *Interpretation of Dreams* was published in 1900, Jung read it on Bleuler's recommendation. It was not until three years later, however, that he realized the book's potential for explaining the mechanism of repression, which he had encountered in his word association experiments. In 1906 Jung sent Freud a copy of the first volume of *Diagnostische Assoziationsstudien: Bieträge zur experimentellen Psychopathologie* (*Diagnostic Association Studies: Contributions to Experimental Psychopathology*), which Jung had edited and which contained six studies by Jung and other doctors at the Burghölzli Hospital. Freud responded with a note (*FJ*, p. 3) and a copy of the first volume of *Sammlung kleiner Schriften zur Neurosenlehre* (*Collected Short Papers on the Theory of the Neuroses;* see *SE*). Jung replied (*FJ*, pp. 4, 6), expressing his thanks for the book but questioning Freud's theory that repressed contents are invariably rooted in sexual traumas.

When Jung and Freud met for the first time on March 3, 1907, in Vienna, they talked for thirteen consecutive hours. During the next six years, they wrote many letters to each other and met on numerous occasions. Through their letters and meetings Jung became increasingly aware that he held conceptions that differed from Freud's. Despite these differences Jung, at Freud's urging, assumed the presidency of the International Psychoanalytic Association in 1910. Freud wanted Jung to hold the position for life, and, thus, to be Freud's "heir apparent."

Two years later, Jung's differences with Freud came to a head with the publication of his *Wandlungen und Symbole der Libido* (*Transformations and Symbols of the Libido;* translated by Beatrice Hinkle as *The Psychology of the Unconscious;* revised and republished as *Symbols of Transformation, CW5*). At the 1913 meeting of the Association in Munich, a stormy discussion centered on the book. Seven months later Jung resigned the presidency of and, subsequently, his membership in the Association. Jung and Freud never met again after that Munich meeting. (In 1938 Jung sent an emissary to convey his offer to help Freud leave Hitler-dominated Austria, but Freud refused the assistance. Through the intercession of the American ambassador and others, however, Freud and his family were permitted to emigrate to England, where he died in 1939.)

Both Freud and Jung were physicians whose starting point was the observation of data. Freud was eager to arrive at a comprehensive theory that would withstand the test of any and all subsequent data, one that would be to psychology what the theory of gravitation, for example, has been to physics. Jung, on the other hand, from the very beginning, saw psychological phenomena as different from physical phenomena and as needing a theoretical framework that was adaptable and flexible enough to take into account the infinite variety of human experiences. The result was two theoretical frameworks with very different flavors. Freud's theory developed as more precise and definable—and quite rigid. Jung's evolved as more receptive to new possibilities and easily modified—but often vague. Freud seemed to reach for conclusions, for a closed system, as if there were nothing new to learn about human behavior and experiences; many people regard him as dogmatic. Jung continuously suggested hypotheses to be tested because he believed that psychology was still at the stage of amassing data rather than drawing conclusions. Because he included many data that are difficult to observe and to replicate, he is often charged with being "mystical."

Freud and Jung both went through inner experiences, which Ellenberger (1970) dubbed "creative illnesses." Freud's "illness" seemed to have been marked by physical symptoms and intense emotional attachments to other people, especially to Wilhelm Fliess and Josef Breuer. Jung's "illness" was characterized by the threat of being overwhelmed by powerful unconscious contents, which he described as archetypal. Freud's creativity was focused on describing the structure of the mind; Jung's on understanding a dimension of the unconscious beyond the personal unconscious and its once-conscious contents. Indeed, interest in the unconscious brought the two men together and divergent concepts of it drove them apart.

In attempting to comprehend the mind's structure, Freud hypothesized an unconscious composed entirely of contents acquired from an individual's experiences. Some of these contents are thoughts and memories that are readily accessible to consciousness; Freud called these the preconscious. Other unconscious contents are repressed—barred from consciousness with considerable force—and hence can be made conscious only by considerable effort. Jung, in contrast, posited an unconscious composed only partly of such personal contents; it included also, in his view, archetypal contents that were generated outside the realm of the individual's experiences (see Chapter 3). Thus, to Freud the unconscious was equated with pathology; to Jung it contained healthy, even creative resources as well as some pathological contents.

The development and structure of the mind was the focus of further divergence between Jung and Freud. Freud concerned himself almost exclusively with early development; he emphasized early childhood and seemed to consider development to stop with adolescence. To Jung development was lifelong. Indeed, as he grew older, he became increasingly interested in the development occurring during the second half of life.

If there remains any doubt that Jung was an independent investigator and was not merely reacting to Freud, it may be based on Jung's referring to himself as a "pupil of Freud's" (e.g., CW4, par. 553) and, in some of his letters, declaring his allegiance to Freud. He also referred to the psychoanalytic group he organized in Zurich as "Freudian" (FJ, p. 93). Nevertheless, a persistent theme throughout the correspondence is Jung's doubt about Freud's overgeneralized theories, especially the conceptualizations of all neuroses as rooted in polymorphous, perverse, infantile sexuality. Clearly, Jung was working independently of Freud before, after, and, to a large extent, during their association, and much of his work did not bear the Freudian imprint. Although popular opinion has tended to ascribe to Jung mere deviations from Freud's theories, there is no question that Jung was an original thinker who developed systems of psychology, psychotherapy, and dream analysis that are markedly different from those of psychoanalysis.

The relationship between Jung and Freud is recognized as that of "a collaboration between independent scientists working in the same field" (Ellenberger, 1970, p. 820). However, during his association with Freud, Jung called his treatment methods "psychoanalysis" and himself a "psychoanalyst." These terms later became identified solely with Freud's theories and followers. (Freud had coined the term psychoanalysis in 1896 to distinguish his system from Pierre Janet's "psychological analysis.") Because Freud had wanted only "disciples who would accept his teaching en bloc or develop it under his control" (Ellenberger, 1970, p. 820), a condition which Jung could not accept, the split between the two innovators was inevitable. Most accounts of the end of the association between Freud and Jung are biased by the loyalties of the writers. With the publication of the Freud/Jung Letters (1974), however, new perspectives on the ill-fated association have been provided. For example, Winnicott (1964), a Freudian psychiatrist, hypothesized that although the break between the two men was precipitated by ideological and personal differences, it can be seen also as the destiny of two intellectual giants; any reconciliation of their differences would have meant a loss to the world of the maximum creativity of one or the other or both.

Analytical Psychology and Other Psychologies

Psychoanalysis

Despite the differences over which Freud and Jung parted, their students are finding increasing points of convergence in their approaches. Many members of the London group of Jungian analysts, for example, make substantial and effective use of the work of Melanie Klein; her roots are in Freudian theory but her ideas have been modified in the direction of Jungian theory. For instance, she saw the child as "reacting not so much to a reality situation as to a system of fantasies based on the archetypes" (M. Fordham, 1957, p. 167).

In addition, the attribution of Jungian concepts to Freud is not uncommon. For example, Jung's attitude was that the dream means what it says; that is, the manifest images can be understood directly. This view of the dream has come to replace Freud's view that an underlying "latent" content of the images must be discovered. That the change was not initiated by Freud himself is recognized by relatively few Freudians today.

Academic Psychology

Academic psychologists have criticized Jung on the ground that he did not deal sufficiently with observable behavior, statistical norms, or controlled experiments. Many of these psychologists seem to have overlooked the fact that these criticisms can also be applied to Freud. Among the reasons that academic psychologists consider Freud's thought to be more acceptable may be that (a) Freud presented the unconscious as basically amenable to rational explanation, whereas Jung conceptualized the unconscious as the source of creativity and, hence, as ultimately nonrational; (b) Freud wrote in a straightforward manner, for the most part, and was relatively easy to understand as compared with Jung, who complicated his writing with poetic descriptions of the complexities of the psyche; (c) Freud provided a fairly consistent and closed theory, whereas Jung never ceased his investigations and insisted that available knowledge was still too elementary to formulate an enduring theory; (d) Freud's theory was accepted by the logical positivists of Vienna who were trying to apply scientific principles to all human intellectual endeavors, including philosophy; and (e) Freud's followers tended to malign colleagues who disagreed with Freud and left his circle.

Perhaps because of these factors the empirical base of Jung's work has escaped the notice, largely, of academic psychologists. Gradually, however, these psychologists have come closer to Jung's view in broadening the range of admissible data. Hypnosis and phenomenology, for example, are providing bridges to connect the externally observable data of academic psychology with the dreams and other subjective data of Jung's researches.

The ignoring of Jung's theories can be likened, moreover, to earlier attitudes toward Jean Piaget's work. Piaget's failure to carry out controlled studies and to establish statistical norms kept American academicians from paying attention to his writings. However, when American child psychologists could no longer deny the relevance of Piaget's theories, they quickly developed appropriate empirical studies. The variables of Jung's hypotheses may be more difficult to manipulate than those of Piaget's but certainly observation, the basis of Piaget's theories, can also be used to test Jung's hypothesis. The studies that are presented in this book demonstrate that research based on Jungian theory is possible.

Indeed, even the experimental method, which is valued highly by academic psychologists, was used by Jung—when it was applicable—primarily in his work on the Word Association Test. This work brought him early recognition, including G. Stanley Hall's invitation to lecture at Clark University in 1909. The test is considered to be "the progenitor of the majority of our modern non-questionnaire-type of personality tests" (Bell, 1948, p. 15), including projective tests such as the Rorschach Psychodiagnostic Inkblot Test and the Thematic Apperception Test. Since 1950, interest in the word association method has undergone a revival, but for purposes different from those of Jung's early professional life. Now, the focus is on the study of verbal behavior and a variety of cognitive processes; Jung's interest was in clinical diagnosis and his theory of complexes.

Still another of Jung's methods that has influenced academic psychologists is the use of the psychogalvanometer, especially in criminology. Jung's attempts to use the Word Association Test to detect criminal behavior failed but the psychogalvanometer succeeded and became the forerunner of biofeedback and other uses of galvanic skin responses to monitor emotional responses.

One of the best known of Jung's theories, and the one which has had the greatest impact upon academic psychology, is that of the attitude types, introversion and extraversion (also spelled extroversion). An enormous literature, most of it using introversion-extraversion as a dimension rather than a typology, has been compiled. Eysenck, for example, studied attitude types extensively (e.g., 1947, 1956, 1960, 1971), although his definitions of the terms differed somewhat from those of Jung. The function types (feeling, intuition, sensation, and thinking) have generated less research than attitude types but are beginning to be recognized as useful in investigations of personality (see Chapter 4).

Recently, academic psychologists have been paying more attention to Jung's theories. This increased interest seems to be based on three developments: (a) Jung's theories are having an increased influence on other theorists and on lay people who look to psychology for help in understanding their subjective worlds; (b) Analytical Psychology is more applicable to the continuing development of adults than is psychoanalysis; (c) Jung's concepts, especially those of archetypes and the collective unconscious, are significant for the creative aspects of human endeavor.

Adlerian Psychology

Although Alfred Adler, like Jung, differentiated himself from Freud, his theories differed largely from Jung's but the commonalities in their work have received little attention. Nonetheless, a major commonality is in the concept of the complex. Jung developed the general concept through his work on the Word Association Test and in his clinical studies. Consequently, Jung has been incorrectly credited with one of Adler's major concepts: the inferiority complex, the response of a person to his bodily (organ) defects.

Another striking similarity between Jung's and Adler's theories is the concept of purposiveness. Adler's theory of neurosis was based on the idea that psychic life is future-oriented; that is, symptoms appear as the means to various goals.

Jung shared Adler's view that psychic life is purposive but he stressed the healthy, constructive nature of the purposes more than their neurotic qualities.

Both Jung and Adler used the term *compensation*, although with quite different meanings. Adler saw it as a neurotic way of dealing with weakness, especially organ inferiority, whereas Jung saw compensation as a resource of the creative psyche (see Chapter 6).

Humanistic Psychology

Because academic psychology is of little value in guiding people to self-understanding, a number of schools of psychology have appeared in response to popular demand for such help. These schools are known generally as humanistic. Some of them, such as Abraham Maslow's, with its hierarchy of needs, arise out of academic psychology and are based on empirical studies. Others, such as Eric Berne's Transactional Analysis, are modernizations of older concepts: Freudian, in Berne's case. Still others, such as some of those that produced the encounter-group movement, are derived from the subjective experience of the originators.

Humanistic psychologies share with Jung's theories the quality of holism; that is, they are based on the assumption that the whole person is more than a combination of elements—such as perceptions—and should be treated as a totality. A further characteristic that many of these psychologies have in common with Jung's is that they are phenomenological—concerned with experiences, rather than with assumptions regarding inner dynamics.

Many of the insights of humanistic psychologies were present in theories Jung formulated decades ago. Maslow's "peak experience," for example, was anticipated by Jung's "numinous experience" (see Chapter 12). The widely popular concept of androgyny depends on a concept of Jung's (and Adler's) that physiological and psychological gender is complemented by its opposite in hormones as well as in unlearned and learned behaviors (see Chapter 5). The "here-and-now" approach to psychotherapy was practiced in the Jungian consulting room long before it was so named by such humanistic psychologies as Gestalt.

The Scope and Significance of Jung's Work

Although Jung's contributions to the history of psychology have become widely recognized relatively recently, he received considerable recognition over much of his lifetime. An honorary degree awarded in 1909 by Clark University was only the first of many such honors. Among others were professorships at the Federal Institute of Technology in Zurich and at the University of Basel, memberships in the Swiss Academy of Sciences and the (British) Royal Society of Medicine; and honorary doctorates from, for example, Oxford University and the University of Calcutta.

Jung's influence on fields other than psychology has been recognized and appreciated for decades. People in the arts, the humanities, history, anthropology, and even physics have found in Jung's works significant contributions to their understanding of their own fields. In recent years his place as a major psychological theorist has received increasing appreciation. Elkind (1970) stated, "In many domains . . . Jung offered pro-phetic insights about modern man which are only now coming to be widely appreciated" (p. 102).

Part I

Structure of the Psyche

2

The Components of the Psyche

The word *psychology* means, literally, the study of the psyche. *Psyche* has been translated variously as mind, soul, or spirit. Many psychologists appear to have forgotten the origin of the word; the academic definition of psychology is "the science of behavior." Jung, a classical scholar as well as a psychiatrist, was fascinated with the study of psyche, which, for him, was the infinitely varied composite of all human nonsomatic capacities, both conscious and unconscious. He developed his description of the psyche empirically by observing images and other cognitions, as well as behaviors, in himself and others. The commonalities and varieties of human personality that he saw led him to the identification of the components of the psyche.

The psyche, or personality—Jung used the terms interchangeably—is made up of several major components, each of which can be envisioned as a combination of contents, mental and emotional. These components are *ego, persona, shadow,* and *animus* or *anima*. There is also a superordinate Self, which is not a component but has a significant relation to the components.

The psychic components are not physical entities, of course. They are combinations of mental contents that are manifested in observable behaviors, emotions, and attitudes. The components of the psyche bear the same relation to Analytical Psychology as the id, ego, and superego bear to psychoanalytic theory, and as traits and characteristics bear to other personality theories.

The Conscious and the Unconscious

To understand the structure of the psyche it is necessary to distinguish between its conscious and unconscious contents. The term *conscious* has come to mean, in common parlance, cognitive awareness. *Unconscious*, to many people, means motives and other contents of which one is not aware, and it has become a widely known concept. Thus, even ten-year-olds may be heard to say, "Consciously or unconsciously, I wanted . . ."

Jung used the terms *conscious* and *unconscious* somewhat differently. For him, *conscious* meant "under the control of the ego" (see later section); *unconscious* meant "not under ego control." For example, a man can be aware that the reason he forgets his wife's birthday is that he is angry at her, but he still forgets; that is, he is aware but not conscious of his motive for forgetting. If the motive becomes conscious—under ego control—he still may be angry but he remembers and can choose whether to observe her birthday.

Most of the mental contents forming the psyche are unconscious, that is, not conscious. The unconscious part of the psyche is not a single entity but is composed of many kinds of contents that vary from person to person and from time to time. Some of these contents are products of individual and cultural experiences, whereas others seem to be general to all humans, that is, shared with all members of the human race and, hence, collective. Usually, we refer to the conglomerate of unconscious contents as "the unconscious" even though the word probably should not be used as a noun; "unconscious psyche" or "unconscious contents" would be more accurate. However, the practice of using "unconscious" as a noun is so common and convenient that it is followed here.

The term *subconscious* is used frequently in nontechnical discussions to denote mental contents that are "below" the level of consciousness. Jung rejected the use of this term as a synonym for "unconscious" because to him the unconscious sometimes has a superior wisdom. When he used the term *subconscious* it was to refer to the "momentarily unconscious contents" (*CW8*, par. 383), which Freud called "preconscious."

The term *personal unconscious* was used by Jung to denote the experiences, thoughts, and memories that slip out of consciousness and become unconscious. Thus, the personal unconscious contains some contents that are simply too unimportant to remember; some subliminal impressions and perceptions that never entered awareness; other contents that are "waiting in the wings," that is, that are available to consciousness if one's attention turns to them; still others that have been suppressed—pushed out of consciousness—but are capable of being recalled; and some repressed contents, those that have been banished virtually irrevocably from consciousness, presumably because they are painful.

Although sometimes it is said that Jung's "personal unconscious" is synonymous with Freud's "unconscious," the two conceptions differ importantly: (a) Freud included more unconscious contents than did Jung in the category of the repressed by making clear that not only the id but parts of the ego and superego are unconscious; (b) Jung's personal unconscious includes contents that have "not yet reached the threshold of consciousness" (*CW7*, par. 441); evidently he was of the opinion that some psychic "acquisitions," or learnings, pass directly into the unconscious.

Jung wrote relatively little about the personal unconscious, not because he was uninterested in it but because he felt that Freud had covered the topic very well. Jung found that the contents of the personal unconscious "constitute integral portions of the personality, they belong to it, and their loss to the conscious mind puts it in a state of inferiority. . . . Whoever makes progress along the path of self-realization must inevitably bring into consciousness the contents of his personal unconscious, thus enlarging considerably the domain of his personality" (*CW7*, par. 446).

The *collective unconscious* was hypothesized by Jung and denied by Freud. Jung found that the nonpersonal material of the collective unconscious was reflected in his and others' dreams, visions, and fantasies. He pointed out that if there were nothing in the unconscious beyond contents of a personal nature it would be possible to empty the unconscious by means of the process of analysis and to halt the production of further fantasies. In that event, he argued:

> The analysis should be capable of making a complete inventory of unconscious contents. . . . But, as we have convincing evidence every day, this procedure seems to have no effect whatever upon the unconscious, which persists no less than before in its creative activity and, as we see, produces the same infantile sexual fantasies which, according to the original theory, should be the effects of personal repressions. (CW7, par. 442)

Thus Jung postulated an underlying unconscious that is shared by all humans and, hence, is collective.

The components of the psyche are expressions of both consciousness and the unconscious. The ego is the center of consciousness. The shadow, persona, and animus or anima are largely unconscious and exist partly in the personal unconscious, partly in the collective unconscious. Jung saw the conscious and unconscious aspects of the psyche as mutually interdependent; the conscious needs the unconscious for continuous renewal and the unconscious needs the conscious as a channel for expression in everyday life.

The Ego

Ego, which means "I" in Latin, signifies approximately the same in analytical psychology. The ego is by no means the entire personality. It is the center of consciousness, that is, the point of reference for one's conscious experiences. The center of the whole personality, which includes both consciousness and the unconscious, is the Self (see later section).

As the center of consciousness, a well-functioning ego perceives reality accurately and differentiates the outer world from inner images. Such an ego also is capable of initiating and directing thought and action.

The ego of Jungian psychology should not be confused with the ego of common parlance. The latter, which often is used to denote selfishness or conceit, is used to mean "egocentric" or "big ego." However, such an ego is not big; rather, it is underdeveloped, insecure, and in need of protection. The healthy ego of which Jung wrote does not need protection; it can tolerate criticism from other people as well as from within.

The formation of the ego, according to Jung, begins with a "collision" between bodily needs and the environment. In order to survive, an infant must make his or her needs known; when the infant does this, an embryonic ego has differentiated itself from the environment. Moreover, Jung hypothesized that at birth the infant is enveloped in the collective unconscious and that ego development includes the child's becoming differentiated from the archetypal world.

In addition to being the center of consciousness, the ego provides continuity for the personality. The fact that one can say, "When I was three years old . . . ," and have some understanding that the three-year-old child was in some sense the same person who now says, "I," is a function of the ego.

Freud's view of the ego is similar but not identical to Jung's. Masserman (1946) summarized Freud's definition of the ego as "that portion or stratum of the 'mind' or personality which is in contact with the environment through the senses, perceives and evaluates the milieu through intellectual functions, and directs behavior into acceptable compromises between the blind drives of the *Id* and the inhibitions (conscience) and idealizations of the *Super-Ego*" (p. 274). In short, both Freud and Jung saw the ego as directing behavior, but Freud regarded the ego as the mediator in the inevitable conflict between id and superego, whereas Jung viewed the ego's direction of behavior as relatively conflict-free.

The ego is characterized, in Jung's view, by the dominant one of two attitudes—extraversion or introversion—and the dominant one or two of what Jung labeled "functions"—thinking, feeling, sensation, and intuition. This attitude and these functions are expressed consciously. The uncharacteristic attitude and functions, that is, those that are not developed, are part of the unconscious.

The Shadow

The shadow consists of psychic contents which a person prefers not to show. They are the parts of oneself that one considers unpresentable, because they seem weak, socially unacceptable, or even evil. Manifestations of the shadow are often embarrassing; for example, one suddenly may be unable to name the guest of honor at one's party or may hear oneself blurting out a hostile remark during a friendly conversation. Expression of the shadow is most likely when a person is in the grip of anxiety or other emotion, under the influence of alcohol, or otherwise subject to a lowering (diminishing) of consciousness. In dreams, according to Jung, the shadow often appears as a person of the same sex as the dreamer.

It is possible for one to be acquainted with one's shadow and even for it to be at least partially conscious, that is, under ego control. Many people, however, reject, or repress, their shadows so completely that the ego is not aware of shadow behavior and thus has no possibility of commanding it. Under these conditions, the shadow is autonomous and may express itself in inexplicable moods, irritability, and cruelty, and in physical symptoms.

A classic example of the autonomous shadow is that of Otto von Bismarck, the leader who unified Germany in the nineteenth century. A strong, brutal military man outwardly, he is said to have been overcome sometimes by hysterical weeping spells. These spells were manifestations of his shadow. Also exemplifying the shadow is the universal experience of being "beside oneself," that is, of behaving occasionally in an excited or agitated way that is contrary to one's usual personality. In such a situation it is the shadow that is "beside" the conscious personality.

The content of the shadow varies with the person; in each, a large part of the shadow consists of idiosyncratic qualities. In everyone, however, these qualities are undifferentiated, that is, undeveloped, awkward, unattractive, even crude. If the same qualities appear in differentiated form (developed, graceful, attractive, and refined) in another person, one often becomes jealous of that person, probably without understanding why. Thus, a given quality can be part of one person's shadow and another person's ego, but it will be awkward in the one, refined in the other.

Although the shadow is usually perceived as negative it can also be useful. It contains qualities that are awkward and perhaps destructive when they are unconscious but that can be valuable if they are made conscious and developed. Thus, Jung viewed the shadow not only as necessary for wholeness (see Chapter 13) but also as capable of yielding treasure. For example, out of the shadow the quality of anger can become assertiveness and the quality of vulnerability can become sensitivity to the needs of others. Jung stated repeatedly that inasmuch as a two-dimensional substance casts no shadow, the shadow is a necessary component of a three-dimensional body. Indeed, the shadow "displays a number of good qualities, such as normal instincts, appropriate reactions, realistic insights, creative impulses, etc." (CW9–II, par. 423). In addition, von Franz (1964), using the generic he to denote the shadow, pointed out: "The shadow is not necessarily always an opponent. In fact, he is exactly like any human being with whom one has to get along, sometimes by giving in, sometimes by resisting, sometimes by giving love—whatever the situation requires. The shadow becomes hostile only when he is ignored or misunderstood" (p. 173).

Usually the shadow is negative, but some shadows are positive. They take one of two major forms: (a) seeing oneself as inadequate or bad, that is, being unconscious of one's good qualities, or (b) prizing one's negative characteristics. The first category encompasses primarily neurotics, persons with low self-esteem who live on a more constructive level than they think they do but believe that other people are superior to them in ethics and ability. The second category includes mainly criminals; they let the world see their cruelty and destructiveness and are ashamed of their tenderness and generosity.

In addition to individual contents, the shadow also contains some collective contents. The history of Nazi Germany provides an example. Jung puzzled long and unsuccessfully over the question of how a presumably civilized and Christian nation could allow and, indeed, support the collective evil of Nazism. He could only conclude that each of us is linked through the collective unconscious to a collective shadow. In Germany this archetypal image was Wotan, "the ancient god of storm and frenzy" (CW10, par. 373), a compensatory force to the one-sided goodness and loving kindness preached by Christianity.

Some people dispute Jung's contention that criminality and evil mass movements such as Nazism reflect unconscious contents that are potential in all of us. Whatever one may believe about the idea of a collective shadow, it is indisputable that each of us has a personal shadow. Awareness of one's personal darkness helps a person to understand that other people's shadows do not make them totally evil. This understanding can prevent the "we-they" mentality that often produces hostile and punitive attitudes toward people who are outside one's social group.

The term *shadow* is sometimes used in Analytical Psychology to refer to the entire unconscious, not just to the part of the personality described here. In my view, such usage adds nothing to the understanding of the psyche and should be avoided in favor of the more precise meaning presented in this section.

The Persona

Persona, the Latin word for mask, designates the part of the personality that one presents to the world to gain social approval or other advantages, and to coincide with one's idea of how one should appear in public. Thus, the persona reveals little of what a person is; it is the public face, determined by what one perceives to be acceptable to other people. An example of the persona is the polite behavior of most adults; we go through the motions of consideration for others, saying, "Excuse me" and "Thank you" even if we do not feel apologetic or grateful. The persona is composed primarily of positive behaviors that conceal the negative qualities of the shadow. Hence the persona, more than the ego, is the "presentable" alternative to the "unpresentable" shadow.

No one wears the same mask on all occasions. The persona is made up of many masks, each of which is assumed as the appropriate response to a specific environment and set of conditions. Often a particular mask corresponds to a certain status. (The combination of behaviors that reflect any one status is called a role by anthropologists.) The sum total of masks used by the individual makes up the persona.

Produced by a compromise between the demands of the environment and the necessities of the ego, the persona appears to be unique to each person. The professional (occupational) persona, for example, reflects one's particular interests and hence, to a considerable extent, the true personality. Nevertheless, Jung stated that the persona is a compromise between individual and society as to what a man should appear to be. He takes a name, earns a title, represents an office, he is this or that. In a certain sense all this is real, yet in relation to the essential individuality of the person concerned it is only a secondary reality, a product of compromise, in making which others often have a greater share than he. (*CW7*, par. 246)

Jung used also the term *collective psyche* for the source of the persona, although he did not differentiate between the universally human and the collectivity of a particular culture. His explanation that the persona is "a compromise between individual and society" seems to suggest that "collective" in this context includes the cultural dimension. Thus, the tendency to form a persona is universal but the content is specific to the culture and the individual. For example, there seems to be a "Mother archetype," but the specific persona of a good mother varies from culture to culture and individual to individual.

The negative aspects of the persona are often the most obvious. For example, a role identification is likely to require forms of behavior that are adapted more to the demands of the role than to the demands of individuality. This adaptation becomes a problem when one feels that one exists only in that role, whether it be parent, counselor, scientist, community leader, or whatever. According to Jacobi (1976), "The characteristics of such a persona are superficiality, boringness, stiffness, and mediocrity" (p. 42). Ultimately, this state of affairs can be destructive. In Arthur Miller's play, *Death of a Salesman*, Willy Loman was identified with his persona: "a smile and a shoeshine." When he was no longer allowed to function as a salesman he felt empty, and the feeling became so intolerable that he committed suicide. Many people have a similar problem, although to a lesser degree. The consequences of persona identification were indicated in a study by Fehrenbach (1972). He found that retired college faculty men who described themselves as "high-dominant-low-affiliative" evidenced more state anxiety than other personality groups of retirees. The investigator (Fehrenbach, 1980) interpreted the results in Jungian terms as meaning that such professionals who overidentify with their work roles have more difficulties in retirement than do those who have other sources of a sense of identity.

The persona is much less conscious than it seems. Subjectively, it seems highly conscious; a person makes decisions regarding the way one presents onself to the world and then finds that this view is consonant with the terms in which one is described by other people. Yet Jung described the persona as unconscious; he included the aspects of the persona that are known to the ego as well as those that are not known. The discrepancy in the perception of consciousness becomes less baffling when the nature of consciousness is considered: A characteristic can be known to the ego without being under ego control.

Much of the persona is so far beyond ego control that many people who seek psychological development through psychotherapy or other means find that the persona is the most difficult part of the psyche to change. This difficulty is proportionate to the stake one has in the roles one plays in family, community, and occupation. The special persistence of the occupational persona is reflected in Jung's half-humorous statement that "the temptation to be what one seems to be is great, because the persona is usually rewarded in cash" (CW9–I, par. 221).

Sometimes, a person's various "masks" are so incompatible that they cause severe discomfort. An older adolescent, for example; may present a compliant "good boy" persona to his parents and a tough, swaggering persona to his peers. When he is in the presence of both his parents and peers he may behave in a way that is inappropriate to either role, such as crying or talking like a small child.

A common mistake is to regard the persona as purely concealing and, hence, undesirable. Actually, the persona is necessary for adaptation to the world. Consequently, it is necessary for adequate psychological functioning. Without a developed persona one is likely to be socially inept and, thus, unable to achieve the objectives that depend on making a positive impression on other people.

At the same time, the persona is largely autonomous and may function without regard for the wishes of the ego, often to the point of conflicting with them. Indeed, if the ego is very weak, the persona may function nearly always in its stead. This situation is described as "identification with the persona." An example is the person who is, appropriately, a parent with his or her own children but who seeks, inappropriately, to be mother or father to adults. A strong, well-functioning ego, however, makes use of the persona appropriately. Such an ego can decide, for example, to function as a parent to sons and daughters and as a companion to one's peers.

Animus and Anima

The remaining components of the psyche, as Jung described them, are the animus and anima, the respective contrasexual contents of the male and female. He postulated that a woman has a primarily feminine consciousness and a primarily masculine unconscious while a man has a primarily masculine consciousness and a primarily feminine unconscious. The animus and anima exist partly in the personal and partly in the collective unconscious. Because these components function differentially in the female and male psyches, they are discussed in Chapter 5.

The Self

Superordinate to all the components of the psyche is the Self.* The Self is so all-encompassing a concept that it is difficult to characterize; hence it has been described in various ways. The phrase that seems to designate the concept best is "the total personality," conscious and unconscious. Thus, it becomes evident that the ego is "subordinate to the self and is related to it like a part to the whole" (CW9–II, par. 9). Jung also referred to the Self as the center of the personality, comparable to the sun in the solar system—the source of all the system's energy. In this image the ego is to the Self as the Earth is to the sun.

As the totality of the psyche, the Self combines in potential all the mental processes, contents, and characteristics, from positive to negative, constructive to destructive. These contents do not exist in chaos, however. They are the parts of a pattern for the development of a whole person. Thus, as the conscious personality encounters the problems and possibilities of life, the Self draws upon the collective unconscious to provide the necessary resources to meet life's demands.

Subjectively, the Self is not experienced as readily as are the ego, persona, and shadow. Nevertheless, it is glimpsed sometimes in dreams, for example, as the image of a person whom the dreamer sees as embodying wholeness. As the individuation pro-

---

* The spelling of the word *self* with a capital or lower-case S is a matter of disagreement among Jungians. It is not capitalized in the *Collected Works*. It is capitalized in this book, however, to indicate its importance and to differentiate it from the concept of "self" in other psychologies (e.g., Cattell, 1957; Rogers, 1959). In these other systems "self" usually means what Jung meant by "ego."

cess results in greater psychic integration, more frequent experiences of the Self occur.

Empirical Evidence for Components of the Psyche

Most of the empirical evidence for the delineation of the various components of the psyche is clinical. An example is a case of multiple personality; each of the "personalities" seems to correspond to one of the components of the psyche. A well-known instance is the case described in *The Three Faces of Eve* (Thigpen and Cleckley, 1957). "Eve White," a timid, conscientious housewife, manifested behaviors that belong to the persona; "Eve Black," who wore low-cut, black evening dresses and stayed out most of the night, acted the part of the shadow; and "Jane," who was personable and outgoing but still fulfilled her responsibilities, seemed to represent the emerging ego. It is said that after *The Three Faces of Eve* was published, a fourth personality appeared. Such a personality may have been identifiable as the Self.

Experimental evidence, although not available for the separate components of the psyche, is available for the existence of the unconscious. Penfield (1952) and other neurophysiologists have demonstrated that the brain retains many memories that are not available to consciousness. Patients whose temporal cortices were stimulated electrically remembered experiences they had not been able to recall prior to the stimulation. After the electrodes were withdrawn the subjects could remember the general outlines of the newly-recalled experiences but not the details. One of Penfield's examples was the case of S. B.:

> Stimulation at [a point] in the first convolution of the right temporal lobe caused him to say: "There was a piano there and someone playing. I could hear the song, you know." When the point was stimulated again without warning, he said, "Someone speaking to another, and he mentioned a name, but I could not understand it. . . . It was just like a dream." The point was stimulated a third time, also without warning. He then observed spontaneously, "Yes, 'Oh Marie, Oh Marie'—Someone is singing it." When the point was stimulated a fourth time, he heard the same song and explained that it was the theme song of a certain radio program.

When [another point] was stimulated, he said, while the electrode was being held in place, "Something brings back a memory. I can see Seven-Up Bottling Company . . . Harrison Bakery." He was then warned that he was being stimulated, but the electrode was not applied. He replied, "Nothing." (p. 179)

Penfield pointed out, "In [this and other] examples it seems to make little difference whether the original experience was fact, dream, or fancy; it was a single recollection that the electrode evoked, not a mixture of memories or a generalization" (p. 180). It is quite possible that all of a person's past experiences are recorded in his or her brain although no way has been found, as yet, to test the possibility.

Further evidence for the existence of the unconscious was reported by two psychologists, Shevrin and Fritzler (1968). They used an electroencephalograph (EEG) to detect and measure electrical currents in the brain, a computer to select meaningful EEG responses, and a battery of psychological tests. They found that subjects participating in the study could discriminate between two objects that had been flashed on a screen for a millisecond but which they were not aware they had seen. The investigators concluded that "in the absence of a conscious discrimination, there may nevertheless be present an electrocortical discrimination" (p. 298). The latter discrimination could be called an unconscious one.

Indeed, in several areas of psychology, investigators have arrived at explanations which incorporate concepts that seem indistinguishable from unconscious processes. Shevrin and Dickman (1980) found "a number of different sources of evidence and a variety of theories, all of which appear to involve an implicit assumption of psychological unconscious processes. These areas of research and theory are (a) selective attention, (b) subliminal perceptions, and (c) certain visual phenomena involving perceptual processing, namely retinal image stabilization, binocular rivalry, and backward masking" (p. 423). Thus, although it is called by various names, the existence of the unconscious is rapidly becoming recognized as indisputable.

3

The Collective
Unconscious

The idea of the collective unconscious did not originate with
Jung. It had been present for a long time in philosophical,
literary, and even psychological works as well as those of
religious history. Even Freud, who explicitly denied the existence
of the collective unconscious as it was described by Jung, seemed
to accept it implicitly. For example, Freud wrote about "archaic
remnants," by which he seemed to mean myths that are replayed
by each individual, such as the Oedipus myth.

Jung made his enormous contribution by defining the collective unconscious and describing its function and its contents,
which he called archetypes. Thus, the concepts of archetypes
and the collective unconscious are interdependent. Indeed, they
form one theory so that Jung's use of "collective unconscious"
implies "archetypes."

The theory was developed empirically and its truth or
falsehood can be judged only on an empirical basis. Because
Jung insisted that anyone who had his experiences would come
to his conclusions, the discussion here begins with some of the
experiences that led Jung to the conclusion that there was indeed
a collective unconscious.

Development of the Theory

The theory of the collective unconscious originated, Jung said, in a dream that he had in 1909. He recounted it as follows:

I was in a house I did not know, which had two stories. It was "my house." I found myself in the upper story, where there was a kind of a salon furnished with fine old pieces in rococo style. On the walls hung a number of precious old paintings. I wondered that this should be my house, and thought, "Not bad." But then it occurred to me that I did not know what the lower floor looked like. Descending the stairs, I reached the ground floor. There everything was much older, and I realized that this part of the house must date from about the fifteenth or sixteenth century. The furnishings were medieval; the floors were of red brick. Everywhere it was rather dark. I went from one room to another, thinking, "Now I really must explore the whole house." I came upon a heavy door, and opened it. Beyond it, I discovered a stone stairway that led down into the cellar. Descending again, I found myself in a beautifully vaulted room which looked exceedingly ancient. Examining the walls, I discovered layers of brick among the ordinary stone blocks, and chips of brick in the mortar. As soon as I saw this I knew that the walls dated from Roman times. My interest was by now intense. I looked more closely at the floor. It was of stone slabs, and in one of these I discovered a ring. When I pulled it, the stone slab lifted, and again I saw a stairway of narrow stone steps leading down into the depths. These, too, I descended, and entered a low cave cut into the rock. Thick dust lay on the floor, and in the dust were scattered bones and broken pottery, like remains of a primitive culture. I discovered two human skulls, obviously very old and half disintegrated. (MDR, pp. 158–59)

The dream occurred during the trip with Freud to Clark University; the two men were together every day for seven weeks and were analyzing each other's dreams. When Jung told Freud this dream, Freud urged him to find the repressed wish indicated by the two skulls. Knowing that Freud assumed that the skulls indicated death wishes—perhaps for Freud's death—Jung complied outwardly (naming his wife and his sister-in-law as possible objects of his death wishes). He did so, despite his "violent resistance" to such an interpretation, because he "did not then trust [his] own judgment, and wanted to hear Freud's opinion" (MDR, p. 159). Jung also feared that if he insisted on his own point of view he would lose Freud's friendship. This experience, however, forced Jung to recognize the basic incompatibility of his and Freud's ideas. Jung evidently had no clear idea of the dream's interpretation at the time but remembered the experience as his "first inkling of a collective a priori beneath the personal psyche" (*MDR*, p. 161). He saw Freud as taking refuge in doctrine and unable to comprehend Jung's mental world. Nearly fifty years later he elaborated these impressions:

> It was plain to me that the house represented a kind of image of the psyche—that is to say, of my then state of consciousness, with hitherto unconscious additions. Consciousness was represented by the salon. It had an inhabited atmosphere, in spite of its antiquated style.
>
> The ground floor stood for the first level of the unconscious. The deeper I went, the more alien and the darker the scene became. In the cave, I discovered remains of a primitive culture, that is, the world of the primitive man within myself—a world which can scarcely be reached or illuminated by consciousness. . . .
>
> The dream pointed out that there were further reaches to the stage of consciousness I have just described: the long uninhabited ground floor in medieval style, then the Roman cellar and finally the prehistoric cave. These signified past times and past stages of consciousness. . . .
>
> My dream thus constituted a kind of structural diagram of the human psyche; it postulated something of an altogether *impersonal* nature underlying that psyche. . . . This I first took to be the traces of earlier modes of functioning. Later, with increasing experience and on the basis of more reliable knowledge, I recognized them as . . . archetypes. (*MDR*, pp. 160–61)

Subsequent experiences contributed further to Jung's hypothesizing the collective unconscious. His clinical work exposed him to the dreams, delusions, and hallucinations of his patients at the Burghölzli Hospital. The contents recounted to him convinced Jung that there existed a realm of the unconscious beyond the repressed representations that were the object of Freud's dream investigations. Several times in his *Collected Works* Jung repeated one patient's particular delusion. One version reads as follows:

> One day [in the hospital] I came across [a patient] there, blinking through the window up at the sun, and moving his head from side to side in a curious manner. He took me by the arm and said he wanted to show me something. He said I must look at the sun with eyes half shut, and then I could see the sun's phallus. If I moved

my head from side to side the sun-phallus would move too, and that was the origin of the wind.

I made this observation about 1906. In the course of the year 1910, when I was engrossed in mythological studies, a book of Dieterich's came into my hands. It was part of the so-called Paris magic papyrus and was thought by Dieterich to be a liturgy of the Mithraic cult. It consisted of a series of instructions, invocations, and visions. One of these visions is described in the following words: "And likewise the so-called tube, the origin of the ministering wind. For you will see hanging down from the disc of the sun something that looks like a tube." (*CW8*, pars. 317–18)

Although the first edition of the book had appeared in 1903, the patient could not have had access to it because he had been committed several years earlier; nor was it likely that he could have learned of the Mithraic material from other sources. Although there was no way to prove that the patient had not been exposed to the idea at some time in his life, Jung concluded that the image in the book and the image seen by the patient had a common unconscious source.

Jung's experience with the patient's vision of a sun phallus was only a suggestion of the hypothesis which was to come into being with the accumulation of more and better evidence. For a while, Jung thought that these contents, which were related to the past, might be explained by racial inheritance. He investigated this possibility by studying the dreams of blacks in the southern United States. When he found motifs from Greek mythology in their dreams he concluded that these images belong to humankind in general and not to particular racial groups. The motifs included, for example, the image of a man being crucified on a wheel. The black male who reported this image had had minimal education and was unlikely to have had conscious knowledge of such an image. Jung explained:

If he had not had any model for this idea it would be an *archetypal image*, because the crucifixion on the wheel is a *mythological motif*. It is the ancient sun-wheel, and the crucifixion is the sacrifice to the sun-god in order to propitiate him, just as human and animal sacrifices formerly were offered for the fertility of the earth. The sun-wheel is an exceedingly archaic idea, perhaps the oldest religious idea there is. We can trace it to the Mesolithic and Paleolithic ages, as the sculptures of Rhodesia prove. Now there were real wheels only in the Bronze Age; in the

Paleolithic Age the wheel was not yet invented. . . . The Rhodesian sun-wheel is therefore an original vision, presumably an archetypal sun-image. (CW18, par. 81)

Despite Jung's impression that the collective unconscious was a phenomenon waiting to be identified, some years were required for the idea to crystallize in his mind. The concept of archetypes first appeared in Jung's work in 1912 in the term *primordial image* (*The Psychology of the Unconscious*, republished as *Symbols of Transformation*, CW5, the publication that precipitated his break with Freud). Jung used the term to designate mythologems, legendary and fairy-tale motifs, and other images that express universal modes of human perception and behavior. In 1916 Jung introduced the term *dominants of the collective unconscious* (*Two Essays on Analytical Psychology*, CW7). The culmination of the theory of the collective unconscious came in 1919 when he introduced the term *archetype* ("Instinct and the Unconscious," CW8-III).

The Contents of the Collective Unconscious

To distinguish it from ego consciousness, which is subjective, Jung characterized the collective unconscious as the "objective psyche" because it is nonpersonal and, in its power to generate images and concepts, independent of consciousness. The personal unconscious also functions autonomously, that is, independently of the ego, but it is dependent on consciousness for its contents, which have been repressed. "Collective" contents are so designated because they are common to all humans and far broader in significance than the repressed remains of each person's experience.

Archetypes

The word *archetype* did not originate with Jung. The term had been used earlier by several philosophers, with different meanings, often including that of an ideal form. For example, "In Platonic philosophy, *archetypal* is applied to ideas or forms of natural objects held to have been present in the divine mind prior to creation" (*Oxford English Dictionary*). Writers in the popular press sometimes use the word *archetype* to mean a stereotype, that is, a fixed image.

In Analytical Psychology, the term refers neither to perfection nor to fixed images. Jung described archetypes as "*typical [uniform and regularly recurring] modes of apprehension*" (*CW8*, par. 280), that is, modes of perception. Thus, the archetype is a "possibility of representation" (*CW9–I*, par. 155), a predisposition to an image, that underlies and shapes a variety of specific images.

Thus, it is not the archetype itself that is experienced but, rather, its effects. Perhaps the concept would be understood better if the adjective *archetypal* were always used rather than its noun; images may be archetypal but are not in themselves archetypes. It is true that Jung sometimes used *archetype* to mean images and emotions but essentially he distinguished between the archetype as such and the images, emotions, and other behaviors effected by the archetype.

Archetypal material is often difficult to identify because it is intertwined with personal material. In Jung's view, however, such material appears in virtually pure form in fairy tales (see von Franz, 1970). Evidence of their collective nature is the fact that before modern communications joined all peoples in the world, almost identical motifs and tales appeared in widely separated cultures.

Instincts

Archetypes are not the only contents of the collective unconscious. Also included are instincts. Indeed, the collective unconscious is the source of instincts, in Jung's view. But whereas archetypes are typical modes of apprehension, instincts are *typical modes of action*: "*uniform and regularly recurring modes of action*" (*CW8*, par. 273).

Writing in 1919, Jung gave no indication of being aware that American academic psychology, with the advent of behaviorism in 1913, had rejected the concept of instincts in humans. Like Freud, Jung assumed that motives such as hunger and sex are accompanied by behavior patterns that are shared by humans generally. It is interesting to note that the idea of instincts has reappeared in academic psychology in such terms as *drive* and *species-specific behavior.*

Jung's view of instincts differs significantly from that of academic psychology in ways other than terminology. He saw instincts as reflections of the collective unconscious and, hence, as more predispositions to behaviors than the behaviors themselves.

Archetypes and instincts are related to each other like the colors in a spectrum of light: Archetypes can be said to be at the ultraviolet end, instincts at the infrared end. Both are expressions of the same "vital activity"—energy—in the unconscious. Jung maintained that it is impossible to say which is primary, archetypes or instincts; that is, apprehension of the situation or the impulse to act. Nevertheless, Jung sometimes described instincts as a subspecies of archetypes.

The Nature of Collective (Archetypal) Material

It is a mistake to think of a specific image, idea, or motif as inherited. Jung wrote:

> It would be absurd to assume that such variable representations could be inherited. The archetype is, on the contrary, an inherited *tendency* of the human mind to form representations of mythological motifs—representations that vary a great deal without losing their basic pattern. (CW18, par. 523)

He sometimes seemed to say that archetypes are specific to various cultures. He modified this idea considerably, however, with the observation that the archetypes are general to humankind but the images are shaped by specific history and culture. For example, individuals or cultures may have different images of the good mother or hostile brothers but the motif is the same whatever the image. Kettner (1967) provided a useful summary of the manner in which an archetype works: "a basic theme, recognizable patterns of variation, and the unique individual twist taken in a specific case" (p. 35).

Each category of archetypal contents can produce a variety of culture-specific images. For example, depending on the interests and experience of a twentieth-century dreamer, the "hero" could take the form of a medieval knight, a football player, a military leader, or an antiwar protester. Jung noted also that archetypal images often take mythological form. In Western culture, Greek mythologems are cited frequently as examples.

Comparable images often appear in modern form, however; "for instance, instead of the eagle of Zeus, or the great roc, there is an airplane; the fight with the dragon is a railway smash; the dragon-slaying hero is an operatic tenor; the Earth Mother is a stout lady selling vegetables; the Pluto who abducts Persephone is a reckless chauffeur, and so on" (CW15, par. 152).

Whatever the archetypal content, it is always bipolar in significance. "Just as [they] have a positive, favourable, bright side that points upwards, so also they have one that points downwards, partly negative and unfavourable, partly chthonic, but for the rest merely neutral" (CW9–I, par. 413). The specific image, however, can be either positive or negative, at least in the view of consciousness. Thus, although many people have a tendency to consider an archetypal dream to be favorable, it is not always so. It can reflect the destructive side of the personality as readily as the constructive.

Wherever archetypal images appear—in dreams, waking visions, or events—they tend to arouse intense emotions. Usually, they are numinous, that is, awe inspiring. Thus, they seem to come from a "different level" (CW17, par. 209) of the unconscious. (Some people believe that psychedelic drugs plunge individuals into transpersonal layers of the psyche.) An archetypal image may even have a cosmic quality: temporal or spatial infinity, movement at tremendous speeds or for enormous distances, astrological associations, or changes in the body's proportions.

Do we know how many archetypes there are? The question may not be meaningful because archetypes are patterns and processes rather than entities. Nevertheless, Jung offered at least two answers: (a) There is only one archetype, the collective unconscious, which is the producer of all archetypal images, and (b) there is an unlimited number of archetypes, as many as the typical situations in life. Some of the image-categories he listed, many of them in personified form, are: the Hero, Dragon, helpful animals, demons, Wise Old Man, Divine Child, Great Mother, anima and animus, anthropos (original human), Christ, duality, mandala, marriage, death and rebirth, hidden treasure, and transformative processes of alchemy.

A Jungian-oriented anthropologist, Jennette Jones (1979), has developed a classification of archetypal categories that organizes and augments Jung's list. Her first classification is that of geometric figures: mandala, tetrahedron, and pyramid. The second includes patterns and natural forms (adapted from Stevens, 1974). The patterns are spiral, meander (connecting same set of dots as efficiently as spiral), branching (compromise between spiral and meander), and explosion (longer total length, shorter average length in connecting dots); the natural forms are sun, moon, stars, earth, mountains, the four elements (earth, air, fire, water), plants, and animals. Jones's third category contains the personifications that Jung listed.

Jones's fourth category is that of alchemical processes. Although the medieval alchemists worked tirelessly at the concrete processes of transmuting base substances, such as lead, earth, water, or dung, into more valuable substances, such as gold, Jung saw their work as a projection of their own psychic individuation processes into the alchemical work. These intrapsychic processes are archetypal, just as are the inner psychic components, the shadow, for example, that presumably are the participants in the processes. An example is *calcinatio,* "the intense heating of a solid in order to drive off water and all other constituents that will volatilize. What remains is a fine, dry powder" (Edinger, 1978b, p. 17). The process of *calcinatio* corresponds to drying-out periods of life and dried out or dead areas of the psyche. There are many versions of the list and descriptions of the alchemical processes (e.g., Edinger, 1978b, 1978c, 1979).

Inferential Support for the Concepts

Jung arrived at his concepts of the collective unconscious and archetypes empirically and he upheld them primarily by arguments based on analogies with different fields of knowledge. As a physician he observed the tendency of people to lack awareness not only of the common psychic structure but, also, of the common physical structure. He pointed out that not knowing a body part or a psychological characteristic does not negate its existence. "Does [man] know he ought to have an appendix? He is just born with it. Millions of people do not know they have a thymus, but they have it" (CW18, par. 84). These organs and our entire bodies, in fact, are in their current forms because of our biological evolution. Indeed, the vestiges we carry within tell us of changes that have occurred in the human body over the aeons. Similarly, people do not know that they carry "psychic organs"—archetypes.

The human brain also has evolved over the millenia, and with the changes came new dimensions of the mind: " . . . there is no doubt that the strengthening of mental power came with the vast expansion of the cerebral cortex of New Brain in man" (Hawkes, 1963, p. 165). Some of the potential for images produced by minds when the brain was less developed seem to be vestigially present now. If the body has retained vestiges of organs, why should not the mind retain vestiges of thought patterns?

To clarify the concept of archetypes, as a way of looking at a body of data, Jung used the parallel of the botanical system. He stated emphatically:

> Critics have contented themselves with asserting that no such archetypes exist. Certainly they do not exist, anymore than a botanical system exists in nature! But will anyone deny the occurrence and continual repetition of certain morphological and functional similarities? It is much the same thing in principle with typical figures of the unconscious. They are forms existing *a priori* or biological norms of psychic activity. (*CW9–I*, par. 309n)

Consonant with his understanding that archetypes are recognizable only by the effects they produce, Jung likened them to "the axial system of a crystal, which, as it were, preforms the crystalline structure in the mother liquid, although it has no material existence of its own" (*CW9–I*, par. 155). Archetypes can be said to "arrange the psychic elements into certain images" (*CW11*, par. 222n) by a comparable process.

Further support for Jung's theories of archetypes and the collective unconscious can be inferred from the fact that they appear under various names in scholarly works of many disciplines. In anthropology, for example, "the term 'représentations collectives' used by Lévy-Bruhl to denote the symbolic figures in the primitive view of the world, could easily be applied to unconscious contents as well, since it means practically the same thing" (*CW9–I*, par. 5. The recognition that the customs of preliterate peoples reflect underlying archetypes has occasioned the inclusion of the study of "primitive practices" in the training of Jungian analysts.).

Another anthropologist, Claude Lévi-Strauss (1967) and a psychologist, Jean Piaget (1970), "are embarked on parallel scientific enterprises" (Gardner, 1974, p. xii), which together comprise structuralism; it seems to provide additional confirmation for archetypal theory. These two investigators hypothesized that the mind has preformed categories that enable humans to acquire language and produce similar organizational forms in widely separated societies. Lévi-Strauss was convinced "that human societies, like individual human beings (at play, in their dreams, or in moments of delirium), never create absolutely; all they can do is to chose certain combinations from a repertoire of ideas" (cited by Gardner, 1974, p. 118). This repertoire is yet to be identified completely but seems indistinguishable from the concept of archetypes. Similarly, "Piaget has developed a theory of perception which emphasizes the amount of active construction involved in judging visual arrays and illusions" (Gardner, 1974, p. 105). This active construction seems to be the equivalent of a predisposition to an image; that is, an archetype.

Noam Chomsky (1968) and other psycholinguists focused on the human capacity to learn language as evidence of universals in mental content. They pointed to the fact that children, by the age of five or six, can understand and produce a much larger number of phrases and sentences than they have actually encountered. The ability to do so appears to stem from a preformed mental pattern, a predisposition to an image.

Some of the most enthusiastic support for the concept of the collective unconscious has come from people in the arts. This acceptance is due, apparently, to the fact that much of the subject matter of all the arts is based on archetypal themes and forms. The common ground for Jungian psychology and the arts is also found in the Jungian writings that include analyses of works of art, especially of literature, which contain remarkable psychological insights. For example, the archetypal themes developed in such books as Herman Melville's Moby Dick (see Edinger, 1978) and Emily Brontë's Wuthering Heights (see Hannah, 1971) are rich lodes for exploration. Some Jungian writings take specific themes and trace them through works of art, for example, "Poetry and the Anima" (Hough, 1973).

The theory of the collective unconscious can be inferred further from human creativity and its origin in a source beyond personal experience. Examples abound, not only in the arts but also in science, human relations, and other fields of endeavor. One example is the solution of a difficult problem by a flash of insight after extensive, methodical, but seemingly unfruitful work, such as the discovery of the structure of the DNA as a double helix. (This event was described by Watson, 1968.) Such insight cannot be explained by previous learning; it seems to come from a source deep within the mind, perhaps the collective unconscious. If scientists eventually find a specific seat of creativity in the brain, that finding could confirm Jung's hypothesis that the capacity for creativity is innate to humans but depends on the interaction of experience with capacity.

Living as we do in an age of individualism, with its emphasis on the ego, rather than on the Self, we have lost sight, largely, of the commonalities that bind all of mankind into one species and of the history that links us irrevocably to our common origins and development. Perhaps if Jung had used a term more compatible with individualism, such as "creative unconscious" rather than "collective unconscious," the concept would have a wider acceptance.

Empirical Support for the Collective Unconscious

The appearance of similar archetypal images in widely divergent cultural settings helped Jung to hypothesize the concept of the collective unconscious. He validated his findings to some extent by studying, for example, themes and images of the myths and fairy tales of geographically separated cultures. However, because of the enormous leaps in communication in the twentieth century, it has become virtually impossible to continue the use of this method of validating the concept; commonalities in various cultures are easily explained today by direct communication. It seems likely that future achievements in validating the existence of the collective unconscious must come from studies of brain structure and function. Some such evidence has been found. When Penfield (1952) applied electrical stimulation to the brains of human subjects, he found that the patterns in the sensory area differed from those in the memory areas, and concluded that the sensory patterns are innate. Penfield reported:

Stimulation of the visual cortex produces bright, lighted objects, such as stars or squares or streaks, or the opposite, i.e., black forms. . . . They have form and movement but they do not resemble anything which the subject has seen in his environment. He sees no people, no remembered object, no panorama.

The responses from stimulation of sensory areas follow what may be called inborn patterns. They are the same regardless of what an individual's past experience may have been. (p. 181)

More recently, Rossi (1977) hypothesized that the differences in functioning of various parts of the brain are related to the now-familiar discrepancies between the left and right hemispheres. He wrote, "In sharp contrast with the concepts of ego and complex which are so closely associated with the use of words and the left hemisphere, Jung's concepts of archetype, collective unconscious and symbol are more closely associated with the use of the imagery, gestalt and the visuospatial characteristics of right hemispheric functioning" (p. 42). Rossi's hypothesis is intriguing but it seems largely speculative, whereas Penfield's hypothesis is supported by experimental data.

Although its investigators do not use the word *instinct* as Jung did, the rapidly developing field of ethology is providing evidence for innate behavior potentials which may be examples of archetypelike predispositions. For example, ethologists' findings give evidence of imprinting, the phenomenon in which the experience of an animal at a critical period of early development determines its primary affective attachment and, therefore, determines much of its lifelong social behavior. Imprinting is known best through the work of the Austrian zoologist Konrad Lorenz. He showed that goslings become attached—as evidenced by what or whom they follow—to whatever object is in their line of vision at the critical period of about fifteen to seventeen hours after hatching. Although most goslings were imprinted to their mothers, some were imprinted to adult males of their species, and others, to Lorenz himself. The phenomenon is observed most clearly, of course, in young birds, which can be kept apart from their mothers in the first few days of life. Something similar seems to happen, however, in other animals, including mammals (which usually are with their mothers for a time after birth), and is conceivably present in human beings (see Hess, 1958). Thus, ethology, with its concept of "innate releasing mechanisms," which Tinbergen (1963) equated with an animal's being "selectively responsive" (p. 425), seems virtually equivalent to the Jungian concept of a "predisposition of 'readiness'... to apperceive a universal, emotional core human experience, myth, or thought-image-fantasy" (Maduro and Wheelwright, 1977, p. 94). That the ethological findings are compatible with, and perhaps supportive of, the concept of archetypes was confirmed by Konrad Lorenz. He assured von Franz (1975) that "he [accepted] Jung's theory of archetypes in principle" (p. 127).

Further empirical support for Jung's theory of the collective unconscious is found in the fact that people in different parts of the world who were not in communication with each other "invented" the same artifacts. One example is the pyramid, which was conceived of in such widely separated places as Egypt, Thailand, and Mexico. Another example is the wheel; it appeared in the Mediterranean area during the Bronze Age and was put to use for vehicles pulled by animals. In Central America, the Mayans (or their predecessors) also invented the wheel but, perhaps because they had no draft animals, they used the wheels for toys. Anthropologist Jacquetta Hawkes (1963) upheld Jung's theory by arguing that

> When two peoples at some distance from one another possess some peculiar implement, design, myth, in common, it may well have been transferred by trade, migration, or a spreading influence. These contacts should always be looked for, but if they cannot be detected, then there remains the alternative that the trait represents two independent expressions of a common mental pattern. (p. 168)

One form of this common mental pattern is the tendency to impose on stimuli a perceptual structure that is more defined than is warranted by the raw stimuli. The research of Ross (1976) provides an example. When targets were squares in a general way, adult subjects perceived the targets as "more perfectly square, with more perfect edges than any real square" (p. 86), that is, the subjects imposed on them a kind of ideal squareness (reminiscent of Plato's ideal forms). The ideal squareness went beyond observation to a mental source that seems equivalent to Jung's archetype.

Another example of a common mental pattern was described by Fodor and his associates (1975). They found that infants of fourteen to eighteen weeks old can discriminate syllables that have a similar consonant sound from those that lack such similarities. Thus, the infants seemed to draw on an unlearned resource that provides the kind of pattern that Jung identified. Indeed, the field of comparative linguistics is full of examples of mental functioning that is similar in all humans.

A third way of imposing perceptual structures on stimuli is in the kinds of images that are stimulated by projective tests. Mc-Cully (1971) found that many responses to the plates of the Rorschach test, for example, reflected archetypal themes. In one instance, a twenty-two-year-old woman responded to Plate I (one detail of which is often seen as a woman's figure) with the words: "Two griffins, wings, heads, four feet; half-bird, half-lion" (p. 86). The fact that griffins are mythological figures contributed to McCully's interpretation of this response as being archetypally based.

Further examples of archetypal responses to projective tests are provided by the thematic apperception test (TAT). Murray (1938), the originator of the test, found that "the biographical facts did not convince us that external occurrences . . . were the major determinants of infantile complexes. . . . We are finally driven, I think, to Jung's conception of [archetypally] determined sequences of fantasy" (pp. 737–38). Spiegelman (1955) also found that many TAT responses can be understood archetypally. For example, "the 'father card' in the Thematic Apperception Test (Card 7BM) may be assumed to constellate the individual's father archetype and its derivative (e.g., his actual father, father surrogates, or other individuals upon whom he has projected the father archetype)" (p. 256).

Much of the latter half of Jung's *Collected Works* is made up of instances of archetypal images, along with the amplification and interpretation of them in terms of human experience. A classic example is the following:

> The idea of a second birth is found at all times and in all places. In the earliest beginnings of medicine it was a magical . . . experience; it is the key idea in medieval, occult philosophy, and, last but not least, it is an infantile fantasy occurring in numberless children, large and small, who believe that their parents are not their real parents but merely foster-parents to whom they were handed over. Benvenuto Cellini also had this idea, as he himself related in his autobiography. (*CW9–I*, par. 94)

Evidence for the archetypal nature of the rebirth image was also presented by Krimsky (1960). He found that catatonics are more strongly preoccupied with rebirth fantasies than are non-catatonics. If, as Jung suggested, psychosis (e.g., catatonic schizophrenia) is a state of being overwhelmed by archetypes (see Chapter 9), then Krimsky's data tend to support the archetypal nature of images of rebirth. Some people seem to experience rebirth in Christian baptism or conversion, others, in the belief in reincarnation. However, like all archetypal images, those of rebirth are possible in each person but are not necessarily manifested in everyone.

Uses of the Concepts

The centrality, to Analytical Psychology, of the concept of archetypes may be attributed, in part, to the archetype's role in relation to complexes, which were all-important to Jung. He specified an archetypal core for each complex. In addition, the concept affords vastly increased possibilities for understanding dreams and other human behavior. Its significance is emphasized further by James Hillman's (1970) proposal that Jung's psychology be renamed archetypal psychology:

> To call this psychology today archetypal follows from its historical development. The earlier terms [Complex and Analytical Psychology] have, in a sense, been superseded by the concept of the archetype, which Jung had not yet worked out when he named his psychology. The archetype is the most ontologically fundamental of all Jung's psychological concepts, with the advantage of precision and yet by definition partly indefinable and open. (p. 216)

The uses of the concept of archetypes, however, can be seen as both theoretical and practical. Jung spent a great proportion of his time, especially in his later years, in studying archetypal material in order to understand better the workings of the psyche. Many of his students, past and present, continue this work and glean many insights that enrich the Jungian theory of personality. For example, von Franz (1972), from her study of creation myths of various cultures, gained understanding of creative persons and creativity in personality. She noted, for example, that some myths tell of creation from above, others from below. When someone dreams of creation from above, that person is in danger of inflation (grandiosity), perhaps that "he has had a great illumination about which he must tell the world" (p. 48). If creation in the dream is from below, it is likely "that if some sudden instinctual urge should come up to do something, [the dreamer] should not repress it" (p. 47) but should carry it out.

The usefulness of the concepts of archetypes and of the collective unconscious makes it regrettable that so much controversy surrounds them. At the opposite extreme from the people who reject the idea of archetypes, however, are those who consider everything to be archetypal, perhaps on the ground that everything that is actual had to be potential first. Such a view seems less than helpful; archetypal loses meaning if there is nothing that is not archetypal.

The practical application of the concepts of archetypes and the collective unconscious is extensive. Some specifics of this application, amplification of dreams, are presented in Chapter 17.

Part II

Varieties of
Psychic Structure

4

Attitude and Function Types

Everyone, according to Jungian personality theory, has an ego, a shadow, and the other components of the psyche, each with individual characteristics. In addition, from observations of himself, his patients, and other persons, Jung identified several dimensions that combine variously to create what he called personality types. These dimensions are the *attitudes*—extraversion and introversion—and the *functions*—sensation, intuition, thinking, and feeling. Although Jung referred to them as "types," he treated them as personality dimensions. Each person has all of them but in different degrees; one attitude and one or two functions tend to be dominant. To distinguish a "type" of personality, consequently, one must look to the attitude and function(s) that are most developed in a given individual.

Some people reject the idea of Jung's typology on the ground that it results in consigning all individuals to pigeonholes. If such categorizing were the intent or even the inevitable effect of the types schema, it would be unacceptable to virtually every Jungian and most other persons who are concerned with individual development. Jung's typology is not a confining set of categories but, rather, an aid to understanding and appreciating the individual ways in which people view the world.

Attitude Types

After parting from Freud, Jung was deeply distressed over the break; indeed, many years elapsed before he could achieve a significant degree of objectivity about it. In trying to analyze the reasons for it, he devoted a great deal of thought to the quarrel between Freud and Alfred Adler, which had led to Adler's withdrawal from Freud's circle in 1911.

Adler, eleven years younger than Freud, had been a valued member of the Vienna psychoanalytic group from its inception in 1902. When his differences with Freud became irreconcilable, he and six of his adherents resigned from the Viennese Psychoanalytic Society and formed what became known later as the Society for Individual Psychology. Adler's disagreement with Freud arose over the etiology of neurosis. To Freud, the origin was sexual conflict; to Adler, the origins lay in the individual's relation to society and, especially, in the will to power.

Why, Jung pondered, had such insuperable ideological differences emerged between Freud and Adler? Both men had been reared in Jewish homes on the outskirts of Vienna, both were products of Vienna's intellectual environment, and both had pursued the same interests for at least a decade. Yet Adler developed a theoretical stance that was unacceptable to Freud. Their differences, Jung hypothesized, must lie in different ways of perceiving the world. His explorations of history and literature revealed comparable pairs of ideological rivals among the church fathers (see later section of this chapter); among writers, such as Spitteler and Goethe; and in mythological characters, such as Apollo and Dionysus. To Jung, these rivalries indicated two basic and conflicting perceptual modes. He labeled them "attitudes" of "introversion" and "extraversion." In applying his theory to Freud and Adler, Jung identified Freud as extraverted, Adler as introverted:

> The basic formula with Freud is . . . sexuality, which expresses the strongest relation between subject and object; with Adler it is the power of the subject, which secures him most effectively against

the object and guarantees him an impregnable isolation that abolishes all relationships. Freud would like to ensure the undisturbed flow of instinct towards its object; Adler would like to break the baleful spell of the object in order to save the ego from suffocating in its own defensive armour. Freud's view is essentially extraverted, Adler's introverted. (CW6, par. 91)

Not everyone agrees that Freud was the extravert and Adler the introvert, but there is little dispute that there were personality differences between them.

Description of the Attitude Types

The extraverted attitude is characterized by a flow of psychic energy toward the outer world, an interest in events, people, and things, a relation with them, and a dependence on them. Thus, the flow of psychic energy is toward the *object*. The extraverted person is likely to adjust well to the environment: to be sociable, enthusiastic; and optimistic. However, such a person also may tend to be superficial, too ready to accept conventional standards, dependent on making a good impression, afraid of the inner world, and, perhaps, disinclined to be alone.

The introverted attitude is characterized by a flow of psychic energy inward, the concentration on subjective factors and inner responses. Thus, the energy moves toward the *subject*. An introvert prefers his or her own thoughts to conversation with others and, consequently, enjoys being alone. Such a person tends to have only a few friends but to be very loyal to them. An introvert is likely to be clumsy in a social situation, perhaps too outspoken or ridiculously polite, and may be overconscientious, pessimistic, and critical.

In each person either extraversion or introversion is the "attitude of consciousness." Thus, one attitude is dominant in the person's behavior, thoughts, and feelings, and it is largely under the control of the ego. Jung posited, however, that both attitudes are potential in every personality. The attitude that is not under the control of the ego remains in the unconscious and, hence, is quite awkward. For example, an introvert who attempts to communicate may chatter about rare birds to someone who has no interest in them; an extravert who seeks to reflect on a variety of feelings may focus only on morbid fears.

Historical Evidence for the Attitude Types

Jung found convincing evidence of the existence of the two attitude types in the histories of many periods and countries, suggesting that the classification is not limited to a time and place. He traced the phenomenon in some detail in *Psychological Types* (*CW6*), beginning with the church fathers at the end of the second century and the early part of the third, and continuing with religious and secular intellectual leaders in subsequent centuries. For example, in the ninth century, Abbot Paschasius Radbertus propounded the doctrine of transubstantiation (that the wine and bread of communion are transformed into the actual blood and body of Christ). Inasmuch as this doctrine emphasized the external and concrete in religious experience, Jung classified Radbertus's view as an extraverted one. Scotus Erigena, a philosopher of the early Middle Ages, took the opposite view of communion. Jung saw his view as introverted and "nothing more than a commemoration of that last supper which Jesus celebrated with his disciples, a view in which all reasonable men in every age will concur" (*CW6*, par. 36). Thus Jung disclosed his own preference for an introverted attitude.

Box (1966) added a recent historical observation that echoes Jung's researches. In a study of the contrasting doctrines of freedom in the works of the English philosopher William Temple (1881–1944) and the Russian philosopher Nikolai Berdyaev (1874–1948), Box discerned an underlying extraversion-introversion dimension. Temple, who seemed to be at home in the outer world, was evidently an extravert; he had grown up in a relatively flexible social milieu in which freedom was not a problem. Berdyaev, on the other hand, grew up under the rigid, restrictive regime of the czars; he was alienated from the world and had to struggle to win his inner freedom from the objective world. He was an introvert.

Formal Scientific Evidence for the Attitude Types

Many years after Jung hypothesized, on the basis of clinical and historical evidence, that individuals differ on the introversion-extraversion (IE) dimension, several psychologists tested the hypothesis and defined the dimension with the help of factor analysis. For example, Eysenck (1969), who is British and has a different theoretical orientation from Jung's, found that extraverts are high on sociability and impulsiveness, whereas introverts are low on these factors. Eysenck and some other investigators usually mentioned extraversion first (EI); Jung's practice was to list introversion first (IE).

In addition to defining the dimension somewhat differently, some theorists have used different terminology, such as Rorschach's (1964) "introversive" and "extratensive." Also, some investigators (e.g., Carrigan, 1960) doubted that IE is a unitary dimension. Nevertheless, the evidence for one underlying dimension exists.

Steele and Kelly (1976), for example, found a high correlation between the Myers-Briggs Type Indicator (MBTI), a self-report forced-choice inventory derived from a type theory very similar to Jung's and the Eysenck Personality Questionnaire (EPQ), an unpublished self-report inventory that is based on the Eysenck personality inventory. The EPQ measures EI according to Eysenck's particular definition. The subjects of Steele's and Kelly's study were ninety-three paid volunteer undergraduates (fifty-four females, thirty-nine males), 18 to 22 years old, with a mean age of 19.7 years. The EPQ was given first, followed by the MBTI. One week later, the subjects were retested with the same instruments given in the same order. Because the male and female initial correlation matrices showed no significant differences, the final correlations were based on both sexes combined. Reliabilities on the two tests were .88 for the EI scale on the EPQ, and .89 for the EI scale on the MBTI. The EI scales on the two tests had a correlation of .74. The investigators noted, "Despite the differences in the theoretical orientations of Jung and Eysenck, the high correlation of the MBTI and EPQ Extraversion-Introversion scales demonstrates an area of equivalency at the self-report questionnaire level" (p. 691).

An additional type of evidence for the EI dimension is "construct validity," the confirmation by experiment of predicted differences in attitude or behavior between introverts and extraverts. For example, Palmiere (1972) studied the hypothesis that introverts produce a larger quantity of fantasy than do extraverts. Using the MBTI she selected 25 "extreme" introverts and 25 "extreme" extraverts from a pool of 114 undergraduates and analyzed their responses to selected cards of the Thematic Apperception Test. These responses were quantified according to numbers of words and ideas. Higher "fantasy scores" (both more words and more ideas) were produced, as expected, by introverted subjects.

Frequency of Introverts and Extraverts

Although we cannot determine unequivocally what determines attitude type in an individual, three studies, conducted at widely separated times and in different locations, have given some indication of the relative incidence of introverts and extraverts in the general population. In their study of two hundred responses to an early version of the Gray-Wheelwrights Test (GWT; Jungian Type Survey), Gray and Wheelwright (1946) found that 54% were more introverted, while 46% were more extraverted. Myers and Briggs (1962) used the MBTI to study 8,561 subjects, ranging in age from junior high school students through adults. In this large sample 55% were extraverted, 45% introverted. Neither set of investigators specified the sources of their subjects.

Determinants of Attitude Type

Even investigators who affirm the existence of the attitudes do not agree on what determines the predominance of one attitude over the other in an individual. There is considerable agreement, however, that introversion and extraversion are equally normal. Jung's concept of introversion is not the same as the "Social Introversion" scale of the Minnesota Multiphasic Personality Inventory (MMPI), which, like other scales making up the Inventory, measures a pathological factor. Jung's perception that neither introversion nor extraversion is pathological has been confirmed repeatedly by Eysenck (1952) and his associates, using the Eysenck Personality Inventory. Other investigators, using different instruments, have obtained similar results. Two studies (Lovell, 1945; North, 1949) used the Guilford Personality Inventory. A third study (Reyburn and Raath, 1950) used a rating scale. In all three, EI and neuroticism were found to be orthogonal—relatively independent—factors.

Determinants of attitude type may include "some kind of biological foundation" (CW6, par. 558), although Jung did not specify what this foundation might be. There is a possibility that it is a difference in brain function, a hypothesis that is suggested by two studies.

Savage (1964), an Australian, used the Maudsley Personality Inventory (MPI), the precursor to the EPI, to obtain measures of extraversion (E) on twenty female students with an average age of eighteen years eight months. The respondents scoring high on E were classed as extraverts, those scoring low, introverts. When the electrocerebral activity for each subject was measured by amplitude of alpha rhythm with eyes closed in an EEG, the alpha amplitude of extraverts was found to be significantly higher than that of introverts.

Gale, Coles, and Blaydon (1969) replicated and extended Savage's results. These English investigators tested five male and nineteen female undergraduate students who had a mean age of twenty-one years four months. The subjects were divided into two groups: twelve extraverts with a mean E score on the EPI of 17.3 and twelve introverts with a mean E score of 8.1. It was found in this study that when the subjects' eyes were closed the extravert EEG was higher in integrated output across the whole measured range, with the divergence in output being greater in the lower alpha range. Moreover, when the subjects' eyes were open even a gross filter discriminated between extraverts and introverts.

Some investigators have found the biological foundation for attitude type to be genetic. Under Eysenck's (1956) direction, his associates McLeod and Blewett studied twenty-six pairs of identical twins, thirteen male and thirteen female, and twenty-six pairs of fraternal twins, also thirteen male and thirteen female, averaging thirteen years ten months in age. All were secondary school students in London, England. EI was measured by a factor analysis of several tests of intelligence, personality, and autonomic functioning. The identical twins, who had 100 percent common heredity, were significantly more alike in EI ($r = .499$) than the fraternal twins ($r = 1.331$), who had the more limited genetic similarity of ordinary siblings. The investigators had no explanation for the negative correlation between fraternal twins, except possible measurement error. (Another possible reason is that pairs of twins, especially same-sex twins, may tend to develop different skills in order to differentiate themselves from each other.)

Gottesman (1963) studied thirty-four pairs each of volunteer identical and same-sex fraternal twins from three school districts in the Minneapolis–St. Paul area. The MMPI Social Introversion Scale showed a "predominance of variance" (H = .71) accounted for by heredity. That is, the pairs of fraternal twins differed so much more from each other that the findings indicate that Social Introversion is 71 percent due to genetic factors. Although the Social Introversion Scale measures introversion according to a definition that is quite different from Jung's, Gottesman's results suggest that personality factors such as introversion and extraversion can have a large degree of heritability.

Despite the importance of biological factors in determining whether a person is more extraverted or more introverted, environmental factors also play a significant role. Siegelman (1965) studied two sample groups of fifty-seven males and ninety-seven females who made up the total enrollment in six sections of a child-development course at The City College of New York. The mean age was twenty-two for males and twenty for females. The Roe-Siegelman Parent-Child Relations Questionnaire, which is designed to measure adult retrospective reports of early parental behavior, was administered, together with the Cattell Sixteen Personality Factor Questionnaire (16PF). The investigator found that parental behaviors correlated significantly with EI in the grown children. Introverted males reported rejecting fathers and mothers, and extraverted females reported loving fathers. Although correlation does not demonstrate causation (a child's introverted behavior may elicit as well as result from parental rejection), the results support the influence of environment on the development of introversion and extraversion.

One important factor, cultural influence, has been tested little in controlled studies. An exception is a study by Gray (1946) which produced some results that seem to' reflect differences among cultures and some that do not. According to their scores on the GWT, 882 natives of the United States were more extraverted to a significant degree than 118 persons of several other nationalities. There were no differences in attitude type, however, between 26 natives of the United Kingdom and the dominions as compared with 92 control subjects who were born neither in that confederation nor in the United States. Another result was that among 47 Jews who were compared to 953 Gentile controls, there was a slight but not statistically significant tendency to introversion. A study by Cattell and Warburton (1961) found that Americans are more extraverted than Britons. These investigators administered the Cattell 16PF Questionnaire to 112 British and 604 American university students. The Americans were more extraverted at the .01 level of confidence.

Significance of the IE Dimension

The attitude types have great significance for the psychology of individual differences and for clinical work. Practitioners in the applied fields have benefited greatly from understanding the different modes in which people normally perceive and respond to their worlds. In counseling and psychotherapy, for example, many problems are alleviated when clients can be helped to understand that interpersonal conflict often arises out of different perceptions of the world rather than out of malice or egocentrism.

A study related to vocational choice was conducted by Greenfield (1969). He found that 125 Jewish "clergymen" who persisted in their vocational choice were more extraverted, whereas 194 nonpersisters were more introverted.

Appropriate personnel placement and job selection often can be expedited by attention to attitude differences, according to empirical studies such as Pardes's (1965). He found that when presented with repetitive, monotonous tasks, extraverts tend to report boredom more than do introverts. The investigator measured extraversion with the MPI, boredom by a ten-point boredom scale. The tasks were the "Cancellation of A's" and the Partington Pathways Test, which requires subjects to draw lines between scattered numbers.

Monotony seems not to be on the same continuum as sensory deprivation. In two studies (Rossi and Solomon, 1965; Tranel, 1962) introverts were found to be less tolerant of sensory deprivation than extraverts. Rossi and Solomon hypothesized that this difference is related to introverts' greater inclination to be passive and to follow instructions, in contrast to extraverts' greater action-orientation and inclination to modify external conditions to alleviate discomfort.

The Function Types

The IE typology, which Jung had identified by 1913 (*CW3*, pars. 418–21 and *CW6*, pars. 858–82), proved rather quickly to be insufficient to account for all the dimensions of conscious personality. Jung described his experience, in part, as follows:

> Scarcely had I published the first formulation of my criteria when I discovered to my dismay that somehow or other I had been taken in by them. Something was amiss. I had tried to explain too much in too simple a way, as often happens in the first joy of discovery.
>
> What struck me now was the undeniable fact [that] while people may be classed as introverts or extraverts, this does not account for the tremendous differences between individuals in either class. So great, indeed, are these differences that I was forced to doubt whether I had observed correctly in the first place. It took nearly ten years of observation and comparison to clear up this doubt.
>
> ... To observe and recognize the differences gave me comparatively little trouble, the root of my difficulties being now, as before, the problem of criteria. How was I to find suitable terms for the characteristic differences? . . .
>
> I realize that no sound criteria were to be found in the chaos of contemporary psychology, that they had first to be created, not out of thin air, but on the basis of the invaluable preparatory work done by many men whose names no history of psychology will pass over in silence. (*CW6*, pars. 943–45)

Jung then launched into a description of the function types: sensation, intuition, thinking, and feeling.

Characteristics of the Function Types

Initially, Jung thought of thinking and intuition as introverted, and feeling and sensation as extraverted. By the time he wrote *Psychological Types* (*CW6*, first published 1921), however, he recognized that either attitude could be associated with any function.

Sensation is the function by which one perceives—ascertains—that something exists. Indeed, the German word *Empfindung*, which Jung used and which has been translated as "sensation," can also be translated as "perception." (The *MBTI Manual*, 1962, has substituted the word *sensing*, possibly because the term implies the five senses and "sensation" has a connotation of excitement.) A person with dominant sensation (sensate) is interested in facts and things, that is, in the objective universe. The term *sensate* is not used much but seems to be an apt parallel to "intuitive," "thinker," and "feeler." In my view, bodily experiences, including kinesthetic ones, are of great importance to a sensate. People often see such a person as matter-of-fact, down-to-earth. Many scientists probably are sensates; they tend to be fascinated with facts and with discovering and observing how things work. Sensation focuses on specifics in the here and now, however, often to the point of not being able "to see the *woods* for the trees."

In an extraverted person, sensation functions to make objects the important elements. The extravert with dominant sensation is likely, for example, to notice and remember everything in a room, and to take delight in material things, perhaps because of their beauty and orderliness.

In introverted persons, sensation functions to make the effects of objects more important than the objects themselves. For example, a favorite color arouses a subjective emotion, such as joy or sadness. Many artists and musicians are probably of this type as well as people who enjoy physical activities such as athletics and dancing.

Intuition tells what the possibilities are; it "sees around corners" and produces hunches. As Jung explained, intuition "presents a content, whole and complete, without our being able to explain or discover how this content came into existence" (*CW6*, par. 770). Thus, this function mediates perceptions by way of the unconscious. According to Wheelwright (1973), intuition "works when there are no facts, nor moral supports, no proven theories, only possibilities. . . . In conversation, intuitives leap from point to point, [leaving other people to] fill in all the gaps. They live in the future or in the past, and are most uncomfortable in the present" (pp. 12–13). Thus, intuitives are unable "to see the *trees* for the woods."

Persons with dominant intuition sometimes feel that their perceptions are considered by other people to be inferior because it is difficult to specify the source of intuitions. Well-developed intuition may produce perceptions that are as correct as sensation-derived perceptions, although each kind is obtained in a different way.

An extraverted person who has dominant intuition enjoys anything new in the outer environment, is imaginative and innovative, and may become completely absorbed in a project for a time. Completing the plans may be difficult, however, because the person's attention is easily sidetracked by new possibilities. An introverted person with intuition as the dominant function is concerned with the dark background of experiences: the subjective and strange. Inner images are all-important; they may include visions, exotic fantasies, and extrasensory perceptions.

Thinking is the function that categorizes and assigns meanings to the elements perceived. A person with a developed thinking function can analyze cause and effect, define alternatives, and ascertain truths and falsehoods. When thinking is functioning well, the person can reason objectively.

The thinking of an extraverted person serves to put order into the external world. The person's interest is in the result, not in the idea behind it. Pragmatic politicians, who are concerned more with finding ways to reach their goals than with the goals themselves, are likely to be extraverted thinking types. The thinking of an introvert makes the person interested in abstraction, principles, and putting order into the bases on which one acts, that is, defining goals. Many philosophically minded people are of this type.

Feeling is the function that evaluates the object, determines whether it is desirable or undesirable and its degree of importance. In this technical sense feeling is quite different from some of the commonly understood meanings of the term. The phrase "It feels soft (or hard)," expresses what Jung called sensation; "I have a feeling that something is going to happen," reflects intuition; and "I feel depressed," refers to emotion. Feeling must be distinguished from emotion, especially. Developed feeling is a function of consciousness, under the control of the ego, whereas emotion (see Chapter 6) is a response that arises out of the unconscious and is likely to be connected with whichever of the four functions is inferior.

An extraverted person with a dominant feeling function places a high value on harmonious interpersonal relations, serves them by being aware of what is happening to other people, and thus is perceived as warm. Such a person is enthusiastic, spontaneous, and imaginative but holds traditional values and can be so nice that the niceness is a burden to others.

In an introvert the feeling function may give an impression of coldness because the person is undemonstrative. When the feeling of an introvert is expressed, however, it tends to be disconcertingly genuine, contrasting with the conventionality of extraverted feeling. Introverted feeling is probably intense, moreover, and may carry deep compassion.

Frequencies of Function Preferences

Two studies in which different instruments were used give some indication of the frequency of each function preference in the populations tested. Gray and Wheelwright (1946) obtained two hundred responses to an early version of the GWT, from respondents who were mostly physicians; 71% preferred sensation over intuition and 29% preferred intuition over sensation, whereas thinking was preferred over feeling by 60% and feeling over thinking by 40%. Wheelwright (1980) hypothesized that physicians tend to prefer sensation and thinking even more than the general population. This hypothesis seems to be supported by the Myers and Briggs (1962) study of 8,561 persons from the general population, of whom 51% preferred intuition over sensation and 56% preferred thinking over feeling.

Interrelations among the Functions

Usually, one function is especially well developed in each person. It is known as the *superior* function. Many persons have a fairly well-developed *secondary* function and relatively few have some conscious use of a third function. The fourth, and least developed, hence *inferior* function, remains unconscious —part of the shadow.

According to Jung's observations, the paired functions are incompatible, thinking with feeling, sensation with intuition. That is, each pair tends to be mutually exclusive; if a person is determining whether something is true or false (thinking), evaluation of its relative importance (feeling) must be postponed. Similarly, if one is ascertaining facts (sensation), consideration of their possibilities (intuition) is likely to produce inaccuracies.

Despite being opposites, each pair has the common characteristic of perception or judgment. That is, sensation and intuition are both ways of perceiving; thinking and feeling are both ways of judging. Sensation and intuition are nonrational in the sense that they simply receive perceptions without selection or bringing order to the perceptions that are received. Thinking and feeling are both rational in the sense of ordering and judging: Thinking judgment works on the basis of true-false; feeling judgment, on the basis of desirable-undesirable. Each pair can be seen as a dimension: introversion-extraversion (IE), thinking-feeling (TF) and sensation-intuition (SU on the GWT; SN on the MBTI).

Jung's evidence for the pairing of the functions was clinical. He observed that persons with developed feeling or intuition, for example, tended to be especially undeveloped in thinking or sensation. Some students of types theory have come to question, however, whether Jung's pairings are quite so clear-cut.

In part, the questioning is based on recent developments in the study of brain function. Goodman (1978), a non-Jungian psychologist, stated, "There are two brains in your head: one linear, logical, conforming to precedent; the other, integrative, holistic, and creative" (p. 44). These "two brains" are not strictly identified with the left and right hemispheres, although they were discovered as a result of "split brain" surgery. At first glance, they seem to correspond to thinking and intuition, which are not opposites in Jung's schema. However, it is possible to view the two as corresponding roughly to Jung's thinking-plus-sensation and intuition-plus-feeling combinations. Alternatively, they can be seen as corresponding to the judgment-perception dimension which is hypothesized by the designers of the MBTI. Zaidel (1978) cautioned, however, that hemispheric specialization falls on a continuum: "a matter of degree rather than an all-or-none concept." Rossi (1977) hypothesized that introversion, intuition, and sensation are right hemispheric. He found supportive emphasis in the work of Fischer (1975) in which 90 percent of the college subjects who enjoyed volunteering to explore and "travel into inner space" scored high as introverts, intuitives, and feelers on the MBTI.

All these dichotomies should be taken as merely suggestive, however. Additional variables, such as right-handedness and left-handedness and the back and the front of the brain on simultaneous readings must be taken into account. Goleman (1977) pointed out that "brain lateralization [does] not work the same for everybody. . . . The truth is that during different mental tasks, one hemisphere is only *relatively* more active than the other" (pp. 149, 151).

The Auxiliary Function

"Function type" usually refers to a second, auxiliary, function as well as to the primary function. According to Jung, "another, less differentiated function of secondary importance is invariably present in consciousness and exerts a co-determining influence" (CW6, par. 666). He saw the secondary function as supplementing the first; if the primary function is one of judgment, the secondary is one of perception, and vice versa.

Jungian theorists seem to agree generally on the importance and nature of the auxiliary function, but whether the first and second functions are of the same or opposite attitudes is not clear. That they are of the same attitude seemed to be Jung's assumption, on the basis, perhaps, that the more conscious attitude is linked with the two more conscious functions, and the more unconscious attitude is linked with the more unconscious functions. My clinical experience generally supports this hypothesis.

Other Jungian analysts take a different position, however, as do the developers of the *Preliminary Guidelines for MBTI Workshops* (Center for the Application of Psychological Types, 1979). These people contend that successful adaptation requires that an introvert have an extraverted auxiliary function, and an extravert, an introverted auxiliary. Quenk (1978) generally supported the view of analysts who find the first two functions to be of opposite attitudes, but he seemed to consider this generalization to need modification. He wrote, "For the extreme introvert, both the dominant and auxiliary functions take on an introverted attitude. The extreme extravert would be one for whom both dominant and auxiliary take on an extraverted attitude" (p. 13).

The Inferior Function

The inferior function is the opposite of the superior (first) function, according to Jung's clinical findings. Thus, if the first function is thinking, feeling is the fourth function, and vice versa. If sensation is the first function, then intuition is the fourth, and vice versa. Again, not everyone agrees with this hypothesis. Bradway and Wheelwright (1978) asked 172 Jungian analysts (who could be assumed to be thoroughly familiar with types theory and able to ascertain their own types) to indicate their superior and inferior functions. Of the 172 analysts queried, almost one in four found the inferior function to be other than the function opposite the superior function. To discover whether these analysts were mistaken, or Jung was, more evidence is needed.

Whichever specific function is inferior for a particular person, it is likely to have the same characteristics: undifferentiated, emotion-charged, and capable of erupting suddenly. It is not under ego control; indeed, it is awkward, embarrassing, slow, and likely to be the focus of one or more complexes. As Wheelwright (1973) put it, "A man can run the superior [function], whereas the inferior one runs him" (p. 10). The obverse of these undesirable characteristics, however, is that the fourth function has a great deal of vitality and even creativity. Von Franz (1971) explained this positive role by the fact that the inferior function is

> the door through which all the figures of the unconscious come into consciousness. Our conscious realm is like a room with four doors, and it is the fourth door by which the Shadow, the Animus or the Anima and the personification of the Self come in. . . . The inferior function is so close to the unconscious and remains so barbaric . . . and undeveloped that it is . . . the weak spot in consciousness through which the figures of the unconscious can break in. (p. 54)

The unconscious contents often enter consciousness first in their negative guises. For example, a person with superior extraverted sensation has inferior introverted intuition—dark hunches, perhaps, about possible misfortunes. The positive side of intuition is that it may anticipate coming events correctly. When intuition is an inferior function it is very unreliable, however, and no one knows which premonition is correct and which is merely the most negative possibility imaginable.

Emotion and the Functions

The relation of emotion to the functions is a frequent source of confusion. The feeling function is not the same as emotion. Indeed, a developed feeling function is no more emotional than any other developed function. The fourth function, and sometimes the third, however, are likely to be highly emotional. An apt example is the thinking function of a person with primary feeling; when his or her ideas (products of thinking) are questioned by another person, the effect can be emotionally devastating.

The hypothesis of the emotionality of the inferior function was tested by Bachant (1972). She administered the MBTI to forty-three subjects (source of subjects was not specified in *Dissertation Abstracts*) and asked them to report their experience of an argument. The subjects' dominant functions as determined by the MBTI were correlated with the function judged prevalent in the argument protocol; the expectation was that during emotion there would be an increased manifestation of the individual's inferior functions. The results supported the hypothesis that with increasing emotion there was an increasing influence of the inferior functions.

Determinants of Function Type

How the dominant function(s) of a person is (are) determined is even more difficult to ascertain than the determinants of a person's attitude type. Early environment almost certainly plays an influential role in strengthening or discouraging the development of each function. It seems likely, however, that Jung was correct in his opinion that each person has an innate tendency to develop certain functions; otherwise, a culture or family that encourages, for example, thinking and sensation would produce no intuitive or feeling-type offspring. Yet every culture and virtually every family produces children with identifiably different dominant functions.

An early hypothesis advanced by Jung was that thinking is a male function and feeling a female function. He discarded the hypothesis when it became evident that thinking could be the primary function of either a man or a woman. In Jung's clinical experience, however, male feeling types and female thinking types were in the minority, perhaps because of the prevailing culture. Today, the trend seems to be toward the development of thinking *and* feeling in both women and men (see Chapter 5), perhaps because of the changes in cultural conceptions of male and female roles accompanying the growth of the women's movement (see Chapter 18).

Empirical Evidence for the Attitude and Function Types

Addressing himself to the question, "Is Jung's typology true?" Cook (1971) examined the eight personality types (i.e., introversion versus extraversion as modified by each of the four functions) both experimentally and theoretically. Selecting nine indices for each of Jung's eight personality types, Cook phrased the indices as declarative statements to form a seventy-two-item structured Q-sort. Thus, a sample of 183 introductory psychology students were asked to describe themselves by sorting the seventy-two statements into nine piles ranging from "fits me best" to "fits me least well." A student's measure of resemblance to a particular type was taken to be the level at which that student endorsed the nine indices for that type. When the subjects' scores were compared with a computer simulation of ten thousand random Q-sorts, they were found to show a stronger resemblance to one or another of Jung's types than would be expected by chance. The investigator concluded that the findings "suggested that the Ss tend to resemble one or another of the eight types, that the types appear to be products of two sets of variables reminiscent of 'attitudes' and 'functions,' and that a S's tendency toward describing himself in terms of one of the attitudes seems to be associated with a tendency to disavow traits reflecting the opposing attitude. However, a similar opposition of functions was not found" (p. 78).

Gorlow, Simonson, and Krauss (1966) examined the hypothesis, similar to Cook's, that "within the domain of self-report, individuals will order themselves into the types postulated by Jung" (p. 108). The volunteer subjects from an introductory psychology course at Pennsylvania State University were ninety-nine males and females between the ages of seventeen and twenty-two and representing various curricula at the university. A large pool of self-regarding propositions was derived from Jung's descriptions in *Psychological Types* and one hundred statements were finally selected. The latter represented the extraverted-thinking person (twelve statements), introverted-thinking person (twelve), extraverted-feeling person (thirteen), introverted-feeling person (twelve), extraverted-sensing person (thirteen), introverted-sensing person (twelve), extraverted-intuiting person (thirteen), and introverted-intuiting person (thirteen). The statements were reproduced on cards and given to groups of subjects who were instructed to sort them into eleven piles along the dimension "least like myself" to "most like myself." In addition, the subjects completed items providing demographic data on themselves.

To identify the characteristics of persons clustering together (i.e., types), correlations between factor scores and placements of one hundred self-regarding propositions were computed. Five types clearly emerged from the analysis; the three that did not emerge were introverted-feeling, introverted-sensing, and introverted-intuiting. The reasons proposed by the investigators for the apparent absence of three types are that young persons of such types are not found in large state universities, that they are reluctant or unable to identify themselves, or that the instrument was not sufficiently sensitive. Despite the absence of the three types, the investigators concluded that the results of the study support the hypothesis that "individuals in their self-reports order themselves into types postulated by Jung" (p. 117).

Somewhat similar results were obtained by Hill (1970) in a study considering whether the eight subtypes would be evident within a sample of variables from different instruments that are theoretically consistent with Jungian typology. The instruments used were the MBTI, the 16PF questionnaire, and the Holtzman inkblot technique. A Q-sort was used to factor twenty-two selected subjects across sixty-nine variables. The factor analysis was rotated to eight factors to investigate for the existence of the eight Jungian subtypes. Six of the eight factors could be interpreted within the Jungian system: (1) intuition versus thinking; (2) introversion; (3) perceiving introvert versus perceiving extravert; (4) sensing extravert; (6) feeling extravert; (7) thinking. Factors 5 and 8 could not be interpreted within the Jungian framework and thus were not named. Two second-order factors were extracted from the eight-factor solution: (1) extraversion and (2) perceiving-judging. Although the results do not fit the Jungian typology completely and the investigator admitted that the Q-methodology has limitations, the results give some support for the Jungian schema.

Ball (1967) examined Jung's personality typology for stylistic dimensions by means of which divergent behaviors could be conceptually related and understood. Two dimensions, introversion-extraversion and thinking-feeling, were selected for study, using measures that included such variables as perceptual and cognitive style, response style, personality, and occupational preference. The subjects were 143 students in undergraduate psychology courses at Pennsylvania State University. Correlations were obtained between all possible pairs of variables; the resulting matrix was factor analyzed and a varimax rotation was performed. Six factors were obtained that accounted for 42 percent of the total variance: (1) rejection of business extraversion; (2) introverted thinking, practical; (3) introverted thinking, abstract; (4) neurotic acquiesence; (5) occupational intuition; and (6) introverted control. Ball concluded that the dimensions postulated by Jung have some utility for understanding many divergent behaviors by organizing them conceptually.

Four studies were conducted by Carlson and Levy (1973) to examine the relevance of Jung's typology to behavior. Two basic questions were addressed: "(1) Is Jungian theory capable of providing novel and testable insights into person-situation relationships? (2) Can theoretically guided research employing categorical constructs offer a clearer, more differentiated—and more humanly economical—understanding of person-situation interactions than is afforded by current concerns . . . with establishing general laws?" (p. 559) The first three studies used a sample of Howard University undergraduates selected on the basis of their MBTI scores.

Study I, Type Differences in Memory Task Performance, made the following predictions: "(1) Introverted thinking types should be more effective in remembering interiorized, neutral stimulus material; (2) Extraverted feeling types should be more effective in remembering novel, social, emotionally toned stimulus material" (p. 564). The subjects, twenty-four females distributed among four groups of six subjects each, had been identified as introverted thinking, introverted feeling, extraverted thinking, and extraverted feeling. Two memory tasks, the Digit Span subtest of the Wechsler Adult Intelligence Scale and twelve pictures selected from the Lightfoot facial expression series (Engen, Levy, and Schlosberg, 1957), were administered. The findings clearly supported both predictions: Introverted thinking types were significantly (p < .002) superior on the Digit Span task; extraverted feeling types were significantly (p < .002) more accurate in recognition of facial expressions.

Study II, also Type Differences in Memory Task Performance, made the same predictions as Study I. The subjects, thirty-two females in equal groups of the two types, were given ten geometric forms prepared in two versions: In one set, each form contained a two-digit numeral; in the other set, each form contained a fictitious proper name of a male or female. Comparison of discrepancy scores (numbers score minus names score) provided highly significant (p < .003) confirmation of the predicted differences: Introverted thinking types were clearly more effective in remembering objective, impersonal material; extraverted feeling types were far more effective on the names task.

Study III, Type Differences in Social Perception, was based on the prediction that intuitive-perceptive types who are open to latent possibilities will be more successful in interpreting emotional expressions as compared with sensing-judging types who emphasize concreteness and closure. The subjects were forty female and sixteen male intuitive-perceptive types, and twenty-eight female and fourteen male sensing-judging types. An emotional recognition task, developed by the investigators, included two pictures in each of ten categories: anger-annoyance, contempt, despair-distress, determination, fear, guilt-shame, happiness, love, pride, and surprise. The findings clearly confirmed the prediction that intuitive-perceptive types were significantly (at the .01 level of confidence) more accurate in interpreting emotional expressions than were sensing-judging types.

Study IV, Personality Type and Volunteering for Social Service, turned to a field situation (in place of the laboratory situation of the first three studies) to examine the types of people that participate in volunteer service. The prediction was that extraverted intuitives would be overrepresented among volunteers as compared with nonvolunteers. The subjects were twenty Howard University students: ten volunteers in a halfway house for disturbed adolescents and ten nonvolunteers matched to the volunteers for age, sex, parents' occupations, number of siblings, and ordinal position. The findings clearly confirmed the hypothesis: seven of the volunteers, as compared with only one of the nonvolunteers, were extraverted intuitive types on the MBTI ($p < .025$).

The significance of these four studies lies in the fact that (a) they clearly support Jung's theory of psychological types and (b) they suggest ways in which the theory can be exploited to deepen our understanding of complicated personality characteristics and their interaction with social-situational variables.

Ross (1966) reached conclusions that, in his view, were opposite to those cited here. He administered a battery of thirty-two tests, including the MBTI, to 319 male and 252 female high school students. Factor analyses for males and females separately showed that the indicator scales as a set were linked (correlated) with ability, interest, and personality variables. Ross interpreted the results to indicate that all four scales (extraversion-introversion, sensation-intuition, thinking-feeling, and judgment-perception) reflect some surface characteristics other than the typological differences for which they were constructed. His reasoning is questionable, however. In order for the Jungian types to be validated, they must be linked with observable traits. Ross found that they were so linked; extraversion-introversion was correlated, for example, with talkativeness and gregariousness. In my view, these traits are some of the surface manifestations of typological differences.

In addition to the studies that evidence the existence of Jung's typology, additional support is available in the form of construct validity. For example, MacKinnon (1971), a non-Jungian, found that a person with introverted intuition was more likely to produce active, creative fantasy than were persons of other function types. Thus, the construct of introverted intuition appears to exist, as evidenced by its performing in the manner expected.

Discovering One's Attitude and Function Type

Some people, after reading descriptions of the types, know immediately which are theirs; others still do not know after years of study. For many of the latter, it is helpful to think of the attitudes and functions as preferences rather than types. For others, no explanation makes the concept of types acceptable.

Anyone who seeks insight into his or her typology, however, can have access to several ways of obtaining some indication of which attitude and functions are dominant.

The Jungian Type Survey
(Gray-Wheelwrights Tests)

The Jungian Type Survey was first formulated in 1944 by Jungian analysts Horace Gray, Jane Wheelwright, and Joseph B. Wheelwright. Later, Elizabeth Wilson Buehler and John Buehler collaborated in its development. The Survey is usually referred to as the Gray-Wheelwrights Test (GWT). It was developed from three hundred questions and given to persons whose preference types were ascertained by clinical observation. The questions were then scored according to the way they were answered by persons of the various types. Thus, the survey was developed empirically. It now consists of eighty-two "forced-choice" items which can be answered on score sheets in twenty minutes or less. It provides a measure of preference on the three dimensions introduced by Jung: introversion-extraversion (IE), sensation-intuition (SU), and thinking-feeling (TF).

Although the GWT has been used extensively by Jungian analysts and other clinicians, little work has been done on the measure's reliability and validity. A split-half reliability study was conducted on the GWT by the developers of the MBTI. The reliabilities of the IE, SU, and TF scales were .64, .58, and .30, respectively. The small number of items per scale (34, 26, and 21), however, makes split-half a less than optimally effective method of testing reliability for the GWT. More useful information on the test was provided in a study by Davis (1978), which examined reliability by test-retest and validity against the criterion of self-typing. The subjects were forty-two undergraduate and graduate students (twenty-one men, twenty-one women) in an evening class in Jungian psychology at the University of Minnesota. The test was found to be most reliable (.834) on SU, almost as high (.798) on IE, but only moderately reliable (.449) on TF. All three coefficients were significant at the .01 level. Validity of the GWT was measured by a self-typing instrument devised by the investigators but based on "Effects of Each Preference in Work Situations" (Myers, 1976). Subjects responded to the GWT at the beginning of the term, before most of them had studied the Jungian theory of types. Some had previous familiarity with the theory, however. All subjects completed the self-typing instrument and the second administration of the GWT near the end of the term, after reading about types, spending one class period of two and one-half hours discussing the theory, and after learning the results of their earlier responses to the GWT and the MBTI. The validity coefficients for self-typing in relation to the first and second administrations of the GWT were all relatively low: introversion, .301 and .526; extraversion, .303 and .529; sensation, .425 and .396; intuition, .417 and .408; thinking, .282 and .417; feeling, .306 and .427.

It seems likely that the self-typing provided an inadequate criterion. To test validity adequately, criterion groups, composed of persons whose types are known, are needed. At least two such attempts have been made, one by Bradway (1964), the other by Bradway and Detloff (1976). The investigators compared GWT scores with self-typing. The subjects were the twenty-eight Jungian analysts practicing in California at the time in the first study, and ninety-two California analysts and advanced trainees (85% of the total number possible) in the second study. Concordance between the GWT and self-typing on IE was 96% and 87% in the two studies, 79% and 83% on SU and 79% and 76% on TF. The level of statistical significance was beyond the .001 level on all three dimensions for the first study, and .0000 for all three on the second.

The studies would be good tests of validity of the GWT if the subjects were not "contaminated" with knowledge of the theory. Unfortunately, these subjects were contaminated. Most analysts are thoroughly familiar with types theory and can guess many of the items that are scored in each direction on a particular dimension. In addition, many Jungians have a preference for which type they would like to be (often introverted with intuition and thinking as the first two functions, as were Jung and many of his early students). It seems probable that some test responses were distorted in the directions desired by the subjects.

What is needed, in my view, is a method of self-typing or peer-typing that is more objective. One possibility would begin with a translation of definitions of types into observable behavior (including verbal behavior, which reflects attitudes) that could be subjected to the scrutiny of persons who know the subjects well enough to describe their behavior. An informal kind of self-typing occurs when persons who respond to the survey agree, as most of them seem to do, with its results.

The Myers-Briggs Type Indicator

The development of the Myers-Briggs Type Indicator (MBTI) was the work of Katherine C. Briggs and her daughter, Isabel Briggs Myers. They began in 1942 to construct the Indicator and made changes over the years, including the construction of a form appropriate for college and high school students. The Indicator, like the GWT, was developed empirically, using the responses of persons who appeared to be of one type or another, and selecting the items that discriminated among persons of various types.

Two forms of the MBTI are currently in use: Form F has 166 forced-choice items; Form G contains 126 of the same items. Both forms provide scores on the three dimensions described by Jung: EI, TF, and SN, (the MBTI uses N for intuition), and a fourth dimension, judgment-perception (JP) that was implicit in Jung's writings. TF is scored somewhat differently for males and females, to allow for the fact that, in American culture at least, males are given more encouragement to develop their thinking, females to develop their feeling.

The reliability of the MBTI has been established quite well by split-half correlations of tests from several groups of varying academic achievement—from underachieving seventh graders through Pembroke College students. Except for the TF correlations for "under-achieving 8th" and "Mass. Non-prep 12th," all split-half reliabilities were .7 and over, and most were .8 and over. Gerald A. Mendelsohn (1970), assistant professor of psychology, University of California, Berkeley, acknowledged that "the reliabilities of the test are like those of similar self-report inventories" (p. 1126).

No predictive or concurrent validity studies seem to be available except the one by Davis (1978). As in her GWT validity study, the correlations with self-typing were below .5 on all dimensions: introversion, .316; extraversion, .343; sensation, .494; intuition, .475; thinking, .232; feeling, .312. Again, the criterion probably is faultier than the test; as with the GWT, the MBTI results ring true to most of the persons who use it.

The Eysenck Personality Inventory

A third paper-and-pencil instrument measures only the EI dimension. It is the Eysenck Personality Inventory (EPI), a revision of the Maudsley Personality Inventory. It has been used a great deal in research but, to my knowledge, not clinically.

Despite the fact that all three tests are highly correlated with each other, some investigators have expressed doubt that the tests actually measure what they purport to measure. Stricker and Ross (1964) found that the intuition scale of the MBTI describes an interest in abstract ideas, which, they pointed out, is "at best, only one facet of intuition" (p. 637). Wozny (1966; cited in Meier and Wozny, 1978, p. 226) concluded that the thinking-feeling scale on the GWT measured introverted thinking-extraverted feeling, rather than simply thinking-feeling, as the test authors claimed.

Additional Types Tests

Two other tests are in the process of development. The Detloff Psychological Types Questionnaire has been in the process for a number of years. Its author is attempting to make use of items from the GWT and the MBTI, as well as the results of the accumulated research on and clinical experience with these tests, in order to construct the new measure (Detloff, 1966).

The second new test, the Singer-Loomis Inventory of Personality (SLIP), is based on Jungian theory and the hypothesis that the attitudes, perception functions, and judgment functions are not pairs of opposites but separate dimensions. The hypothesis is derived from the fact that when agree-disagree responses were requested in place of the forced-choice items of the GWT and the MBTI, nearly half (48 percent) of the respondents had inferior functions that were not the opposites (as defined by Jung) of their superior functions.

For example, an item such as:

At a party, I
  a) like to talk.
  b) like to listen.

was replaced by two scaled items separated in the test:

At a party I like to talk.
At a party I like to listen.

The subject was asked to use a scale from 1 to 7, where 1 is never and 7 is always (Loomis and Singer, 1980).

Following this format, 120 subjects responded to a test composed of such items generated by the GWT and to the GWT itself. The finding that 72 percent of those using the GWT and 36 percent of those using the MBTI scored a different superior function (on the tests that were derived by using free choice instead of forced choice) suggested that some significant distortions of personality functions were being manifested in the GWT and MBTI. The SLIP was designed to make more subtle differentiations. It is composed of fifteen questions, each with eight possible responses and each response representing one type of cognitive mode: introverted thinking, extraverted thinking, introverted feeling, and so forth. The resulting profile shows the relative strengths of the eight cognitive modes in the individual. Construct validity and predictive validity of the SLIP are being studied.

Self-Typing

Self-typing, which has been used to validate types tests, is an alternative method to ascertain one's type. For many people, Jung's descriptions (CW6, Chapter 10) are the most useful; others find that the descriptions based on a listing and rephrasing of the personality characteristics associated with each type are more helpful. One set of descriptions is "Effects of Each Preference in Work Situations" prepared by Myers (1976, pp. 17–18). It includes the perception-judgment dimension.

Typing by Others

For one person to type another is difficult. Although the person doing the typing often can observe a great deal of the other person's verbal and other behavior, the first cannot know all of the second's thoughts. This fact is important because cognitions are important manifestations of typology. Better than behavior they reflect directions of energy, by which type is defined.

Nevertheless, at least one study has indicated that typing by others can be an effective method. Peavey (1963) used the MBTI to identify four twelfth-grade students who were extreme sense (sensation) types and four who were extreme intuitive types. Using brief paragraph descriptions of the types as a guide, a teacher who had known all eight subjects for one year was able to type correctly six of the eight.

A study by Harrison (1976) failed to demonstrate the validity of typing by others. The subjects were thirty-seven undergraduate students who had been tested with the MBTI and who each saw one of the counselors in two sessions. After the initial session, which was structured toward conscious, reality-oriented, here-and-now topics, the counselor rated the student for superior type. The second session was structured to gather material indicative of unconscious processes: discussions of dream records kept by each client and the administration of an abbreviated version of the TAT. After the second session, the counselor classified the client for inferior type. There was no significant correlation between the clients' scores on the MBTI and the counselors' typing of the clients. In comparison with the teacher's interactions with the students in the Peavey study, however, the counselors interacted minimally with the students in the Harrison study.

Whatever the method, it is often difficult to discover a person's primary function and especially to distinguish which of the two developed functions is superior. Sometimes the decision can be made with less difficulty by ascertaining the inferior function. With that decided, the opposite of the inferior function is presumably the superior function.

A question that often arises is whether it is possible for a person to express one attitude or function in one situation and the opposite in another. It is not only possible, but probable. Different situations require the use of different functions. Thinking is likely to be required in a mathematics class but feeling is needed at a funeral. If the needed function is not a developed one, the person is likely to behave awkwardly and ineffectively. It is important to keep in mind, however, that attitudes and functions are not behaviors but preferences—preferred directions of interest and energy. These may remain stable even while life circumstances, and the person's values, require behaviors that arise out of the less preferred attitude and functions.

Developing the Nondominant Attitude and Functions

People often ask how one can develop one's second, third, and perhaps fourth functions. The Jungian literature affords very little commentary on this question. The assumption seems to be that, as psychological growth occurs, development of the nondominant attitude and functions will take place concurrently. Indeed, changing life situations, including the aging process, often force the development of the nondominant attitude and functions. It is helpful to recognize that one's inferior function is only marginally available and that it works slowly, awkwardly, and largely autonomously. Thus the best prescription for its development may be patience.

Significance of Jung's Typology

The theory of types is probably the theory of Jung's that has attracted the most interest and understanding from non-Jungians. For example, Leona Tyler, a leading psychologist of individual differences, recognized introversion and extraversion as "not traits or dimensions to be measured, but rather directions of development" (p. 70).

Jung's typology is outstanding among his theories in its heuristic value. The research thus far has focused largely on the construct validity of the types. The typology is also of great clinical value: (a) The nondominant attitude and functions are aspects of the shadow that are relatively easy to identify and in which one can find positive values; (b) problems of interpersonal relations are often elucidated and alleviated by determining that differences in typology have given sets of spouses or friends different ways of perceiving and responding to the world (see Chapter 15); (c) the problems and complexes of some clients in psychotherapy can be understood better when it is discovered that the clients are "distorted types." That is, environmental influences, especially family constellations, may have pushed the client into functioning in terms of an attitude and/or function that is not naturally dominant.

Gerhard Adler, a leading analyst and interpreter of Jung, described Jung's typology as "so often misunderstood as a schematic pattern of personality, but in reality revealing the dynamic interplay of opposites" (1975, p. 14). The far-reaching impact of this view was expressed by C. A. Meier, Jung's successor as professor of psychology at the Federal Institute of Technology in Zurich: "Individuation begins and ends with typology. . . . [Jung said that in his typology he had intended] to give nothing less than the clearest pattern for simply all the *dynamics* of the human soul" (1971, pp. 276, 278–79).

5

Females and Males

Jung hypothesized a psychic structure that corresponds to the different chromosomal makeup of men and women: a predominantly feminine conscious personality in a woman, masculine in a man, together with a predominantly masculine or feminine component, respectively, in the unconscious. He used *masculine* and *feminine* not to describe roles or stereotypes but, rather, to denote archetypal principles: the feminine principle, *eros*; the masculine, *logos*. Both terms are Greek words.

Eros signifies relatedness, the attitude that works for harmony through conciliation and reconciliation. It fosters both interpersonal relationships and integration within oneself. It values subjectivity and the concerns of individuals rather than collective society. Eros is rooted in the concrete, material universe; thus, it has an earthy quality. Like the earth, it is passive, receptive, and creative.

Logos can be translated as word, power, meaning, and deed. It signified for Jung "objective interest" (*CW10*, par. 255): structure, form, discrimination, and the abstract. He often equated logos with the spiritual, not necessarily in the religious sense of the term but in the sense of the nonmaterial.

Repeatedly, Jung stressed the idea that eros and logos are equally necessary in human life. Each is needed to complement the other and, therefore, is insufficient alone. Logos is necessary for differentiation, whereas eros "unites what logos has sundered" (CW10, par. 275). For a man or woman to achieve wholeness, it is essential that each develop both the feminine and masculine sides of his or her personality.

The logos and eros principles have broader implications than the psyches of individuals. Their Chinese counterparts, for example, are linked to the phenomena of nature, such as the sunny and shady sides of a stream. "Yang is of the sunny side; yin, the shady. On the sunny side there is light, there is warmth and the heat of the sun is dry. In the shade, there is the cool . . . of the earth, and the earth is moist. Dark, cold, and moist; light, hot, and dry; earth and sun in counteraction" (Campbell, 1972, p. 116).

Female Psychology

The Jungian view of female psychology opposes Freud's notion that women are incomplete men. In general, Jung had a positive perception of women's natures; the women who knew him evidently perceived him as positively disposed to their possibilities for development, a perception that is attested to by the disproportionate number of early Jungian analysts who were women.

The Animus

Probably Jung's greatest contribution to female psychology is his concept of the animus, the contrasexual (male) archetypal component of the female psyche. Clinical experience suggested the existence of the animus and the bases for its variations in content. The content of the animus in each woman, Jung hypothesized, is determined by the combination of archetypal images and her early experiences with men, especially her father. Jung said little about the influence of national or tribal culture but it seems impossible to deny this influence; the animus of a French woman is likely to differ markedly from that of a Japanese woman.

Both the archetypal and learned (personal and cultural) aspects of the animus are largely unconscious. Jung stated, however, that the animus is "a mediator between the conscious and the unconscious" (CW9–II, par. 33). By this he seemed to mean that this content makes available to consciousness the previously unconscious logos capacities. He did not explain, however, how the animus is a mediator, any more than is the shadow, for example, nor how logos can be a mediator between consciousness and the unconscious.

If the animus has acquired a bad name it is because Jung tended to emphasize its negative aspects. He described the animus as hostile and power-driven and especially given to producing irrational opinions, "rather like an assembly of fathers or dignitaries of some kind who lay down incontestable, 'rational' ex cathedra judgments" (CW7, par. 332). He seemed to assume that this opinionatedness was archetypal and the mark of an undeveloped (immature) animus. In my view, however, such a quality is characteristic of men more than of women; daughters probably acquire the quality from their fathers more than from their mothers. Indeed, opinionatedness is perhaps undifferentiated thinking more than negative animus.

Too little has been written about the positive side of the animus. Jung mentioned its "*discriminative* function" (CW16, par. 505), which "gives to woman's consciousness a capacity for reflection, deliberation, and self-knowledge" (CW9–II, par. 33). The animus is also "creative and procreative" (CW7, par. 336). It is possible, further, to identify desirable qualities, such as assertiveness (which is not the same as aggressiveness), and the ability to initiate action, as manifestations of the animus.

Jung's view of the animus, even its strengths, lacks full appreciation of women's capabilities. He explained the creative power of the animus as an analogue to the male role in producing new life. However, he described male creativity as being complete in itself: "A man brings forth his work as a complete creation out of his inner feminine nature." In contrast, female creativity must work through the male: "The inner masculine side of a woman brings forth creative seeds which have the power to fertilize the feminine side of the man" (CW7, par. 336). It seems as if any independent functioning by a woman was treated by Jung, in theory (as distinguished from his positive treatment of woman students and colleagues), as an aberration. He wrote, for example, that "by taking up a masculine profession, studying and working like a man, woman is doing something not wholly in accord with, if not directly injurious to, her feminine nature" (CW10, par. 243).

From the perspective of the late twentieth century, such statements read like severe depreciations of women. Yet, at the time Jung wrote them he was expressing a prevailing view, and he expressed other views (such as the equality of the masculine and feminine principles) that were advanced not only for his time but remain so. Even in his most conservative moments, moreover, he did not subscribe to the idea that every woman suffers from "penis envy" until she learns to accept her role as subservient to men. The difference between Jung's attitude toward women and Freud's was reflected in the fact that Jung encouraged his wife, Emma, to become an analyst and to share his interests, whereas Freud, writing to his fiancée, Martha Bernays, described the position of women as "in youth an adored darling and in mature years a loved wife" (Jones, 1953, p. 177).

Empirical Evidence for the Animus

Empirical verification of the existence of the animus is primarily clinical; Jung and his students found ample evidence of the animus in women's problems (see Chapters 7 and 15) and in their dreams. One quantitative study (Bash, 1972), however, sought to demonstrate the existence of the animus, along with the anima (see next section), through their projections in subjects' perceptions of the Rorschach inkblots. The subjects, four hundred residents of German Switzerland, were each assigned to one of four equal groups: neurotic women and neurotic men (drawn from psychiatric institutions, outpatient services, and private psychiatric practices), and "healthy" women and "healthy" men. The latter groups of subjects "were tested as opportunity presented itself, a considerable number of the males having been referred for selection as candidates for the Zurich police force . . . while a substantial proportion of the females were nurses trained or in training at Bernese hospitals" (p. 341). The diagnosis of neurosis was based on clinical psychiatric criteria (excluded were borderline or doubtful cases, neuroses complicated by psychopathy, mental deficiency, or organic dementia). "Healthy" was interpreted broadly to mean the absence of apparent psychic disorder of more than a trivial degree. Human movement responses were taken as indicators of projection on the ground that "Rorschach himself stated, and all authors since then have confirmed him, that the . . . movement responses (M) are preferential bearers of projections" (p. 340). Bash hypothesized from Jungian theory that neurosis favors an increase of projection and that "we should find more human movement responses of the opposite sex in Rorschach records of neurotic subjects of both sexes than in records of normal subjects" (p. 346). The hypothesis was confirmed. Of neurotic women 50.5% saw male movement, as compared with 39.3% of healthy women. Similarly, 26.3% of neurotic men saw female movement, as compared with 15.1% of healthy men. For nonmovement human responses, which are assumed not to reflect projection in the Jungian sense, the percentages of opposite sex responses were nearly equal for the four groups, ranging only from 35.3% (healthy men) to 40.6% (healthy women). The results provided evidence for an unconscious contrasexual figure: animus in women and anima in men.

Jung acknowledged his limitations in understanding the psychology of women. Consequently, he deferred to his female co-workers, especially M. Esther Harding, Emma Jung, and Toni Wolff, for presentations of the specifics of female psychology. All three women wrote on the subject.

M. Esther Hardings's "Animus Women" and "Anima Women"

Harding (1970) developed the thesis that the animus functions differently in different women. Some women, whom she designated animus-type, tend to express the animus positively, seemingly from childhood, or at least from adolescence, by being active, taking initiative, and often becoming leaders and achievers. Sometimes the animus is manifested primarily in an exaggeratedly negative way in animus-type women, and Harding called them "animus-hounds." Such women are opinionated, abrasive, competitive, and aggressive. Exaggeration of her masculine side may result when a woman has repressed it in order to present to the world a conventionally feminine persona.

In other women, the animus is scarcely perceivable. These women, popularly called "clinging vines," were labeled anima-type women by Harding (1970). They relate easily to men, at least on a superficial level, and sometimes scarcely at all to women. In traditional Western society they probably have an easier time in early life because they are willing to take second place to men. Later, however, the problems of such women increase as they are forced by the stresses of living with men (such women nearly always have husbands or lovers, at least through middle age) to become more conscious of relationships, negatively as well as positively. That is, a woman who has "played the anima"—lived according to men's expectations and assumed that men are always strong, knowledgeable, and competent—often is forced, over the years, to discover men's vulnerability and the fact that her own wishes may not accord with theirs. Such discoveries produce greater consciousness but, as in all human relations, at the cost of emotional pain. In later life, an anima-type woman may have to suffer even further when widowhood leaves her without a man on whom to lean. Whereas the animus-type woman must work to tame her animus when she becomes uncomfortable with its negative effects, the anima-type woman must find and develop her animus after she discovers the need for more independence.

In my experience, there are women who cannot be described by either animus or anima type. Some of them have such balanced personalities that they are well-developed in both femininity and masculinity; in other instances, animus-type women are trying desperately to live the anima role. The discomfort resulting from the distortion of personality in the latter case is likely to produce depression, anxiety, hostility, or other indications of maladaptation. The reverse—an anima woman living as an animus type—is rare because the culture does not encourage it.

A study by Bradway (1978) yielded empirical evidence for Harding's categories of animus- and anima-type women. Bradway found that, of the thirty-one women over twenty years of age whom she had seen in therapy in the preceding five years, all but one fell into one of two contrasting groups. "One group consisted of eighteen married women, sixteen with children, all with at least one year of college and only one with an outside job; the other group consisted of 12 women with graduate degrees in nursing, social work, psychology or medicine, and actively engaged in their professions. Only two had been married and only one had a child. None of this group was married at the time of beginning analysis" (p. 30). Bradway struggled to give names to the two groups that were more psychologically descriptive than "family women" and "career women." She had started to use the terms Hearth Tender and Warrior when she came across an article (Kotschnig, 1976) that personified the two categories as Hestia (goddess of the hearth) and Athena (who had many functions, including that of goddess of various kinds of workers). The two groups henceforth were designated Hestia and Athena. Bradway found differences between them that describe generally the differences between anima women and animus women: Hestia women were more introverted, more predominantly feeling (both according to the Gray-Wheelwrights Test), and more likely to be first-born in their families of origin. In contrast, Athena women were more extraverted, more thinking, and more likely to be last-borns.

Emma Jung: Manifestations of the Animus

To spell out the possible developmental course of the animus, Emma Jung (1969) described four major archetypal manifestations, which she saw as stages: power, deed, word, and meaning. The four correspond to the meanings of logos. Each has a positive and a negative aspect and a characteristic personification in dreams. When a woman is developing psychologically, these manifestations are likely to occur approximately in the order specified, although with considerable overlapping. Emma Jung described each animus manifestation in personified form and in terms of behavior.

The animus of *power* may appear in a woman's dreams as the image of a physically powerful male, such as an athlete or a soldier. In its positive form the manifestation gives the woman the capacity to achieve, to be active in her own behalf; in its negative form it seeks to dominate other people.

Closely related to the animus of power is the animus of *deed*. The dream image is the man of action, such as an astronaut or a political leader. Its positive manifestation is likely to be effective leadership in social reform; its negative expression often is an exaggerated concern for rules and abstract justice.

The animus of *word* is reflected in the image of an orator or poet. Its positive form includes the capacity to deal with abstractions; its negative manifestation is reflected in rigid and prejudiced opinions.

Meaning is assumed to be the highest level of animus development. It may be personified in dreams as a priest or philosopher. Experienced positively, the animus of meaning becomes "a mediator between the conscious and the unconscious" (CW9–11, par. 33). Negatively, the animus of meaning may be expressed in religious dogmatism or in such single-minded concern with abstractions that concrete experiences are ignored.

Toni Wolff: Structural Forms of the Female Psyche

A very helpful but little-known contribution to the psychology of women was made by Toni Wolff in her sixteen-page paper, "Structural Forms of the Feminine Psyche" (1956). Despite the title, she dealt only with females, not with the feminine side of men. For this reason, the term *female*, rather than *feminine*, psyche is used here.

Wolff saw each woman's consciousness as taking one or two of four forms. Like the function types, all four probably are potential in each woman but one tends to be dominant, especially during youth; a second may be fairly well developed, and a third somewhat so; the fourth is likely to be quite inferior. Again, like the function types, the four structural forms are paired: Mother and Hetaera (also spelled *Hetaira*), which are primarily "personally related," that is, the major interest and energy of such women go into personal relationships; and Amazon and Medial Woman, which are interested primarily in "objective cultural values" (p. 7), such as ideas. The members of each pair contrast with one another in their manner of relating to other persons or achieving cultural values.

The *Mother* form of the female psyche is composed of the qualities of cherishing and nourishing, helping, teaching, and being charitable. A woman whose psyche predominantly takes this form responds to all that is in the process of becoming, is undeveloped, is in need of protection, or that must be cared for and tended. A woman can live as Mother not only with children but also with adults; for example, she supports a man's weaker side and seeks to protect his position in the world. The positive expression of this aspect of femininity helps weaker beings to achieve independence from her care. In the negative expression, the woman continues to nurture and protect even when the recipient no longer needs her help.

The *Hetaera* (from the Greek work meaning "female paramour, . . . concubine, [or] any woman who uses her beauty and charm to obtain wealth or social position"; *Random House Dictionary of the English Language,* unabridged edition, 1967) shares the Mother's focus on personal relations but is opposite her in ways of conducting such relations (just as sensation and intuition share the perceptive capacity but perceive in divergent ways). Specifically, the Hetaera is unlike the Mother in that she relates more to men than to children and is more erotic than nurturant. The Hetaera focuses on a man's subjective interests rather than on those that are linked to his position in the world. "Her own development demands of her to experience and realize an individual relationship in all its nuances and depths. . . . [The positive side of the Hetaera is that she is] conscious of the laws of relationship. Her instinctive interest is directed toward the individual contents of a relationship in herself as well as in the man" (Wolff, 1956, p. 6). The negative side of the Hetaera is that she may undervalue the persona in herself, the man, and her children. Thus, she may deter the male from adapting to responsibilities which are important to his economic and social security and she may bind her children to her emotionally.

Wolff described the relationships of Mother and Hetaera only with men and children. It seems evident, however, that similar attitudes could operate in any personal relationship, whether with siblings, parents, friends, or co-workers.

The other two structural forms of the female psyche do not center on personal relations. The one Wolff labeled *Amazon* is quite independent of the male; she may have friendships and sexual relationships with men but she does not make them the focus of her life. Her interests are directed, rather, toward objective achievements of her own. The positive side of this aspect of femininity is that the woman can achieve a great degree of psychological independence, make unique contributions to the world, gain satisfaction from her work, and be a stimulating competitor. When she has a relationship with a man she makes few personal demands on him. The negative side of the Amazon is "that of a sister who, driven by 'masculine protest,' wants to be equal to her brother, who will not recognize any authority or superiority, . . . who fights by using exclusively male arms and is a Megaera [Fury] at home" (p. 8). Wolff seemed to mean that the negative aspect of the Amazon is that she brings competitiveness into her personal relations and is, in Harding's terms, an animus-hound.

The fourth structural form of the female psyche, a contrast to the Amazon, is the *Medial Woman*. The extreme expression of this form is the medium, who seems to be rare in our society. She mediates between the concrete world and the unseen world, between the conscious and the unconscious. Medial Women, more numerous than true mediums in our society, have some of the characteristics of the medium in that they are able to express "what is in the air": vague and embryonic possibilities not acceptable to the dominant culture; that is, these women are sensitive to currents of thoughts and feelings not perceived by most people but which become apparent in the future. Because these contents are still unconscious to most people, they often appear to be dark, negative, and dangerous. A few centuries ago a Medial Woman probably would have been considered a witch. A contemporary Medial Woman is apt to be fascinated with such subjects as parapsychology, astrology, spiritualism, and Eastern philosophies. The positive aspect of the Medial Woman is that she verbalizes the unconscious contents needed for the wholeness of an overly rational society such as ours. She may make significant contributions to spiritual concerns, the arts, and, perhaps, psychotherapy. The negative side is the danger that these unconscious contents can overwhelm the woman's ego and put her out of touch with outer reality.

Some Jungian writers (e.g., Ulanov, 1971) have mentioned Wolff's schema, but to my knowledge no empirical research or even scholarly analysis has explored the construct. The reason may be due in large part to the work's being available only in German and English private printings. In order for research to be conducted, it probably would be necessary to develop an instrument (a test) that could identify women according to the four structural forms.

One possible avenue of investigation is that of exploring whether there are any parallels between Jung's four function types and Wolff's four structural forms. This avenue does not seem highly promising, however, because only the Medial Woman appears to correspond to a function type, the intuitive.

A more fruitful exploration might be the parallels between anima and animus women described by Harding and the personally related and nonpersonally oriented women described by Wolff. Such parallels could be based on the fact that the personally related quality seems to bear great similarity to the eros orientation of the anima woman, the nonpersonal quality to the logos orientation of the animus woman.

Variations on Wolff's Forms

Another view of the various forms of the female psyche was offered by Guggenbühl-Craig (1977). He emphasized that "there is not only *one* masculine archetype and *one* feminine archetype. There are dozens, if not hundreds, of feminine and masculine archetypes" (p. 48). The archetypal forms of the female psyche, which he enumerated, resemble Wolff's but make a larger number of distinctions. Like Wolff's forms, Guggenbühl-Craig's are divided between those that are defined primarily in terms of personal relations (the first six) and those that are defined on other terms (the other three):

Maternal: Nourishing and protective (or devouring) in earthy form; inspiring (or threatening) in spiritual form.

Mater dolorosa: The mother who has lost her son in war or in an accident in his youth and who identifies with the role of the bereaved mother.

Hetaera: A woman who is independent but enjoys the company of men and is their uninhibited companion in sexual pleasure, wit, and learning.

Aphrodite: Named for the goddess of love, she is the desirable beloved.

Athene: The woman who is energetic, self-sufficient, nonsexual, nevertheless helpful to men.

Conqueror: Widows and divorced women who are independent and relieved to have the man absent.

Amazon: The independent career woman who rejects men, loves "conquests" (e.g., achievements), and enjoys the company of women.

Artemis: The woman who is hostile to men, except for her brothers. Named for the goddess of the hunt, she has goals to pursue that are incompatible with relations with men.

Vestal Virgin: the nun or priestess. These women devote their lives to God or to a cause, but not to men and children.

Some of the similarities between Guggenbühl-Craig's and Wolff's schemas are obvious; others can be surmised. Thus, the maternal archetype is generally the equivalent of Wolff's Mother, and the Mater Dolorosa is a special case of the Mother. Both schemas include the Hetaera, of which Aphrodite may be a subtype. Guggenbühl-Craig's Athene seems to be a combination of Wolff's Hetaera and Amazon. His Artemis may be a subtype of the Amazon, his Vestal Virgin a subtype of the Medial Woman.

Both writers identified feminine psychic structures (archetypes, according to Guggenbühl-Craig) that are not primarily concerned with personal relations—to husband, lover, or children, for example. (Both still defined these structures in terms of the woman's attitudes toward men, but designated as "nonpersonal" the structures that incorporated the negative of these attitudes.) The archetypes that he saw as not primarily personally related suggested to Guggenbühl-Craig that not all feminine (by which he seemed to mean female) nature is characterized by eros, that is, by relatedness. While it seems evident that not all female nature is eros-oriented, I still see eros as synonymous with the feminine principle. Eros is relatedness but not necessarily personal; it can be relatedness to the inner world, to ideas, or to humankind, for example.

Despite its limitations, Guggenbühl-Craig's schema contributed to a useful beginning for a more differentiated view of female psychology.

Masculine and Feminine Consciousness

An additional observation on the nature of the female psyche was presented by another male writer, Neumann (1964). He offered the hypothesis that "even in a woman, consciousness has a masculine character." That this statement is a matter of definition is made clear by his explanation: "The correlation 'conscious-light-day' and 'unconsciousness-darkness-night' holds true regardless of sex, and is not altered by the fact that the spirit-instinct polarity is organized on a different basis in men and women. Consciousness, as such, is masculine even in women, just as the unconscious is feminine in men" (p. 42; Neumann used "correlation" in the nontechnical sense of a mutual relation).

If Neumann's description of consciousness as masculine has any basis in Jung's theory, it probably is that the development of logos (which Jung designated as masculine), with its capacity for differentiation, is a necessary step in the evolution of consciousness—the separation of the opposites. But Jung defined consciousness unequivocally as "the relation of psychic contents to the ego" (CW6, par. 700). Thus, consciousness is a capacity or function comparable to breathing. Just as breathing is necessary for all animal life, consciousness is often identified with being fully human. It has no limitations of gender or other group identification. In addition, it is not the same as logos, but embraces both logos (the masculine principle) and eros (the feminine principle). Thus, consciousness cannot be said to be masculine.

Male Psychology

In contrast to the rather large and growing Jungian literature on the psychology of women, very little has been written by Jungians specifically on male psychology. The difference may be rooted in an assumption, consonant with that of society, that the male is the norm. Several Jungian writers have pointed out the falseness of this assumption but few have contributed to a specific theory of male psychology.

The Anima

The one aspect of male psychology that has been discussed a great deal by Jungians is the anima, the hypothesized largely unconscious feminine (eros) side of the man. (Anima is the Latin word for "soul.") Jung used the term as "a purely empirical concept, whose sole purpose is to give a name to a group of related or analogous psychic phenomena" (CW9–I, par. 114). Like the animus for woman, the content of each man's anima is determined by a combination of archetypal images, the culture at large, and the man's experiences with actual women, especially with his mother. Also, like animus, the anima was seen by Jung, without explanation, to mediate between a man's ego and the inner world.

Although the anima is mentioned frequently in Jungian literature, it is never described with any degree of precision. It is presented, rather, in clinical accounts, such as its effect on a man's relation with his wife or woman friend, or in analyses of literary figures, such as Rider Haggard's *She*. The latter is a novel in which a man encounters "She-who-must-be-obeyed," the prototype of an anima image by which a man can become possessed.

The archetypal anima is manifested in four major images that a man tends to project onto women. Jung's brief description (CW16, par. 369) is expanded here from my clinical experience and gleanings from several Jungian writers:

Eve personifies the Earth Mother. She might appear in a man's dream as a farm woman who harvests grain, gathers eggs, cooks, and cares for children. In her positive form of nourishing and caring for other persons she is life-sustaining; in her negative form, she nurtures excessively, thus restricting the development of her children, husband, and other people.

Helen (of Troy) personifies the seductress, the sex object. The dream image could be any movie star or pinup girl of the 1930s and 1940s. In her positive form Helen can be delightful company; negatively, she may be manipulative, using her charm to others' detriment.

Mary, the pure virgin, is the spiritual mother. The dream image could be a respected high school or college teacher. Positively, she is a person of integrity and independence, who knows her own values; negatively, she may be remote and demand high achievement at the expense of personal relationships.

Sophia is the figure of wisdom. In a dream she might appear as an elderly woman who is known as wise. The positive side of such a figure seems self-evident; the negative is in the use of wisdom, or knowledge, for destructive purposes.

It is important to keep in mind that the behaviors described are those of the male in whom the particular anima image is manifested. In general, when a man's anima is well connected with his consciousness, he can be related, compassionate, and gentle; when it is entirely unconscious, he may become possessed by it and, consequently, moody and filled "with an unshakable feeling of rightness and righteousness" (CW9–II, par. 34).

Male Conscious Personality

Just as he did with women, Jung gave far more attention to the unconscious psyche of men than to their conscious personalities. We must look to others than Jung for a description of male conscious personality. The most complete attempt, among Jungians, to describe the conscious personality and development of the male was made by Thayer Greene (1967). He saw masculine identity as one of *doing,* in contrast to the feminine *being:*

> The expectations of both nature and cultural tradition are that a man will play an active and aggressive rather than a passive role. . . . Creation for [him] . . . is . . . a process of *making,* of active, moving energy seeking to shape and master the environment. His tendency is to be "on the make," whether it be with a woman, an idea, or the harnessing of natural forces. To win the love of a woman, cut farmland out of the forest, or write a book, he is called upon to risk, initiate, grasp hold of life with all the strength that his mind, his muscles, and his ego can muster. (p. 20)

Like Jung, Neumann, and others, Greene seems to have mistaken cultural stereotypes with innate qualities. Although he gave credit to "uniquely feminine" (p. 19) experiences, especially childbirth, as "reassuring" to a woman, he seems to have overlooked the fact that women as well as men cannot find their identities through events that happen to them; both sexes must be active in order to establish their egos.

The development of the mature male personality, according to Greene, depends on the young man's separating himself from his mother. This necessity arises from the very special bond he has had to her. In preliterate societies, the separation was accomplished through specific initiation rites. However difficult and painful the rite, a youth withstood it and thus transcended the conflict between his yearning to return to his mother and his desire to become an adult. Our culture, in Greene's view, lacks such an arena for the young male to experience the conflict, the resolution of which frees him to become a vigorous protagonist of his convictions, aims, and desires. Our society tends to demand, rather, that he be polite and nonaggressive, even nonassertive in personal relationships. The demand leaves a Western young man with an unfulfilled "hunger to be a hero" (p. 44). Inasmuch as the hero is the image for the developing ego, it is essential for a young man to have some experience in being a hero. The scarcity of channels for this experience—not every young man can be a sports star—probably help to account for the increasing incidence of crime, especially crime that seems unmotivated except by the desire to destroy, that is, vandalism.

Kettner (1968) took the stance that the personality of a man tends to be either "cerebral" or "physical." Because both of these qualities are more on the "doing" than on the "being" side of life, these and much more, especially feminine qualities, are needed by the man for wholeness.

Guggenbühl-Craig (1977) observed that men, as well as women, have a variety of "archetypal possibilities" (p. 53). In his view, however, these possibilities have been more readily available to men, despite each man's being limited by his role as provider. The archetypal possibilities to men have always included, according to Guggenbühl-Craig,

> Ares, the simple, brutal warrior and soldier, . . . [and] Odysseus, the clever warrior and husband. The archetype of the priest, the man of God, has always been viable for men. The archetype of the medicine man, the doctor, that of Hephaistos, the clever technician, that of Hermes the clever trader and thief, and many others. . . . (p. 53)

Puer Aeternus

A specific type of male psychology, which is not shared in its complete form by all men but is found to some degree in many, is the *puer aeternus* (eternal boy). As discussed by von Franz (1970), the *puer* is reluctant to make any kind of commitment (personally, occupationally, and, I would add, in the civic-political sphere), hence, he lives what Jung called the "provisional life." His lack of concern for the future and need for excitement may be expressed in a fascination with dangerous sports, such as stunt flying and mountain climbing. If this complex is pronounced, such a man may die young in an accident arising from his daredevilry.

The positive quality of the *puer* is a certain kind of spirituality which comes from relatively close contact with the unconscious. Many such men are charming and have an invigorating effect on other persons. They ask deep questions and search for a genuine religious experience. However, other *puers* live in a kind of sleepy daze that is often characteristic of adolescence. They work only occasionally and get money wherever they can, often from the government, from women, and perhaps from illegal activities.

Jung and von Franz both saw the *puer* as a man with a

neurosis stemming from a powerful mother complex. The attachment to his mother makes it difficult for him to commit himself to a relationship with a woman his own age. Consequently, he may live as a Don Juan, a gigolo, or a homosexual. As such a man reaches middle age he is likely to experience loneliness and a sense of meaninglessness. Men with varying degrees of *puer* neurosis often enter Jungian analysis; consequently, Jung and his students have had many opportunities to observe them clinically.

Other empirical evidence would be desirable to discover whether the qualities listed as characteristic of *puers* actually are correlated. Some support for the concept can be found in the work of non-Jungian psychologists who identified similar phenomena. Ogilvie (1974), for example, described some people, male and female, as "stimulus addictive," that is, as having "a periodic need for extending themselves to the absolute physical, emotional, and intellectual limits in order to escape from the tensionless state associated with everyday living" (p. 94). Meehl (1966) hypothesized that some persons require more stimulation because they have a genetic lack in the capacity for anxiety. (A thrill is probably a mild, easily tolerated, and pleasurable level of anxiety.) Both descriptions match some of the characteristics of the *puer*.

The cure for the *puer* neurosis is work, according to Jung. Von Franz, although not denying the efficacy of work if the *puer*-type man could and would undertake it, recognized that some strengthening of the ego is necessary, perhaps through psychotherapy, in order for the problem to be overcome sufficiently for the man to be able to persevere in work. Even then, results are probably best when the man undertakes a job that is as congruent as possible with his natural flow of interest and energy.

Whatever the nature of any work, routine must be faced. When the necessity for dealing with routine arises, success for the *puer* depends on support from the unconscious. That support is likely to be reflected in dreams indicating that the man needs to push through obstacles. If he perseveres, the battle is won, at least for a time.

Sex Differences

Quantitative research on sex differences, according to Tyler (1965), "began at about the turn of the century and expanded very rapidly" (p. 239). Only after the advent of the current feminist movement, however, has there been a significant amount of research to distinguish innate from learned differences between males and females. Even yet, little of the research tests specifically Jungian hypotheses, many of which posit innate differences.

Indeed, the quantitative research by Jungians on sex differences, thus far, seems to be limited to studies on frequency of types. Gray (1948) collected 1,000 responses to the Gray-Wheelwrights Test (GWT), evidently wherever he could find students, colleagues, and friends to serve as subjects. In his sample the differences between males and females in attitude type (introversion-extraversion) were not statistically significant. There were significant differences, however, in function type. Among the males tested, 70.0% had more sensation than intuition (p = .03), as compared with 63.4% of females, and 77.8% of males had more thinking than feeling, as compared with 53.4% of females (p = .01).

Schaefer (1974) studied the responses to the GWT and the Myers-Briggs Type Indicator (MBTI) of 96 males and 104 females who had registered for a course in Jungian psychology over a three-year period. She found no significant difference in attitude type or in sensation-intuition in this population. In thinking-feeling, there was a significant difference: 55% of males versus 43% of females were more thinking than feeling on the GWT. The difference was in the same direction but not significant on the MBTI.

Increasingly, Jungian writers are challenging Jung's idea that women have no anima and men no animus. For a woman to have no anima suggests that the feminine part of her personality is entirely conscious. Similar reasoning applies to men and the animus. It seems evident that such claims for consciousness are unwarranted.

The concept of androgyny became quite popular during the 1970s to denote the presence of feminine and masculine qualities in both males and females. It reflects the meeting of a crucial pair of opposites in the formation of a complete—individuated—personality. There seems to be little argument that androgyny is an important aspect of psychological development; indeed, it is the logical conclusion of Jung's hypothesis that consciousness (predominantly feminine in women, predominantly masculine in men) must integrate much of the unconscious (predominantly masculine in women, predominantly feminine in men) in order for individuation to proceed.

As with his theory of types and his views on the second half of life, Jung's theories of the psychologies of women and men constitute a valuable contribution to the psychology of individual differences. If there are general norms, they must be modified by the factors of gender, age, and—I would add—cultural background. Jung made an enormous contribution to our understanding of female and male psychology with his simple yet profound assertions that the feminine and masculine principles are *values* more than they are behaviors, and that both principles must be realized in each person, whether female or male, in order for an individual to achieve any degree of wholeness.

Part III

Dynamics of
the Psyche

6

Psychic Energy and Self-Regulation

Unable to accept Freud's narrow conceptualization of the libido as only sexual energy, Jung redefined the term as a general life force, "the *intensity* of a psychic process, its *psychological value*" (CW6, par. 784). This difference in interpretation may have been the crucial issue in the split between Jung and Freud. Gradually Jung ceased to use the term *libido* in favor of *psychic energy*.

The use of this term makes it clear that the psychological concept which is meant is analogous to a principle of physics. Some psychologists reject the premise that physical principles can be applied to nonphysical phenomena; they maintain that what Jung called psychic energy is described better as motivation, attention, or interest. All these can be subsumed, however, in the energic concept.

The psychological "principle of equivalence" parallels the conservation of energy in physics: "For a given quantity of psychic energy expended or consumed in bringing out a certain condition, an equal quantity of the same or another form of energy will appear elsewhere" (CW8, par. 34). The theory of "symptom substitution," which is held by many Freudians and some Jungians, is based on the principle of equivalence. According to this theory, when a symptom is eradicated without removing the underlying cause, another symptom will emerge. Empirical data do not support this theory, at least in any recognizable form, but their absence does not disprove the principle of equivalence in the sense in which Jung defined it. He maintained only that the energy must go somewhere, not necessarily into a symptom; the energy may become disposable or it may be stored in the unconscious, from whence it can be recalled when external and internal conditions are right. Some of this energy is disposable (at the disposal of the ego), some is "in reserve" in the unconscious and is activated readily by an external stimulus, and some of it—bound up with repressed contents—becomes disposable only when the repressed contents are released. Disposable psychic energy is the equivalent of the "will," which was postulated by some philosophers (e.g., Descartes and Schopenhauer) before psychology separated from philosophy and, of course, before the advent of psychoanalysis and behaviorism.

Evidence for Psychic Energy

Psychic energy often is manifested in values that vary from time to time and from person to person, and are sometimes conscious, sometimes unconscious. Values are often expressed in the expenditure of time and money, which are limited and, thus, require choices. If the energy is disposable or readily available to an external stimulus, the choice can be made with little stress. If, however, the energy is held in the unconscious, the necessity of choice may provoke anxiety or depression. For example, a student who faces a history examination but values learning to play the piano can behave in a variety of ways, each contingent on a way of using the existing psychic energy. If the energy is disposable, the student will spend enough time on history to perform creditably on the exam and the rest of the available time practicing the piano. If the energy is available in response to an external stimulus, the approaching exam will pull the student away from the piano in time for enough preparation to pass the exam. However, if the student has a repressed desire to fail the exam, or plays the piano to please his or her parents, the "study time" may be spent at the piano or in a state of anxiety or depression. Such experiences, which nearly everyone has had, are subjective evidence for psychic energy.

The fact that psychic energy is quantifiable and measurable provides further evidence for the existence of such energy. Thus, the energy manifested in affect or emotion (see later section) can be measured by psychogalvanic devices: pulse, respiration, and skin resistance.

Anthropology also supplies evidence for the existence of psychic energy. In some preliterate tribes energy is generated intentionally through engagement in certain rituals before carrying out tedious or difficult tasks, such as planting crops or going to war.

Transformation of Energy

Psychic energy that is held in the unconscious is not lost forever; it sometimes can be freed by a process of energy transformation. The transfer of intensity of value from one mental content to another was designated by Jung as the "canalization of libido" (CW8, par. 79), which corresponds to the physical transformation of energy. Such a physical process is the conversion of heat in a steam engine into steam pressure and then into the energy of motion, such as moving a train. This transfer of energy is made possible by a difference in potential. It flows from the point of high energy (the steam container) toward the point of low energy (the stationary locomotive); as energy is brought to bear upon it, the locomotive begins to move.

A psychological parallel is the release of energy from a complex into problem-solving activities. The complex uses the energy for repression; thus, the problem is "stationary" until the energy is released from the complex and becomes available to resolve it. For example, a young man who expects himself to do perfect work can be said to have a perfectionist complex. At the prospect of handing in a term paper he becomes frantic because of the conflict inherent in the contrast between the intended perfect paper and the actual product. He may fail to submit the paper or submit it late so that the expected low grade is due to lateness rather than to the incompetence he fears is true of him. In psychotherapy, when the perfectionist attempts to justify the excessive demands he makes on himself, strong emotion arises and changes his view of the situation so that he is released from the need to perform perfectly. The energy that had been tied up in the perfectionist complex thus becomes available for writing the paper and undertaking other projects.

Polarity and Entropy

Inherent in Jung's conception of psychic energy is the principle of opposites. Just as in the physical parallel, a flow of energy is produced by the difference in potential between poles. Jung asserted that "Without [a preexisting polarity] . . . there could be no energy. There must always be high and low, hot and cold, etc., so that the equilibrating process, which is energy, can take place" (CW7, par. 115).

A non-Jungian psychiatrist, Albert Rothenberg (1979), reached a similar conclusion, apparently independently of Jung. In an intensive study of fifty-four creative people, Rothenberg found that many creative achievements begin with a tension between opposites; for example, Joseph Conrad conceived his novel Nostromo out of awareness that a rogue also could be a person of character.

The opposite of a flow of energy is entropy. Jung used the term to mean a static condition in which there is no difference in potential and, hence, no psychic energy. This condition occurs in death, physical or psychic. Jung saw a kind of psychic death in the catatonia experienced by some schizophrenics. The syndrome can be described as an example of entropy—of opposites so nearly equal that there is no flow of energy. A condition of perfect harmony is likely to be equally static. Thus, a mature personality, in Jung's view, is one that is in process of development, not one that is in perfect balance.

Progression and Regression

An individual's adaptive capabilities were described by Jung in terms of alternating "progressive" and "regressive" psychic energy. Energy that is progressive is directed toward satisfying the demands of the person's social environment. Progression, however, should not be confused with development.

Psychological development requires differentiation, that is, the capacity to determine when one's interests are served by adaptation to the environment and when to one's inner necessity.

Regression is required when an individual's qualities no longer satisfy the demands of the environment. One's energy moves "backward" and "downward" and activates unconscious contents that have been excluded from consciousness because they tend to be incompatible with it, perhaps because they are irrational or immoral. These contents are important, however, because they contain the "germs of new life and vital possibilities for the future" (CW8, par. 63). Sometimes, such contents are too incompatible with consciousness to be admissible. They continue to be excluded, and psychic energy is dammed up. The result may be neurosis (see Chapter 11).

An example of regression is seen in the situation of a woman who is ambitious to achieve a certain goal, such as a high-status job, but is rejected. The frustrated job seeker becomes depressed and unable to function in the outer world. The disappointment forces her to reassess her life goals and to explore new avenues of expression, such as different work, revitalized personal relations, or an avocation such as writing or painting. She finds that life takes on new vitality and interest and that "new" inner resources have been tapped. Thus, the unpleasant state of affairs has contributed to the development of the woman's inner life and, hence, to individuation. It becomes evident that the alternation of progression and regression is necessary to continued growth.

Emotion

Emotion was discussed little in Jung's writings. He mentioned it incidentally in relation to such psychological phenomena as complexes, projections, and archetypes, and he indicated that the flow of psychic energy is experienced subjectively as emotion. Thus, despite the relative lack of emphasis on it by that name, emotion is of great importance in Jung's view of the dynamics of the psyche. Indeed, he described it as "the alchemical fire whose warmth brings everything into existence and whose heat burns all superfluities to ashes. . . . But on the other hand, emotion is the moment when steel meets flint and a spark is struck forth, for emotion is the chief source of consciousness. There is no change from darkness to light or from inertia to movement without emotion" (CW9–I, par. 179).

The importance and value of emotions must not be allowed to obscure the fact that usually they are not under the control of the ego. Indeed, they tend to override the ego's intentions. Emotions arise out of the unconscious and "upset the rational order of consciousness by their elemental outbursts" (CW9–I, par. 497). This description does not mean that emotion is never under ego control. Although the ego cannot command emotions, it can direct the energy they carry. As the ego becomes stronger, its capacity to channel emotions increases.

Although emotion is often associated with feeling, just as it can be associated with any function, the two should not be confused. Feeling is a function of valuing, of making judgments. There may be a difference between feeling and other functions with respect to emotion, however, in that feeling turns into affect or emotion more readily; values seem more likely to stir passions than, for example, ideas.

Instinct

Other expressions of psychic energy include "instinctive" impulses. Jung defined instincts as "typical modes of action" (CW8, par. 273) based on physiological urges, and as "[modes] of behaviour of which neither the motive nor the aim is fully conscious" (CW8, par. 265). Thus, although Jung wrote at a time when the concept of unlearned behavior was rejected by nearly all psychologists, he hypothesized that some behaviors are innate to humans as well as to animals. As so often happens in the history of ideas, the pendulum is swinging, this time back toward Jung's view. Although the word instinct is not used, the rapidly developing field of ethology is providing evidence for innate behavior potentials (see Chapter 3).

Self-Regulation

That the psyche is self-regulating is a crucial premise of Jung's theory. Self-regulation is an analogue of the body's homeostatic mechanism, which maintains physiological equilibrium: for example, to produce perspiration when the body is overheated (the perspiration evaporates and cools the body). Similarly, when the psyche is out of balance it produces compensatory contents from the unconscious (e.g., dreams) to balance the one-sidedness in consciousness.

Self-regulation, as Jung viewed it, does not result in a static state but, rather, in a new condition of disequilibrium. This view bears considerable resemblance to the "thesis-antithesis-synthesis" formulation of the German philosopher Hegel (1770–1831). Psychologist Gordon W. Allport (1968) stated his agreement with Jung: "The full unification of personality is never attained. Somewhat after the manner of Carl G. Jung, I assume that the nearest approach to unity consists in the never realized striving for unity" (p. 3).

Homeostasis

The concept of physiological homeostasis was posited by Walter B. Cannon (1932). This concept has been found useful, not only in Jung's psychic self-regulation but also in other schools of psychology. For example, behavioral psychologist G. L. Freeman (1948) stated that "all behavior is an attempt to preserve organismic integrity by 'homeostatic' restorations of equilibrium" (p. 1).

Another application of homeostasis is found in the relatively new science of cybernetics. It makes extensive use of the mechanism of feedback—"the furnishing of data concerning the output of a machine to an automatic control device so that errors may be corrected" (Random House Dictionary of the English Language, 1967). Thus, the biological mechanism of homeostasis has been carried over to machines made by humans; feedback is another name for the principle of self-regulation. In Jung's view, psychological feedback occurs through such experiences as errors, dreams, and emotional pain.

Closed and Open Systems

Whether the system is open or closed seems to be a point of disagreement between Jung and some of the other psychologists who study homeostasis. Jung hypothesized a *relatively* closed system in which the collective unconscious provides the dreams and other psychic contents to correct and compensate the "one-sidedness of our conscious life" (*CW8*, par. 557). C. M. Child (1924), writing a few years before Cannon, held that the living organism "is not a 'closed system' maintaining itself against the rest of the world, but a system open at every point and in continuous and necessary relation to environment" (p. 238). The disagreement is not sharp, however; Jung's "relatively" closed system quite clearly allows for the interaction of the human psyche with the environment. His writings on other topics make it clear that he acknowledged and sometimes emphasized this interaction.

The assertion that the system is relatively closed appears to be a corollary of Jung's purposive view of psychic energy, which he contrasted with Freud's causal view. Causality seems to imply that outside forces determine a person's responses. Jung postulated that causality is less important than purpose, and that purpose arises from within the person.

The purposive view of the psyche necessitates a concept of self-regulation. In response to the loss of stability that results from changing conditions, both inner and outer, the psyche moves toward the goal of reestablishing equilibrium, as well as toward other goals.

Compensation

The psychic mechanism through which self-regulation works is that of compensation. Jung's concept of compensation is not the one described by Alfred Adler (the process of providing reassurance for oneself in the face of inferiority or insecurity); nor is it the same as Freud's concept of wish fulfillment (the gratification of impulses). Rather, Jung conceptualized compensation as the instrument of the drive toward wholeness. Compensation draws upon the contents of the collective unconscious: images, feelings, attitudes, and behaviors that combine with those of consciousness to produce approximations to wholeness. The various ways in which compensation can operate, especially in dreams, are described in Chapter 17.

Compensation, according to Jung, differs from *complementation*, a term derived from the Latin *complere*, which means "to supplement or complete." Complementation "designates a relationship in which two things supplement one another more or less mechanically" (CW8, par. 545). Subliminal perceptions, for example, complement the perceptions that have entered awareness. Complementary contents are likely to be of little or no significance to the individual's psychological development.

Compensation is derived from the Latin *compensare*, which means "to equalize." The derivation suggests a "balancing and comparing [of] different data or points of view so as to produce an adjustment or rectification" (CW8, par. 545) by the unconscious of that which is necessary to correct a one-sided attitude in the conscious mind. In other words, compensation modifies consciousness in a purposeful manner.

Although Jung made a point of distinguishing compensation from complementation, he gave no examples of complementation and did not demonstrate conclusively the distinction between the two concepts. The distinguishing of one from the other by Jung seems to be based on subjective data, such as the presence or absence of a dreammr's personal associations to something or someone that is perceived subliminally. Thus, the separation of compensation from complementation may be what some philosophers call "a distinction without a difference."

Bash (1952) attempted to test compensation directly, using the Rorschach Test. The subjects were five introverts, twelve extraverts, and three "ambiverts." He administered a usual Rorschach to each. A few days later, in a dark room, he illuminated Rorschach Plate IX two hundred times for five seconds each. As in a usual Rorschach, after each exposure the subject was requested to say what he or she had seen and what it resembled, and was asked to pay attention to possible repetitions. Certain subjects, who had fallen into a condition that Bash described as "drowsy," gave responses of a dreamlike character, which the subjects often spontaneously compared with dreams. These responses were compared with those from the ordinary Rorschach tests of the five introverts and twelve extraverts. Of the forty-three "dreamlike" responses, twenty-five indicated a reversal of the experience type (introversion or extraversion), seven showed no change, and eleven were undefined. Bash saw these results as confirmation for Jung's thesis that the unconscious is compensatory to consciousness.

An extreme form of compensation that was mentioned often

by Jung is the principle of *enantiodromia*, which was identified, apparently, by the Greek philosopher Heraclitus. According to this principle, everything tends to turn into its opposite. Jung considered *enantiodromia* to occur psychically when an attitude takes an extreme form, for example, when a person who rigidly follows all the rules of proper behavior "flips" into a totally contradictory action, such as murder.

The hypothesis that a person under stress is likely to lapse into behavior that is more appropriate to that person's non-dominant—unconscious—attitude type was tested by Spare (1968). The subjects were forty-three male and female university and extension and graduate students who tested strongly introversive, strongly extraversive or ambiversive on the Myers-Briggs Type Indicator, the Gray-Wheelwrights Test, and the Social Introversion Scale (Minnesota Multiphasic Personality Inventory). Under artificial stress conditions (the expectation of inescapable pain emanating from such sources as electric shock) the battery of tests was repeated. Evidence of change in the predicted direction was not significant. Two subjects who were undergoing real stress (anticipating radical heart surgery) underwent changes of sufficient magnitude to lend support to the notion that the phenomenon of *enantiodromia* may be more likely with subjects undergoing real stress than with subjects experiencing artificial stress. Despite the lack of conclusive results, the study suggests the kind of research that is possible in the realm of the self-regulation of the psyche.

7

Complexes

The concept of complexes was so central to Jung's ideas that, initially, he labeled his body of theories "Complex Psychology." Although the label was not accepted widely, the term *complex* came into common usage. "Complex" and "Jung" became so closely associated that even the inferiority complex, which was identified by Alfred Adler, has been thought by many people to be a discovery of Jung's. Historically, the term *complex* originated with Theodore Ziehen, a German psychiatrist who experimented with reaction time in word association test responses. Although Jung did not originate the concept, he refined it and devoted considerable effort to the detection and analysis of complexes. This work led to the adoption of the term in general psychology.

To Jung, the complex, "the architect of dreams and symptoms," was the *via regia* (royal road) to the unconscious (*CW8*, par. 210). This statement was phrased as an alternative to Freud's idea that dreams are the *via regia* to the unconscious and that complexes *are* the unconscious. Jung's idea, evidently, was that dreams and symptoms were the observable manifestations of underlying complexes, and that behind or under the complexes is the unlimited sea of the unconscious. The complex, in effect, links the personal unconscious, with its repressed contents, to the collective unconscious and archetypes.

In his later years Jung wrote little about complexes as such. Nevertheless, the concept remained central in his thought because he considered complexes to play a fundamental role in the individuation process.

What Is a Complex?

A complex is an interrelated cluster of unconscious contents which is part of the shadow. It is "strongly accentuated emotionally and is . . . incompatible with the habitual attitude of consciousness" (CW8, par. 201). The emotionality of the complex is so intrinsic that Jung initially qualified the term with the modifying phrase "feeling-toned." Inasmuch as "feeling" designates one of Jung's four function types, the descriptive phrase "emotionally toned" seems preferable. The use of the modifier has been dropped in current practice but it is implied. Indeed, Jung saw emotionality as virtually identical with the complex: "Every affect tends to become an autonomous complex, to break away from the hierarchy of consciousness and, if possible, to drag the ego after it" (CW8, par. 628).

Persons who have a complex about sex, for example, become emotionally upset when they see or hear sexually suggestive material, and they read sexual overtones into words or actions that have no relation to sex. The distortion of their perceptions is due to the emotion, perhaps of anxiety, aroused by the complex. Thus, the complex is "a pair of ill-fitting glasses" through which one sees situations and other people in exaggerated or otherwise distorted form.

When the emotion inherent in the complex assumes overwhelming proportions, it enters the realm of psychopathology in the form of hallucination, illusion, or delusion. An example of the latter is the "savior complex," the delusion that one is Christ. At the same time, the emotionality of the complex serves a function in psychological development (see later section) and it provides the psychic energy that is necessary for the complex to be expressed in overt behavior.

In addition to emotionality and its possible accompanying perceptual distortions, complexes are characterized by a large degree of autonomy; that is, they cannot be controlled by conscious intentions. Hence, complexes take on the guise of "splinter psyches" that appear in waking behavior and are ways of thinking and acting that are foreign to the ego. These ways of thinking include disrupted cognitions, for example, compulsive thoughts and disturbed memory. Ways of acting include accidents and slips of the tongue ("Freudian slips"). Jung described some of the manifestations of complexes as devilish:

> Complexes behave like Descartes' devils and seem to delight in playing impish tricks. They slip just the wrong word into one's mouth, they make one forget the name of the person one is about to introduce, they cause a tickle in the throat just when the softest passage is being played on the piano at a concert, they make the tiptoeing latecomer trip over the chair with a resounding crash. They bid us congratulate the mourners at a burial instead of consoling them . . . these impish complexes are unteachable. (CW8, par. 202)

Its autonomous nature means that a complex is more than "separate but equal." We do not have complexes; they have us. When a complex is activated, the person has a sense of being out of control—"beside oneself." Attempts to get rid of a complex are likely to result in its reappearance at the first provocation, in its original or greater strength.

To the habitual attitude of consciousness, complexes are unacceptable and incompatible, just as are all contents of the shadow. A dream may reflect the unacceptability of a complex; for example, it may appear as a person whom the dreamer dislikes. Often, a complex is rooted in the inferior function (see Chapter 4). Thus, a feeling-type individual may have a "stupidity complex" because thinking is the person's inferior function and, thus, is undifferentiated and slow. (Nevertheless, undifferentiated thinking is not synonymous with stupidity, nor is differentiated thinking the same as intelligence.)

What Makes Complexes?

Complexes are normal phenomena in that everyone has them. They vary in content, number, intensity, and origin. Although a complex may arise from a one-time traumatic incident, it is more likely to stem from an oft-repeated experience, usually in childhood. For example, frequent parental criticism can produce in a child a "criticism complex," which may manifest itself, in adulthood, in perceiving neutral or even complimentary comments as critical judgments.

Another possible basis of a complex is what Jung called a "moral" conflict, that is, the apparent impossibility of reconciling conflicting parts of one's nature. An example is the polarity that can occur between one's sex drive and the belief that masturbation and premarital sexual relations are wicked; the conflict often leads to the repression of the sex drive or the distortion of sexual impulses into hostility or anxiety.

Archetypal Core

According to Jung, every complex, in addition to its base in personal experience, has an archetypal core. This core is reflected in the complex's carrying greater energy than can be accounted for by the experiences from which it stems. The complex is rooted so deeply in the unconscious that it links with an intrinsic (archetypal) factor of the psyche.

An example of an archetypal core of a complex is found in the "child archetype," which was discussed at length by Jung (CW9–I). An expression of this archetype is an image of the "Divine" or "Wonder" Child that is often personified in the Christ Child. The Child's miraculous birth denotes the qualities of creativity and spontaneity that are characteristic of the "inner child" (the childlike part of the personality) just as they are of actual children. It is the negative side of this archetype that underlies various complexes, for example, a "vulnerability complex." An archetypal image of vulnerability is the biblical story of the massacre of the male infants ordered by King Herod, a danger that forced the Holy Family to flee to Egypt. Closely related to the vulnerability complex is the "rejected child complex."

Even Freud, who denied the existence of archetypes, contributed an excellent example in the archetypally based Oedipus or Electra complex (see Chapter 10). Although he sought the source of the complex in the person's actual experience with his or her parents, the presumed universality of the experience and its intensity suggest a more adequate explanation: that the individual parent-child relation reflects an archetypal counterpart.

Jung found that the existence and strength of a complex are "guaranteed" (protected) because the person is unconscious of it. For a complex to be unconscious means that the complex and the responses based on it are not under ego control. That is, one may be cognitively aware of a complex without being able to control it. For example, one may be able to identify one's "criticism complex" yet still perceive much more criticism than is actually being transmitted.

The power of the complex is strengthened further by the individual's reluctance to give it up, even if it is negative. Perhaps because it is familiar, the person is frightened at the prospect of life without the complex. The logic of the situation is, "I'm glad I don't like spinach, because if I liked it, I would eat it, and I hate it."

The Ego as Complex

Despite the unconscious nature of most complexes, the ego is a complex, according to Jung. In order for this idea to be valid, the concept of complex must be broadened to designate any functionally interconnected set of psychic contents, conscious or unconscious. Clearly, the ego can be considered to consist of a cluster of conscious psychic contents, and to have an archetypal core—the image of the hero. It seems evident, however, that the usual characteristics of a complex—emotionality and incompatibility with consciousness—do not apply to the ego complex. The differences between the ego complex and other complexes are extensive enough to suggest that Jung used the term *complex* to convey more than one meaning.

Positive Complexes

Thus far it has appeared that complexes are always negative. In my view, however, there are positive complexes, which are accompanied by positive emotions, such as enthusiasm and joy. Jung did not mention positive complexes but they fit his definition of habitual attitudes or responses.

A positive complex is experienced through positive emotions and results in the constructive, even creative, pursuit of an idea, a goal, or a desired personal relationship. For example, an "achievement complex"—an exaggerated need for achievement—can motivate a great deal of productive work and be rewarded by feelings of satisfaction with the work accomplished. (It turns into a negative complex when no amount of achievement satisfies the achiever.) A positive complex sometimes can be identified by appearing in a dream as a person who is admired by the dreamer.

Empirical Evidence of Complexes

The concept of complexes, like all of Jung's theories, was developed empirically. The theory is unusual among Jungian hypotheses, however, in that the empirical data provided by Jung were not limited to the clinical; they were also experimental. Specifically, Jung developed the theory of complexes out of his work on the Word Association Test, which he undertook at the suggestion of Eugen Bleuler. Indeed, Jung's work on the test led him, independently of Freud, to the discovery of complexes and an understanding of the unconscious.

In Jung's Word Association Test the person being tested is asked to say the first word that comes to mind after each stimulus word is pronounced by the tester. Each response is recorded as well as the time lapse between the presentation of the stimulus word and the response. This time lapse, the *reaction time*, is measured in fifths of a second.

Immediately after the first presentation, the list of stimulus words is presented a second time and the subject is asked to repeat his or her responses. Jung's premise was that the emotion of a complex is present when cognition is disturbed; thus, he designated as "complex-indicators" the stimulus words that were associated with longer-than-average reaction times, perseveration (delayed responses to words immediately following), errors in reproduction (recall) of the response word, and repetition (by the subject) of the stimulus word.

History of the Word Association Test

The word association method was invented by Sir Francis Galton, who published his first article on the subject in 1879.

"He found that answers were not given haphazardly but had some relevance to the thoughts, feelings, and memories of the individual. This aspect of the word association test, however, was overlooked by Galton's followers, and it was C. G. Jung who first ũšed that test as a detector of unconscious representation" (Ellenberger, 1970, p. 313).

Wilhelm Wundt and others in Germany also worked with the word association method but used "certain logical principles of classification" (CW2, par. 871). Wundt's successors, Gustav Aschaffenburg and Emil Kraepelin, attempted to find variables (e.g., educational level) that could account for different types of responses to the stimulus words. Other investigators, such as K. R. Sommer, used the type of response (e.g., irrelevancies) to diagnose a specific mental condition, for example, schizophrenia. However, Ziehen and others had found variations in reaction times that were related to the stimulus words' emotional significance.

Clinical Use of the Test

When Jung and his colleagues began to use the Word Association Test clinically, they first followed Sommer's lead in looking for diagnostic factors in the contents of the responses. This approach was unsuccessful. Consequently, they began to focus on reaction times and incorrect reproductions of stimulus words. Thus, they carried forward Galton's and Ziehen's lines of investigation. As Jung explained it, "We know from the research of Ziehen, and of Mayer and Orth that it is particularly the associations that awaken memories of an unpleasant nature that take a long time" (CW2, par. 889).

Jung developed a list of one hundred stimulus words and "made a major contribution in standardizing the methods of administration and interpretation" (Bell, 1948, p. 16). He developed the concept of "complex-indicators," under which he subsumed the various disturbances in responses.

By about 1906 he was using a psychogalvanometer to note changes in respiration and skin resistance that accompanied responses to emotionally charged words. The word association reaction times proved to be correlated with the psychogalvanic measurements and, hence, with the intensity and duration of the emotion. Thus, the list of complex-indicators was expanded to include changes in respiration and skin resistance.

Jung found that the indicators cluster around stimulus words which indicate the nature of the subject's complexes. For example, a young man displayed complex-indicators in association with the words *woman, home,* and *fight.* These indicators led to the hypothesis that his complex was associated with conflict in his marriage. Subsequent analysis confirmed the hypothesis. The validity of the Word Association Test was established through the discovery by Jung and his colleagues that many of their clinical findings confirmed the existence of specific complexes and their content. Ironically, the clinical data, including dreams, matched the Word Association results so well that Jung stopped using the test. Nevertheless, he recommended its use in the training of young psychologists and physicians who had had little or no previous understanding of the unconscious.

Experimental Use of Word Association Tests

Clinically, Jung's Word Association Test is used primarily to discover an individual's complexes. Experimentally, various word association tests are used to discover emotional reactions that are common to groups of persons. For example, Cermák and Dornič (1961) found that when such a test was administered to tuberculosis patients "the most emotionally effective words were those which did not refer directly to the disease but to its personal and social consequences for the patient" (p. 705). Such "personal and social consequences" may have been linked to complexes. (Because the study was published in a Yugoslavian journal, only an abstract is available in English.)

In a study using a word association test to evaluate the psychoanalytical formulation of "depression . . . as aggression directed against an internalized 'loved-hated' object" (Bodin and Geer, 1965, p. 392), the investigators predicted "that depressed [as compared to nondepressed subjects] will show relative increase in disruptions, or 'complex indicators,' to words of aggressive content"; the study was designed also "to specify the relationship between intensity of aggressive content and the amount of disruption" (pp. 392–93), a return to analysis of content, which Jung had rejected. The subjects were twelve male and twelve female hospitalized patients, half with high and half with low scores on the MMPI depression scale. The test consisted of thirty words, ten from each of three hostility levels: high, moderate, and nonhostile. In the administration, two conditions were followed after the initial trial in which all subjects were asked to respond with the first word that came to mind. In one condition, half the subjects were asked to respond with the same words they had given initially; in the second, the remaining subjects were asked to respond with different words from those given initially. The results "did not support the psychoanalytically derived hypothesis that depressed Ss will show more disturbances or 'complex indicators' to hostile stimuli than nondepressed Ss. . . . The most obvious interpretation is that the psychoanalytic formulation is incorrect" (p. 405).

An interesting employment of a word association test was to measure relationships between EEG abnormalities and the test after prefrontal lobotomies (Liberson, 1949). In the twelve patients whose EEGs showed no change after lobotomy, the average reaction time was faster than in the five patients in whom considerable postoperative effects were found.

A study by Bixler (1952) compared responses to twenty-five words on Jung's Word Association Test with responses to twenty-five words that were selected by each of the subjects—fifty-one women and seventy-eight men who were students in general psychology classes at the University of Louisville. Each subject provided twenty-five nouns of his or her choosing, according to instructions aimed at encouraging the subject to write words that would be "related to his attitudes and experiences without emphasizing the latter" (p. 30). The subjects were placed in five groups by random selection for varying the order of presentation of self-selected words and Jung's words. Two "complex indicators" occurred frequently enough for analysis: long reaction time and defective reproduction of the original response at the second presentation of the stimulus word. There were no significant differences between the responses to the self-selected words and Jung's words. This result seems to indicate that Jung's list can be as useful as a list of words selected by a test subject.

Also using a list different from Jung's, the famous Russian psychologist Alexander Luria, according to Gardner (1980), experimented with a word association technique for measuring a person's emotional state. While associating to each word on the list the subject was asked to squeeze a rubber bulb. "Under normal circumstances, a person will say the word that comes first to mind and will be able, at the same time, to squeeze the bulb in a quick and smooth manner. . . . Luria found irregular rhythms of squeezing in those individuals who had conflicts" (p. 90). Although Gardner cited Luria's work as an unprecedented documentation of "the intricate interplay between a person's knowledge (command of linguistic meaning) and unconscious anxieties (which surround sensitive topics)" (p. 90), the similarity of the study to Jung's work is clear, with Luria's bulb pressing replacing the psychogalvanometer Jung used.

The few studies reported here indicate that word association tests are useful for experimental as well as clinical purposes, whatever the investigator's theoretical orientation. In evaluating Jung's studies of the Word Association Test, Dry (1961) wrote:

> Over and above its practical usefulness, . . . the work is of theoretical significance as the first experimental confirmation of psychoanalytic findings, demonstrating, under conditions which are repeatable and open to all, the existence of inhibition or repression as postulated by Freud in his work on dreams and neuroses, the sexual nature of many complexes, and the value of the association method in detecting them. (p. 29)

Two of Jung's three lectures at Clark University in 1909 dealt with the Word Association Test. In the first, "The Association Method," he described the Test, the method of its administration, and its use for identifying complexes in the persons being tested. The second lecture, "The Family Constellation," presented a rudimentary statistical method for discovering differences and similarities in responses to the Test among members of the same family. (These and other relevant studies compose *CW2, Experimental Researches.*)

In sum, Jung's work on the Word Association Test pioneered the development of projective techniques and the application of experimental method to depth psychology (Freud's data were all clinical). By applying experimental techniques, he developed the crucial concept of complexes and provided an empirical means of identifying complexes. In addition, he established the relation between psychogalvanic measures and emotionally laden words; this work has had wide ramifications, including the development of lie detectors.

How to Deal with a Complex

It is relatively easy to confirm the existence of complexes. It is much more difficult to discover what to do about them.

Maduro and Wheelwright (1977) suggested four ways in which the ego may relate to a complex: "(1) by remaining completely *unconscious* of it; (2) by *identification* or possession; (3) by *projection;* and (4) by *confrontation,* which alone leads to assimilation" (p. 90).

If the complex remains completely unconscious, it may be expressed in behavior which the ego is totally unaware of or at least does not recognize as incompatible with conscious values. In this condition, there is no opportunity for the ego to make choices regarding the complex.

If the ego is "identified with" (dominated by) the complex, the behavior is likely to be even more incompatible with conscious values and there is still less opportunity for ego choices. If the complex is projected, its owner sees a problem but perceives it as existing outside himself or herself, in a situation or in another person, and still no ego choice is possible.

Confrontation is an ego choice. It begins when the owner of the complex suspects that some or all of the problem is internal. This suspicion is likely to occur when efforts to solve the problem externally have failed, when the projectee claims or demonstrates qualities that challenge the projection, or when previous experiences with other complexes suggest that the current problem also may be due to a complex. The confrontation occurs in two steps: (a) withdrawal of the projection and (b) assimilation (integration) of the complex. Withdrawal of the projection means that the projector discovers that his or her perception of the problem situation or other person has been erroneous. Assimilation of the complex can occur when one experiences the inner conflict and sees clearly the part it has played in the outer problem.

This explanation of the process of assimilating complexes may be misleadingly simple. Actually, the process is difficult and painful. It includes a lowering of the perceived power of the ego and giving up some treasured illusions. Moreover, it is not primarily a process of intellectual understanding. Rather, it is a process of outgrowing the complex, and growth means change. However devoted one is to change, it carries loss and pain.

8

Projection

Complexes are most apparent, perhaps, when they are projected onto other persons. Although there are different ways of defining projection, von Franz (1975) seemed to express Jung's view when she wrote that a projection "is the tendency to see in others peculiarities and ways of behaving which we ourselves display without being aware that we do. . . . [It] is an involuntary transposition of something unconscious in ourselves into an outer object" (p. 77). For example, a woman who rarely expressed her wishes directly often achieved her objectives by charming her companion and then casually suggesting what she wanted to have happen. When her rival for male attention was more forthright in seeking to satisfy personal needs, the first woman called her "devious." This anecdote illustrates the Jungian concept of projection: attributing to another person a quality or attitude that is present, albeit unconsciously, in oneself.

Just as complexes are autonomous contents so projection is an autonomous act. Thus, projection is not deliberate; it happens to one. Jung briefly described the process as follows: "People say, 'One makes projections.' That's nonsense. One doesn't make them; one finds them. They are already there . . . in the unconscious" (McGuire and Hull, 1977, p. 323). Although we can and do project onto animals, places, and objects, Jung discussed only projections onto persons. Most of his comments on projection can be applied, however, to the other three categories.

Projections can be either positive or negative. Negative projections are close to Freud's (1938) concept of a defense process, whereby an unconscious negative emotion "is ejected from our internal perception into the external world, and thus, detached from [the projector] and pushed onto someone else" (SE13, pp. 62–63). The content that is detached is one which the projector dislikes or fears in himself or herself and, hence, pushes out of consciousness. Such projection is the process of attributing to another person one's emotion or the cause of one's emotion. For example, a woman who never is aware of her anger projects that emotion onto other people, and frequently perceives them as angry. Another woman, who knows that she "blows up" easily, but who is unable to control her anger, projects the cause of it onto other people: They act in ways that "make her angry." Or such a woman may be fearful, seeing the cause of her fear in others' anger, presumably because she fears her own anger.

Projection is positive when one perceives in another person those desirable qualities that are potential but not developed in oneself. The result may be admiration for the other person, desire for acquaintance and friendship, or infatuation to the point of wishing to possess her or him. The strongest positive projections are experienced as "being in love."

Alternatively, the projection of positive qualities may lead to envy or jealousy. In such a case, one perceives the envied quality to be undesirable. For example, if one is jealous of another person's success one may attribute it to ruthless ambition, nepotism, or chicanery. If one envies a neighbor's new car, one may find reasons to characterize the car as inferior to other makes or to suggest that the new owner overpaid for it.

The object of a projection usually has the projected quality but to a lesser degree than is perceived by the projector. Indeed, Jung stated repeatedly that for every projection there is a "hook," that is, a tendency toward the quality projected or toward behavior that suggests such a quality. For example, when a power motive is projected onto a person, he or she usually displays some measure of power seeking, although probably not as much as is attributed by the projector.

It is fairly easy to recognize the projections of one's family and friends but it is difficult and often painful to recognize one's own. This difficulty in perception may result from the conviction that the source of an interpersonal problem is in the other person; for example, a man who denies his sexual impulses may believe that all women deliberately dress and behave in a sexually provocative manner.

Projection and Complexes

Projection is characterized by strong emotion and consequent overreaction in word or deed. The emotionality of projection reflects an intricate relation with complexes; indeed, it is complexes that tend to be projected. This fact makes projections useful in psychological explorations; together with dreams they are the readiest way of discovering the nature and strength of a person's complexes. Jung even maintained that some complexes can be identified only as they are projected onto other persons.

Projections are not necessarily permanent. For example, one young man perceived an admired older woman as being motherly and speaking in a pleasant, well-modulated voice. After long acquaintance, during which she proved not to be very motherly, he was able to see her behavior for what it was and even to perceive the shrillness in her voice. Thus, he "withdrew the projection." It is difficult to withdraw projections, however, and conscious effort alone is rarely sufficient. Nevertheless, because projections interfere with clear perceptions of other persons and, hence, with genuine relationships, withdrawal not only is important but also necessary in order to integrate the projected content and enhance the individuation process.

The withdrawal of projections is easily thwarted because many are negative and tend to make one dislike and even avoid the object of the projection; the avoidance prevents one from becoming better acquainted with the object and from testing the projection against that person's reality. Consequently, the projection may be maintained indefinitely, however false it is.

Projective Tests

The concept of projection is the basis for a number of diagnostic psychological tests. Probably the best known are the Rorschach Test and the Thematic Apperception Test (TAT). The first consists of ten cards with bilaterally symmetrical inkblots, some in color, to which the subject responds by telling what he or she sees. The tester records all the responses. Inasmuch as the forms are ambiguous, considerable projection enters into the responses. In the TAT, the test taker is asked to tell a story about each of nineteen picture cards and one blank card. Although the pictures are less ambiguous than the Rorschach inkblots, they elicit a wide range of responses, each apparently based on the person's experiences and projections.

Experimental Evidence of Projection

Abundant clinical and some experimental evidence attest to the concept of projections. For example, Schlenker and Miller (1977) studied the attributions offered by group members when the group performed poorly. The subjects, 144 male college students, were divided into four-person groups to solve problems. After the groups recommended solutions to a series of problems, the members of each group were informed that their group had done extremely well, average, or very poorly on the problems. Subjects took less personal responsibility for a group's poor performance and they attributed greater responsibility to other group members for failure than they did for success. The assignment of responsibility to others is a form of projection.

Varieties of Projections

In a review of the literature, Holmes (1968) expanded and subdivided the definition of projection. He found two major dimensions: (a) what is projected and (b) whether the individual is aware of possessing the trait that underlies the projection. "What is projected" can be further subdivided into two categories: one's own trait and a trait different from one's own. Each can be paired with the two dimensions of awareness and un-awareness to create four major categories: (a) similarity (one's own trait without awareness); (b) attribution (one's own trait with awareness); (c) complementarity (a trait complementary to one's own with awareness of one's own); (d) Panglossian-Cassandran (an opposite trait without awareness of one's own; Pangloss was Voltaire's character who denied the harsh realities of his situation and insisted on seeing "the best of all possible worlds"; Cassandra was the Greek prophet who foretold disasters and was not believed.).

The first category, *similarity,* is perhaps the best description of Jung's concept of projection. One study (Sears, 1936) appeared to support the category. Sears separated his subjects according to their degree of insight (as determined by peer observations) regarding the amount of a trait they possessed. He reported that noninsightful subjects tended to attribute a greater amount of that trait to other people than did insightful subjects. The methodology of Sears's study has received considerable criticism, however (Campbell, Miller, Lubetsky, and O'Connel, 1964; Murstein, 1957; Wells and Goldstein, 1964; and Wylie, 1961). These investigators found that a statistical artifact made it appear that insightful subjects, as compared to noninsightful subjects, rated themselves more correctly on a trait relative to their perception of others on that trait. Moreover, Rokeach (1945) was unsuccessful in trying to replicate Sears's findings. Thus, Holmes (1968) concluded that "research support for [*similarity*] projection seems to be wholly lacking" (p. 260).

Attributive projection was supported by studies of such qualities and behaviors as cribbing by students (Katz and Allport, 1931), political beliefs (Calvin, Hanley, Hoffman, and Clifford, 1959; Hayes, 1936; Thomsen, 1941; Travers, 1941; and Wallen, 1941, 1943), ratings of the happiness of photographed individuals (Goldings, 1954), and children's overt generosity (Wright, 1942).

Holmes found considerable evidence for *complementary* projection. Murray (1933) reported that, after playing a frightening game of "murder," five young girls saw photographed individuals as more frightening than they had prior to playing the game. Hornberger (1960) obtained comparable results; male college students who had been frightened by painful electric shocks projected more aggression onto a male whom they observed taking some psychological tests than did subjects who had not been shocked. These studies concur that the projected trait is the complement of the subject's own trait.

Panglossian projection may be suggested in some clinical material, such as responses to projective tests that are interpreted as "reaction formation." Some administrators of projective tests, consequently, assume that a person who sees the world as positive actually has unconscious negative feelings. However, Holmes's review contained no support for the concept of Panglossian projection.

Cassandran projection also has not been investigated; however, it was included because the dimensions suggested by the theories of projection make it logically possible. Holmes advised humorously "that psychologists take a tip from Apollo, who decreed that Cassandra . . . be ignored" (p. 263).

Function of Projection

The function of projection has been even more difficult to investigate than its existence. Jung saw projection as protecting the projecting person from looking within and from being forced to confront the dark side of his or her personality. Thus, each of us resists withdrawing projections because to do so demands awareness of them and "saddles us with new problems and conflicts" (CW11, par. 140). No research has been conducted to test Jung's hypothesis. However, because it is similar to Freud's thesis that the function of projection is to reduce anxiety, some psychoanalytic research is relevant. Stevens and Reitz (1970) chose 120 male university students who indicated the belief that vocabulary and spelling correlated at least "moderately well" with general mental ability, and described themselves as being better than "fair" in both subjects. The investigators manipulated a failure variable with all the subjects using "three proportions" of unsolvable anagrams. The students were divided into two groups. For Group I, projection was encouraged by asking the students to estimate how various groups of individuals might do on solving the anagrams. Group II students were instructed to cross out vowels in a short paragraph to insure that they spent an equal period of time in the experiment; this task was selected as likely to "discourage" projection.

The defensive properties of projection were measured by anxiety scores (palmar sweat index, rating scale of subjective anxiety feelings, and sentence completion test); each subject's estimate of the number of anagrams he successfully unscrambled; and a reestimate of his abilities in vocabulary, spelling, arithmetic, and of the validities of these indices as indicators of general mental ability. The results of the study generally did not confirm the hypothesis that projection reduces anxiety; the students who projected their own failures onto other people did not necessarily become less anxious. The anxiety-reduction results were equivocal because reports from the second group of subjects also estimated others' scores on the anagram task, which they had not been asked to do. The estimates "can be construed as projections of failure and as such to some extent anxiety-reducing" (p. 153).

Although the experiment did not demonstrate that projection is anxiety-reducing, it indicated that projection has a general defensive property. When asked to estimate the number of anagrams they had successfully unscrambled, the first group overestimated their performance to a greater extent than the second group did at the .001 level of significance.

The clinical implications of the research are difficult to assess. If Holmes's similarity projection is indeed less prevalent than attributive projection, clinicians may be required to accept more readily the client's view of his or her own perceptions; instead of completely unconscious projection, clients are likely to be aware that they see in other people qualities they also see in themselves. For lack of awareness of projections the clinician would need to look for more complementary projection (emotional responses rather than personal qualities). Thus, a client who sees another person as dangerous may be making known the client's fear. In any case, it seems evident that the content of projections can be ascertained more easily than the factors that motivate them.

To discover the motivations of projections, future investigators may find case material more fruitful than controlled studies. Stevens and Reitz (1970) suggested, however, that "future experimental studies of the projection construct might best concentrate on means of more effectively discouraging and/or encouraging projection. In addition, more attention might be paid to developing unobtrusive measures of anxiety which would interfere minimally with the experimental operations" (p. 154).

Although it is difficult to validate, the concept of projection is too useful clinically to be discarded. Whether a person is in psychotherapy or not, the concept is the source of many valuable insights regarding human interactions, including transference (see Chapter 16).

Assimilation of Projections

The usefulness of the concept of projection implies a possibility that projection contributes to increased consciousness. Based on a statement of Jung's (CW13, pars. 247–48), von Franz (1975) identified five stages in the assimilation of projections:

> At the first stage, on the level of archaic identity, the human being experiences projection simply as if it were the perception of reality. However, if conscious or unconscious doubts should arise from within and if the behavior of the object conflicts with the individual's ideas about it, then he begins to differentiate between the projected image and the actual object; this is the second stage in the assimilation of the projection. In the third stage there is a moral judgment concerning the content of the projection. At the fourth level the individual usually explains the projection as having been an error or an illusion. On the fifth level, however, he asks himself where that faulty image could have come from; then he has to recognize it as the image of a psychic content which originally belonged to his own personality. However, if it was not and still is not in evidence in his own psychology, then external factors once again have to be taken into account and the circle begins anew. (p. 79)

Considerable individual development seems to be necessary before projections can be withdrawn and assimilated; that is, the ego must be fairly strong before it can take on the burden of acknowledging the contents—especially those that are negative—of a projection and recognizing that it has been mistaken by withdrawing the projection. When both conditions are met, considerable psychological development results.

9

Symbol

The German word for "symbol," *Sinnbild,* expresses more directly than the English the significance of the concept. *Sinnbild* is compounded from two words: *Sinn* (sense, meaning) and *Bild* (image). As conceptualized by Jung, a symbol is a meaningful image which is an instrument of psychic change, and the psyche is likely to produce a symbol when rational resources are insufficient. Indeed, "There is no intellectual formula capable of representing such a complex phenomenon in a satisfactory way" (*CW*18, par. 570).

The term *symbol* has at least three definitions and uses, only one of which was accepted by Jung as adequate.

1. In the semiotic definition the *symbol* is a sign. According to this definition, the symbol is a consciously devised designation for a known object or function, such as the badge of a railroad conductor. It is arbitrary; there is no likeness between the sign and the object or function it designates. That is, the badge has no intrinsic similarity to the office it denotes.

Included in the category of sign is an analogue—an image representing a similar appearing object. Most of Freud's symbols were analogues; for example, to him any phallus-shaped image meant a penis. Jung objected to Freud's interpreting dreams according to this concept of symbol. He insisted that each image conveys its own message; the unconscious is capable of depicting a penis if a penis is meant. A church steeple is phallus-shaped but is not a penis and should not be interpreted as one.

2. The term *symbol* may be used to designate an allegory—a concrete representation of an abstract or spiritual concept or experience. In Bunyan's *Pilgrim's Progress*, for example, the journey of the Pilgrim is an allegory of the inner journey of individuation.

3. The meaning of *symbol* that Jung used was, *the best possible formulation of a relatively unknown psychic content.* The image "kingdom of heaven" is an apt example of symbol in this sense because it expresses a psychic (mental) content which is so unknown that it cannot be described with one metaphor. Several metaphors are required, each with its own import; the kingdom is likened to such images as leaven, a grain of mustard seed, and hidden treasure. Leaven is a substance that seems almost magical in its power to increase the volume of bread dough; thus, it is a metaphor for an agent with transformative powers. Mustard seed "is the smallest of all seeds, but when it has grown it is the greatest of shrubs and becomes a tree, so that the birds of the air come and make nests in its branches" (Matthew 13:32). The treasure hidden in a field is so valuable that "a man . . . goes and sells all that he has and buys that field" (Matthew 13:44). None of these images is sufficient alone to describe the kingdom of heaven. All are necessary so that one can "circumambulate" the symbol; thus, the image of the kingdom of heaven *points to* a meaning that is beyond description.

Experts in fields dealing with symbol support Jung's conception of the term. Thass-Thienemann (1973), for example, wrote, "[A] characteristic of the symbol consists of the fact that the symbolic meaning permeates, sometimes consciously, mostly unconsciously, the physical vehicle which is its carrier" (p. 21).

Sometimes a single object or image serves as both a sign and a symbol, under different circumstances. Jung used the example of the Christian cross: "The interpretation of the cross as a symbol of divine love is *semiotic*, because 'divine love' describes the fact to be expressed better and more aptly than a cross, which can have many other meanings. On the other hand, an interpretation of the cross is *symbolic* when it puts the cross beyond all conceivable explanations, regarding it as expressing an as yet unknown and incomprehensible fact of a mystical or transcendent, i.e., psychological, nature, which simply finds itself most appropriately represented in the cross" (*CW6*, par. 815).

Although Jung's objection to Freud's interpreting every phallus-shaped image as a penis was based, in part, on Freud's translating one image into another, it was based also on Freud's insistence on fixed meanings for images from the unconscious. Jung insisted that an image has a different meaning for each person. For example, the blue sky, which, to one person, is a reminder of an idyllic summer day, to another person recalls that under such a sky a catastrophic accident occurred.

Despite Jung's denial that dream images have fixed meanings, he admitted that some symbols are *relatively* fixed because of their archetypal roots. For example, a dream of a dragon is likely to carry the archetypal significance of a monster to be confronted and subdued, even if the dreamer thinks also of "Puff, the Magic Dragon." The full meaning of a symbol, the relatively fixed and the idiosyncratic, can be ascertained, however, only by means of amplification (see Chapter 17).

Whether fixed or not, a symbol's meaning is likely to be manifold and, in Jung's view, a reflection of both its causes and its purpose. An example is the incest wish. Freud saw in this wish the boy's desire for actual sexual relations with his mother. Jung viewed the wish as primarily symbolic—a yearning for a return to the primordial, paradisiacal state of unconsciousness, to a sheltered state free from responsibility and decision making. The womb is an unexcelled symbol for such a state. Moreover, the urge to return to the womb may be "constructive" (see Chapter 17) as well as backward-looking. In its constructive aspect it reflects the possibility of overcoming the personal bond with the actual mother and transferring the psychic energy stored up in this bond to an inner content.

Symbols are characterized, further, by the fact that they arise spontaneously from the unconscious and, thus, are "grounded in the unconscious archetype" (*CW5*, par. 344). The kingdom of heaven, for example, is archetypal; many religions conjecture a far-off "place" where people do not suffer. At the same time, these images are shaped by acquired experiences; a

Moslem may dream of Mecca as the "city of God," a Christian or Jew, of Jerusalem.

Symbol as Transcendent Function

Understanding that symbols are not fixed and that they are more than signs or analogues is of critical significance because only this understanding recognizes their power to enhance and even bring about psychic development. This power was indicated by Jung in his designation of the symbol as the "transcendent function"; that is, the symbol transcends and reconciles pairs of opposites: for example, dark and light, active and passive, and manifest and hidden.

The symbol as transcendent function is implied in its root word, *symbolon*, which means "that which has been thrown together." Edinger (1962) explained:

> In original Greek usage, symbols referred to the two halves of an object, such as a stick or a coin, which two parties broke between them as a pledge and to prove later the identity of the presenter of one part to the holder of the other. The term corresponded to our word tally, concerning which Webster's unabridged dictionary states: "It was customary for traders, after notching a stick to show the number or quantity of goods delivered, to split it lengthwise through the notches so that the parts exactly corresponded, the seller keeping one stick, and the purchaser the other." A symbol was thus originally a tally referring to the missing piece of an object which when restored to, or thrown together with, its partner recreated the original whole object. This corresponds to our understanding of the psychological function of a symbol. The symbol leads us to the missing part of the whole man. It relates to our original totality. It heals our split, our alienation from life. (p. 66)

The transcendent function is likely to be manifested when a person is embroiled in a severe conflict between seemingly irreconcilable opposites. The conflict is so severe that the person is unable to imagine a resolution of the problem. An image, thought, or feeling then appears, perhaps in a dream. This content provides a "third not given"—an unforeseeable reconciling symbol.

For example, a woman (a composite of several of my clients) is unhappily married but feels that she must stay in an intolerable marriage or face poverty and perhaps the loss of her children because she is not financially independent. Her outer problem is "insoluble." Then she has a dream of a female tiger that is in pain but continuing to care for her cubs. The dream is amplified with the fact that tigers are known for their fighting: the animal "fights like a tiger." The dream image, thus, is of a creature that can fight but is not doing so. The woman comes to realize that she can stand up for her rights and yet bear the pain of the marriage or the divorce while continuing to discharge her responsibilities. A transformation—change of attitude—has been accomplished. Thus, the dream symbol has acted as a transcendent function.

The transcendent function may be rooted in the two sides of the brain. Rossi (1977) hypothesized that "the actual process of integrating left and right hemispheres is what we in analytical psychology would call the transcendent function: the union of conscious and unconscious contents; the interaction of ego and archetype; the integration of the rational and abstract processes of the left hemisphere with the synthetic holistic patterns of the right" (p. 45).

Some symbols not only unite a pair of opposites but embrace the totality of the psyche. These are symbols of the Self. They are most likely to occur when the ego has reached a cul-de-sac, perhaps an "insoluble" conflict. One such frequent symbol of wholeness is the mandala (a Sanskrit word for "magic circle"), one of the oldest religious symbols (see CW9–I, Part VI). To form a mandala, a circle usually is divided into a number of parts on the basis of a multiple of four. There may be a square inside the circle or surrounding it, thus suggesting the squaring of the circle. Designs, often with detailed religious symbolism, are superimposed on the circle.

The concept of symbol is a crucial one in Analytical Psychology but difficult to translate into concrete terms. The understanding of symbol as transcendent function is helpful for comprehending why this difficulty exists. An image or other experience that acts as a symbol for one person has no effect on another. The examples given here may or may not be effective for a particular reader. However, as one gains experience in dealing with symbols—for instance, in dream interpretation, which, by definition, is individualized, the concept becomes clearer.

Support for the Concept of Symbol

Except for such notions as Rossi's regarding the hemispheres of the brain, the phenomenon of symbol remains subjective. The nonexistence (to my knowledge) of empirical studies testing hypotheses related to symbols is probably due to two divergent factors: (a) Symbols are so fundamentally human that their existence is virtually self-evident (it has been said that to be human is to symbolize); and (b) the concept of symbol is so abstract and the experience so subjective that there are no specific hypotheses to test.

Psychology has been separate from philosophy for a relatively short time and has been so busy attempting to mimic the physical sciences that it is only beginning to return to the study of mind. Perhaps the next few decades will see developments in thought and research methods that will make possible the translation of some aspects of symbol into communicable experiences, which then can be studied empirically.

10

Synchronicity

If any Jungian theory is more controversial than that of the collective unconscious, it is the concept of synchronicity. Indeed, the two ideas may be interrelated because synchronistic phenomena seem to be archetypal manifestations (see later section).

Jung defined synchronicity as an "acausal connecting principle" in which events are simultaneous and connected by meaning but not by cause; that is, there is no causal connection whatsoever between or among the events. Indeed, "a cause is not even thinkable in intellectual terms" (CW8, par. 967. By "intellectual" Jung seemed to mean "rational."). Jung also described synchronicity as a "meaningful coincidence," something more than "synchronism," which means simply the simultaneous occurrence of two or more events. Synchronistic events can be physical or psychic but often they consist of one physical event (or series of events) and one psychic event (or series of events).

Jung came to hypothesize synchronicity as the result of several experiences which are described in his essay on the subject (CW8, Part VII). On one occasion (par. 843), for example, which occurred in an analytical situation, the patient was a woman whose therapy had been seriously hampered by her superrationality. That day she had brought in a dream that centered on her being given a golden scarab. While she was telling the dream, a "scarabaeid beetle" or rose chafer (the nearest relative of the scarab in western Europe) suddenly appeared at the window of the consulting room. Here was an acausal coincidence which was meaningful: The coincidence impressed the patient so deeply that her rigid rationality was broken.

In 1930, in a memorial address for his friend Richard Wilhelm, the sinologist who had translated many ancient texts, Jung introduced the "synchronistic" principle in relation to the *I Ching* (*Book of Changes*). He mentioned the concept fleetingly over many years but did not describe it until he wrote the foreword to the Wilhelm-Baynes translation of the *I Ching* (discussed in following section).

Types of Synchronistic Phenomena

Jung classified several types of events as synchronistic phenomena. Each must be discussed separately to evaluate the concept. The evaluation takes into account Jung's three stated criteria: acausality, simultaneity, and meaning. (Often rarity of an event plays a role, but Jung did not include it as a criterion.) Where possible, relevant quantitative evidence is presented.

Coincidence of Psychic State
with Objective Event

The coincidence of Jung's patient relating her dream of a golden scarab and the appearance at the window of a scarab-type beetle exemplifies the coincidence of a psychic state (the dream) and a physical event (the appearance of the beetle). Jung considered the event to meet his criteria clearly: The events were simultaneous, no causal relation was apparent, and the experience was meaningful to the patient.

Not everyone has agreed with Jung's interpretation of the event, however. A philosopher (Jahoda, 1967) doubted that the two events were acausal. Jahoda argued:

It was the season of the year when rose-chafers were about; this fact might well have been causally connected with the patient's dream, the golden scarab being an elaboration of the actual sight of a rose-chafer; since many of them were about it is perhaps not really very surprising that one of them bumped against the window, even though it was darker inside the room. (p. 39)

He admitted that some explanation might be necessary for the rose chafer's appearance at just that moment but, he pointed out, Jung himself stated that ordinary occurrences "must for the present be regarded as fortuitous" (p. 40). Thus, in Jahoda's view, the synchronicity, if it existed, was in the perception of meaning rather than in the conjunction of the two highly unlikely events.

A subtype of the coincidence of a psychic state with an objective event is the basis for the use of the *I Ching*. This book, which Jung called "the experimental foundation of classical Chinese philosophy" (*CW8*, par. 863), impressed him deeply with its basis in the principle of synchronicity. The chance division of a bundle of sticks, or the throw of three coins, establishes a hexagram which corresponds to a section of the book. Jung explained that "whoever invented the *I Ching* was convinced that the hexagram worked out in a certain moment coincided with the latter in quality no less than in time . . . the hexagram was understood to be an indicator of the essential situation prevailing at the moment of its origin" (*CW11*, par. 971). Jung consulted the *I Ching* frequently and many Jungians and other people still do so, usually at times of psychological impasse.

Once again, Jung's criteria seem to be met. Although the time of the objective event (the selection of the hexagram) is determined by the person who consults the *I Ching*, the hexagram that is established is believed to be just right for his or her psychic state at that moment. Even if the person is thoroughly familiar with the contents of all sixty-four hexagram texts (which usually is not the case), it is difficult to imagine how the specific positioning of the coins or sticks can be caused by, for example, a wish of the supplicant. The meaningfulness of the coincidence is implicit in the decision to consult the *I Ching* in order to receive a message.

The coincidence of a psychic state and an objective event has been thought to be exemplified also in astrological constellations. Jung used astrology (*CW8*, Part VII) to test the validity of the principle of synchronicity. (His account of the experiment carried the inaccurate title, "An Astrological Experiment.") The "psychic state" under consideration was the choice of a marriage partner. With his co-worker, Dr. Liliane Frey-Rohn, Jung hypothesized that the married couples chose each other according to predispositions that were indicated by relevant astrological configurations more often than would be the case with male-female pairs who were not married to each other. The investigators studied the combinations of horoscopes of 483 married couples and compared them to all the possible combinations of not-married pairs. The experiment produced favorable results in the first but not the later stages. Jung conceded that the early success was due, in part, to errors favoring the hypothesis. More important, because a similar decrease in positive results had happened in other investigators' experiments with extrasensory perception, Jung concluded that his own early enthusiasm, and lack of it later, influenced the results.

An additional vulnerable point in Jung's and Frey-Rohn's experiment was pointed out by Jahoda (1967). Jung wrote that the marriage horoscopes that were examined came "from friendly donors in Zurich, London, Rome, and Vienna. Originally the material had been put together for purely astrological purposes, so that those who gathered the material knew of no connection between its collection and the aim of the present study" (CW8, par. 873). He therefore considered the sample to be a "random one" but Jahoda questioned the premise on the ground that the horoscopes were of people who were "interested in astrology, as indicated by the fact that they went to the trouble and expense of having their horoscopes cast" (p. 39). It is not clear from Jung's account whether the couples initiated and paid for the casting of their horoscopes. If they did so, the sample was clearly not random.

Arno Müller (cited in Jahoda, 1967) conducted an experiment that replicated the one by Jung and Frey-Rohn, except that Müller eliminated the potential element of selectivity that Jahoda had criticized in Jung's work. Müller selected his cases systematically from the records at the registrar's office in Freiburg, taking all those married within a given time span whose hour of birth was known. Müller's results "failed to fit in with the traditional astrological postulates concerning marriage" (Jahoda, 1967, p. 39) and, consequently, did not confirm Jung's hypothesis.

Although the horoscope experiment was undertaken on the

assumption that astrological observations are synchronistic phenomena, Jung later entertained the possibility that there might be a causal connection between the planetary aspects and the psychophysiological disposition. He acknowledged thereby that sometimes what seems to be synchronicity is in fact a combination of events that are related causally but whose cause has not been identified. In any case, astrology has not been demonstrated to be a source of synchronistic phenomena.

Closely related to the coincidence of psychic state with objective event is the duplication of cases. This category includes combinations of three or more simultaneous objective events which are not causally related but have a common motif that suggests an underlying meaning. Although Jung recognized that some such combinations of events can be attributed to chance, others cannot. He gave the following example:

> I noted the following on April 1, 1949: Today is Friday. We have fish for lunch. Somebody happens to mention the custom of making an "April fish" of someone. That same morning I made note of an inscription which read: "Est homo totus medius *piscis* [fish] ab imo." In the afternoon a former patient of mine, whom I had not seen for months, showed me some extremely impressive pictures of fish which she had painted in the meantime. In the evening I was shown a piece of embroidery with fish-like sea monsters in it. On the morning of April 2 another patient, whom I had not seen for many years, told me a dream in which she stood on the shore of a lake and saw a large fish that swam straight toward her and landed at her feet. I was at this time engaged on a study of the fish symbol in history. Only one of the persons mentioned here knew anything about it. (CW8, par. 826)

The span of time over which Jung's combination of events occurred does not qualify as strictly simultaneous but it is short enough to permit Jung's experiences to be considered related. That they were synchronistic is doubtful in any case, because some of the events appear to be causally connected. For example, the fact that patients often brought him dreams and paintings of fish helped to stimulate his interest in the fish symbol in history. This study, in turn, probably occasioned his making a note of an inscription that included the Latin word for "fish." Although the combination of events was meaningful to Jung, it does not qualify as clearly acausal or even simultaneous and, therefore, is not synchronistic.

Extrasensory Perception

Jung included extrasensory perception (ESP) in his definition of synchronicity, although it seems not to meet his criteria. Each form of ESP he mentioned (telepathy, clairvoyance, precognition, and psychokinesis) lacks one or more qualifications (simultaneity, acausality, and meaning) for synchronicity.

Telepathy is communication between persons with no means of sensory perception. J. B. Rhine was known as the foremost investigator of ESP. The procedures he followed were relatively simple: An experimenter with a deck of cards on which five geometric designs were printed sat on one side of an opaque screen while the subject sat on the other side. The experimenter turned up the cards one at a time and the subject tried to guess which of the designs was exposed. The distance between experimenter and subject was increased in successive experiments from the two sides of the screen to four thousand miles. Positive results were obtained at all distances, often varying with the subject's interest in the task. Jung considered these results to be evidence of synchronicity despite the fact that the events (communication of information about the cards) had no perceptible meaning. They were simultaneous, of course, but the question of causality was not addressed.

Many of the examples of telepathy given by writers on synchronicity (e.g., Bolen, 1979) cite examples of meaningful messages received by individuals who appeared to be particularly capable of receiving telepathic messages. These writers seem to be of the opinion that such individual differences in capability constitute evidence that the telepathic events are synchronistic. It seems to me, however, that the individual differences indicate that telepathy is probably causal; that is, that some kind of psychic causality is at work. In any case, the search for a cause generates more openness to new evidence than does the assumption of noncausality.

Clairvoyance (literally, "clear-seeing") is perception at such a distance that it cannot be attributed to the sense organs. One can make the same observations on clairvoyance as on telepathy with regard to simultaneity (yes) and meaning (sometimes yes, sometimes no); but the hypothesized psychic cause is more problematic: There is no "sender," only a "receiver." Nevertheless, psychic causality is conceivable and should be investigated.

Precognition is perception of an event which has not yet occurred. It seems to meet the qualification of meaning; foreseeing an actual event is doubtless an impressive experience. The event and the cognition are not simultaneous, however. (They *coincide*, in the sense of being in agreement, and thus qualify as a "meaningful coincidence," but it seems strange to define synchronicity without a time factor. And it seems unlikely that they are acausal. Just as in Jung's concept of the prospective quality (see Chapter 17) of some dreams, the future event arises out of present conditions.

Psychokinesis is the influence of a psychic state on the physical world. Rhine conducted experiments in this realm as well as in telepathy. Again, results were positive when the subject's interest was high. Psychokinesis meets the criterion of simultaneity but is equivocal on the criteria of meaning (sometimes yes, usually no) and causality (possible).

A causal explanation for ESP is compatible with some of Jung's thinking. When considering the possibility of "perception at a distance" (CW8, par. 504) he granted that ESP is based on something inaccessible to our present level of knowledge; but he did not always insist that the "something" was synchronicity. Rather, he pointed out that "the psyche's . . . space-time limitation is no longer as self-evident and incontrovertible as we have hitherto been led to believe" (CW8, par. 813). Honegger (1979) hypothesized that synchronicities may be communications of the brain's intuitive capacity (which has come to be identified with the right hemisphere) to its language capacity, which is virtually always included as a left-brain capability.

Points of View on Synchronicity

The controversial nature of synchronicity has elicited responses that range from too-easy acceptance to too-easy rejection. The differences of opinion have centered on the archetypal basis of synchronistic phenomena, whether synchronicity should be examined in terms of determinacy rather than cause (both questions of *causality*), whether synchronistic events must be *simultaneous*, and whether the conjunction of *meaning* is a sufficient basis for calling events synchronistic. In short, Jung's three criteria for synchronicity (acausality, simultaneity, and meaning) are all foci of dispute.

Archetypal Basis of Synchronistic Phenomena

The basis of synchronicity, according to Jung, is that an archetype has been activated which gives meaning to the coincidence of events. The activation of the archetype is a response to a psychological impasse in the life of a person and may point the way out of the impasse. (When the archetypal dimension is lacking, the occurrence may be serendipity but not synchronicity.)

The possibility of an archetypal base for synchronicity is supported by many of Jung's examples (e.g., the scarab dream) and by a non-Jungian psychologist and neurologist, Karl Pribram (cited in Russell, 1979). He hypothesized that "a holographic model of 'reality' is able to explain telepathy, precognition, clairvoyance, psychokinesis, healing, and most other phenomena that appear to contravene the laws of space and time. . . . According to the holographic model, there exist underlying patterns and symmetries" (p. 160) that bear a strong similarity to archetypes.

The hypothesis that synchronicity has an archetypal base casts doubt on the acausality of the combination of events. M. Fordham (1962) denied the problem with the explanation, "It is the archetype which makes the correspondence meaningful, but the synchronicity is essentially the correspondence and is not produced by the projected archetypal image" (p. 207). Frey-Wehrlin (1976) disagreed with Fordham, taking the position that synchronicity must be considered as causal: "If an archetype is constellated, then (frequently) unexpected 'coincidences' ensue which are experienced as affective and meaningful" (p. 42). He found a middle ground with Jung in the view that synchronicity, although causal, escapes the realm of science: Synchronicity is a matter of subjective experience and complements the objective data of science.

Causality and Determinism

Synchronicity does not supersede causality; rather, it hypothesizes a link in which causality is not pertinent. Indeed, some theorists find that the concept of synchronicity has some support in modern physics, which departs in some ways from strict causal determinism. They refer to Heisenberg's principle of "indeterminacy" or "uncertainty," which was drawn from Einstein's work on intra-atomic physics: "that the more accurately the position of a particle could be specified, the less accurately could its velocity be predicted, and vice versa" (Encyclopaedia Britannica, 1965, Vol. 20, p. 123c). The indeterminacy principle highlights the fact that, as Jung pointed out, the demonstration of causality in many natural laws is statistical; that is, the laws have been ascertained to be valid only after the examination of a large aggregate of events has proved that the probability of their occurring by chance was infinitesimally small. A particular combination of synchronistic events occurs so rarely that statistical measures cannot be applied to it and, therefore, probability (a statistical concept) cannot be estimated.

Shelburne (1976) recognized Jung's argument that "natural law possesses a merely statistical validity" but challenged the idea that it "thus keeps the door open to indeterminism" (CW8, par. 828). Shelburne argued that science is based on determinism, which is a broader principle than causality. He pointed out:

> The fact that science is unable to employ causality as a universal principle of explanation does not mean that it concedes that things happen indeterminately, i.e., with nothing determining them. In fact, causality is only one form of determinism which is employed by the sciences. . . . Thus, it is a general principle of determinacy rather than the principle of causality upon which the laws of science rest. (pp. 61–62)

If Shelburne's argument is valid, synchronistic occurrences must be indeterminate as well as acausal. Thus, fewer occurrences can be considered synchronistic.

Must the Events Be Simultaneous?

Some of the literature on synchronicity (e.g., Bolen, 1979; Honegger, 1979) hypothesized that synchronistic experiences are as common as dreams; the argument is based partly on the ground that synchronicity, defined as a series of events that form a meaningful whole, often occurs over time. According to these theorists, precognition, for example, requires only that a thought precede a corresponding event. However, their definition seems too broad. If it is not necessary for events to be simultaneous in order to be synchronistic, then every event can be linked synchronistically to some preceding or subsequent event.

The arguments that are used to affirm the frequency of synchronistic events are based largely on the assumption that ESP is synchronistic. Inasmuch as not everyone accepts this assumption, it is possible to agree that ESP is common without agreeing that synchronicity is common.

Conclusion

The main body of Jung's theory is richer if it is used to discriminate phenomena that differ from each other as well as to link phenomena that are similar. Not all coincidences are meaningful and not all meaningful combinations of events are coincidences, in the sense of being acausal. Thus, a dream that alerts one to the importance of a life situation can be meaningful because it is surprising, even startling, and yet the dream is caused by the event. By the same token, many coincidences, including some that Jung cited, are not meaningful. He mentioned, for example, the appearance in the same day of the same number on his tram ticket, his theater ticket, and a telephone number that was mentioned to him. He did not postulate that there was meaning in the coincidence, however.

Despite all the problems, it seems clear that the concept of synchronicity is valuable as a daring attempt to explain certain phenomena for which no rational explanation is possible. Even persons who challenged experiences that aroused Jung's interest in and sustained his conviction about synchronicity could not entirely discount the possibility of the phenomenon. Jahoda (1967), for example, admitted that "most of us have experienced meaningful coincidences" (p. 38).

The value of synchronistic occurrences lies in the deep sense of meaning they can give to people. For some, the simple perception of a coincidence is often numinous, and numinosity provides meaning. For others, a coincidence is meaningful and therefore synchronistic only if it contributes to an insight or to a broader view of life. For both groups, occurrences are clearly synchronistic when they meet all the criteria and also serve, as Jung suggested they do, to point the way out of a psychological impasse.

11

Psychopathology

From the end of 1900 until 1909 Jung was a practicing psychiatrist, initially in training and then as a professional, at the Burghölzli Hospital in Zurich. Exposed to the full gamut of emotional, mental, and organic diseases, he made many of the careful observations that were to lead him to the development of Analytical Psychology. Most of his earliest articles, consequently, were concerned with mental illness (see *Psychiatric Studies, CW1; The Psychogenesis of Mental Disease, CW3;* and *Freud and Psychoanalysis, CW4*). In *Symbols of Transformation* (*CW5*), originally published in 1912 under the title, *Wandlungen und Symbole der Libido* (*Transformations and Symbols of the Libido*), he reported his studies of the archetypal images that were produced by a woman who eventually became manifestly schizophrenic. When Jung resigned from the Burghölzli and concentrated on his private practice, his writings on psychopathology as such dwindled. Nevertheless, his observations on the subject are still of interest, some only for historical reasons; some, because they are as applicable today as when they were written;

some, because they are currently returning to favor; and some, because they are gaining general acceptance for the first time.

In psychopathology, even more than in other areas of study, Jung's main interest lay in discovering general principles rather than dealing systematically with subcategories. Thus, his major contribution to psychopathology, according to the schizophrenia expert Arieti (1974), was his work on the complex. Jung found that complexes are crucial in the etiology of mental illness; they become dissociated from the ego and act autonomously in the form of pathological symptoms such as delusions and hallucinations.

Diagnostic Categories

At the time that Jung was training to be a psychiatrist, the identification and classification of mental diseases was a major concern of practitioners. Eugen Bleuler, for example, is remembered primarily for his systematic identification of different kinds of schizophrenia and for coining its name, which superseded the use of the older term, dementia praecox. Jung did not follow Bleuler's interests in classification; most of Jung's references to diagnostic categories were incidental. He wanted to understand the totality of the mind and its implications for psychotherapy, not just its pathology. Thus he wrote:

> In flagrant contrast to the rest of medicine, where a definite diagnosis is often, as it were, logically followed by a specific therapy and a more or less certain prognosis, the diagnosis of any particular psychoneurosis means, at most, that some form of psychotherapy is indicated. As to the prognosis, that is in the highest degree independent of the diagnosis. Nor should we gloss over the fact that the classification of the neuroses is very unsatisfactory, and that for this reason alone a specific diagnosis seldom means anything real. In general, it is enough to diagnose a "psychoneurosis" as distinct from some organic disturbance–the word means no more than that. (CW16, par. 195)

The term *organic disturbance* was virtually a synonym for a psychosis; like most psychiatrists of the time, Jung considered psychoses to have organic causes. In general, he made no sharper distinction among mental illnesses than the broad categories of neurosis and psychosis.

The diagnosis of subcategories of neurosis was questioned further by Henderson (1955), a psychiatrist and one of Jung's students. Henderson found that what appears to be pathological may be, instead, a manifestation of the inferior attitude or function. He concluded that psychotherapists who "fail to unearth this root of the personality in their patients . . . must eventually have to rediscover this kind of data and reformulate a theory of typology not unlike that of Jung" (p. 139). Understanding of Jung's typology is a deterrent to a diagnosis of pathology, especially when the client is introverted. In American culture, introversion is sometimes mistaken for pathology (see next section).

Jung was especially interested in schizophrenia and, to some degree, in manic-depressive psychosis. In his writings he also mentioned alcoholism and psychosomatic disorders. A common problem, depression, was not necessarily a pathological category to Jung. He often took the attitude that depression is a damming of psychic energy, which may or may not be pathological.

Neurosis

Neurosis was described by Jung as "a dissociation of personality due to the existence of complexes" (CW18, par. 382). It is normal to have complexes. If they are too incompatible with consciousness, however, a neurotic dissociation results. Consider, for example, a man who has a "rejection complex"—a pervasive fear that intimacy inevitably will lead to rejection. His consistent avoidance of close relationships isolates him so that he feels even more rejected. The result is a complex grown so powerful and dissociated that the ego is helpless in the face of it. A neurosis has come into being.

Jung distinguished between neurosis and a condition that is simply undesirable:

> On certain days, or from time to time, [some people] suddenly lose their energy, they lose themselves, and they come under a strange influence. These phenomena are not in themselves pathological; they belong to the ordinary phenomenology of man, but if they become habitual we rightly speak of a neurosis. These are the things that lead to neurosis; but they are also exceptional condi-

tions among normal people. To have overwhelming emotions is not in itself pathological, it is merely undesirable. We need not invent such a word as pathological for an undesirable thing, because there are other undesirable things in the world which are not pathological, for instance, tax-collectors. (CW18, par. 43)

The contents of most neuroses seem to be idiosyncratic. Nevertheless, some commonalities exist. For example, a frequent type of neurosis was identified by Edinger (1972) and labeled an "alienation neurosis."

> An individual with such a neurosis is very dubious about his right to exist. He has a profound sense of unworthiness ... [and] assumes unconsciously and automatically that whatever comes out of himself—his innermost desires, needs and interests—must be wrong or somehow unacceptable. With this attitude psychic energy is dammed up and must emerge in covert, unconscious or destructive ways such as psychosomatic symptoms, attacks of anxiety or primitive affect, depression, suicidal impulses, alcoholism, etc. (p. 56)

The neurosis known as conversion hysteria apparently was widespread around the turn of the century and evoked a great deal of attention from the French psychiatrists at Nancy and from Freud; Jung was somewhat less interested in it. The symptoms of conversion hysteria—sensorimotor dysfunctions (e.g., blindness or paralysis), which have no organic base—are seldom seen now. The reduced frequency of such reactions, according to some psychiatrists, results from greater psychological sophistication in the general population. Other forms of hysteria appear to be current, however. For example, Guggenbühl-Craig (1963) labeled a person who has a tendency to exaggerate emotions and illnesses as an hysteric. Such a person desires to be the center of attention at all costs, evidently to counteract a weak ego and weak emotions.

Jung mentioned but did not emphasize another fact about neurosis: the pathological interaction between the neurotic person and the environment. He wrote:

> Neurosis is ... a severe illness, particularly in view of its effects on the patient's environment and way of life. ... A neurosis is more a psychosocial phenomenon than an illness in the strict sense. It forces us to extend the term "illness" beyond the idea of an individual body whose functions are disturbed, and to look

upon the neurotic person as a sick system of social relationships. (CW16, par. 37)

In taking this view in 1935, Jung predated the theory that became popular in the 1960s and 1970s, that troubled persons are made so by troubled social networks, such as family "systems."

Causes of Neurosis

The origins of neurosis are difficult to determine. Freud and Jung differed critically on the question of etiology. Freud seemed to assume that every neurosis originates in the trauma of a particular childhood experience, usually sexual, which has been repressed. Jung held that a neurosis is more likely to result from accumulated experiences rather than a single trauma.

A correlation between attitude type and incidence of neurosis has been found by some investigators. Richek (1969) administered the Myers-Briggs Type Indicator and the Bown Self-Report Inventory (SRI) to 365 female undergraduates who were applying for admission to teacher-certification programs. Extraverts (both moderate and extreme) scored higher on the SRI measures of psychological adjustment, and extreme introverts scored lower than moderate introverts. If better psychological adjustment is equivalent to less neurosis, extraverts are the least and extreme introverts are the most neurotic. Moderate introverts fall in between.

The relation between attitude type and incidence of neurosis may be different in a culture that values introversion more than the American culture does. Indeed, several American and British investigators have found that introversion and extraversion are independent of neuroticism (see relevant studies reported in Chapter 4). Nevertheless, extraverts and introverts seem to develop different neurotic symptoms. In a series of studies, Eysenck (1956) found that "extraverted neurotics tended to develop hysterical or psychopathic symptoms, whereas introverted neurotics tended to develop dysthymic symptoms, such as anxiety, reactive depression, or obsessional features" (p. 96).

Neurosis may have different causes at different ages. Childhood neurosis, in Jung's view, is largely a reflection of parental neurosis. One example, which he cited from the work of his student Frances Wickes, was that of a nine-year-old girl who "had run a subnormal temperature for three months, was unable to attend school, [and] suffered from loss of appetite and increasing listlessness" (CW17, par. 216; Wickes, 1966, pp. 42–43). The therapist discovered that the parents were considering divorce and trying to hide their difficulties from the child. When the parents decided to separate, the child's health improved.

In the second half of life there may be an increase in emotional problems because of changed life circumstances. The adaptation to the outer world must give way, at least in part, to attention to subjective concerns. With Jung's explicit endorsement, Bash (1959) described this process:

> While productivity need not cease, cultural aims become ever more important in age. To be significant they must primarily be personal aims, spontaneous steps to self-realization, not such as are forced upon the aging individual by society. (p. 565)

Bash concluded, "The strains set up by the resulting need for a reorientation in life are a fruitful source of mental disorder" (p. 563).

Positive Aspects of Neurosis

That neurosis has a positive side is another major Jungian concept. Jung saw neurosis as an attempt at self-cure, often unsuccessful, just as fever or suppuration in a wound is often an unsuccessful attempt at self-cure by the body. Further, neurosis can be seen as an attempt to broaden the personality by admitting repressed contents to consciousness. Goldbrunner (1964) used the image of the neurotic as a person "who has fallen into a river and is sinking; but [it is important] for him to act like a diver. For the place where [he] suffers is not accidental; it conceals buried treasure which only a diver can raise" (p. 23). Indeed, Jung saw neurosis as reflecting an urge to self-realization and many neurotics as having a greater potential for development than "normal" people. The neurosis may force the person to face a responsibility that has been dodged and, hence, use capacities that are needed for his or her development. Often, the positive aspects of neurosis can be realized only with the aid of psychotherapy.

Psychosis

Jung's concept of the difference between neurosis and psychosis changed over time. In his early work (until about 1920) he saw hysteria, which, at that time, was often equated with neurosis, as the illness of extraverts and dementia praecox (schizophrenia) as that of introverts. Later, however (e.g., CW18, Part I), he described the difference between neurosis and psychosis in terms of the relation of unconscious contents to the ego.

In psychosis, as in neurosis, complexes act autonomously and a dissociation of personality results. In the most clear-cut manifestation of such dissociations, these complexes become multiple personalities. Jung did not take a stand on whether multiple personality is a neurosis or a psychosis. In neurosis, "the dissociated personalities are still in a sort of interrelation, so that you always get the impression of a total person. . . . In the case of schizophrenia . . . you encounter only fragments, there is nowhere a whole" (CW18, par. 224). Thus, in neurosis, the unconscious content does not overwhelm the ego but, rather, affects it strongly by acting contrary to the ego's objectives. (Jung stated that the unconscious "assimilates" the ego in neurosis, but this terminology seems not to provide adequate distinction from the "overwhelming" found in psychosis. Consequently, I take "assimilate" to mean "affect strongly.")

In psychosis, the ego consciousness is overwhelmed by archetypal contents, such as hallucinations or delusions. That is, the person's waking cognitions as well as his dreams are likely to be full of frightening images. One of my patients, for example, had the delusion that if she crossed a threshold the universe would collapse and she would be left all alone. She was rendered incapable of physical movement and, hence, became cataleptic. Such images seem to be what Jung characterized as "overwhelming."

Diagnosis of Schizophrenia

Despite the fact that archetypal mental content is characteristic of schizophrenics, Jung found that the presence of such material in dreams and fantasies does not necessarily mean that the person is schizophrenic. Indeed, such material is present also in the dreams and fantasies of neurotics and "normal" people. Nevertheless, experimental evidence gives some indication that the dreams of psychotics are distinguishable from those of normal people. In studies (Bolgar, 1954; Kant, 1942) using only content analysis, significant differences in dream content were not found between psychotics and normal people. In studies using an additional instrument (e.g., an ego-rating system), differences were found. Sheppard and Saul (1958) conducted a study in which twenty-two dreams were rated by two psychiatrists and one psychologist according to an ego-rating system; ten of the dreams had been obtained from eight psychotic patients and twelve from eight employees of an industrial firm. "Although a group of experienced psychoanalysts had been unable to distinguish between the dreams of psychotics and nonpsychotics by clinical inspection, the scores on the ego-rating system did sharply differentiate the two groups. The dreams of psychotics scored higher for each category and for the total rating system" (p. 243). No test of statistical significance was mentioned.

In a second study (Sheppard, 1963), a different twelve-category ego-rating system for dreams was constructed on the basis of psychoanalytic theory, empirical evidence from dreams, and group judgment by a seminar of experienced psychoanalysts and psychologists. When applied by two judges (graduate students in industrial psychology) to the dreams of twenty-eight psychotic and thirty nonpsychotic subjects, the scores on two categories of the ego-rating system differentiated the groups to a statistically significant degree. In eight additional categories the two groups differed (nonsignificantly) in the predicted direction. In contrast, one psychiatrist and two psychologists who were unfamiliar with the rating system were unable to distinguish between the dreams of the two groups of subjects. The ego-rating system appears to be a potentially fruitful method for using dreams diagnostically. A great deal more work is required, however.

Thought disorders often characterize schizophrenia. One manifestation of such disorders is incoherence of association. Jung's work on word association contributed indirectly to diagnosing such disorders. Astrup and Flekköy (1968) used a word association test (not Jung's) to compare 312 psychiatric patients with 40 normal controls. The patients were in twelve clinical groups, for example, paranoid schizophrenia and reactive depressive psychosis. Subjects were measured for reaction times (RTs) and quality of verbal response. The normal control group did significantly better than all the clinical subgroups. The schizophrenics had more incoherent responses and longer mean RTs, particularly on stimulus words related to psychopathological experiences. The investigators quoted Jung's work and found their results to be compatible with his.

Causes of Schizophrenia

The etiology of schizophrenia—biochemical or psychological—is still a controversial issue. According to Arieti (1974), Jung "was the first to see the possibility of a psychosomatic involvement of the central nervous system although he did not formulate his concept in these words" (p. 25). Jung did not see psychological causes and organic changes as mutually exclusive. Rather, he hypothesized that the emotional disorder produces an abnormal metabolism, which, in turn, causes physical damage to the brain. He introduced this hypothesis at a time (early twentieth century) when the reigning assumption was that mental illness (especially schizophrenia, which Jung discussed most frequently) resulted from structural and probably innate abnormalities in the brain. At the same time, Jung conceded that "an unknown quantity, possibly a toxin . . . may arise in the first place from non-psychological causes and then simply seize on the existing complex and specifically transform it, so that it may seem as if the complex had a causal effect" (CW3, par. 195).

Jung's continued rethinking of the subject is evident from his 1958 statement: "I have now, after long practical experience, come to hold the view that the psychogenic causation of [schizophrenia] is more probable than the toxic causation" (CW3, par. 570). His seeming vacillation on the subject is due partly to changes in prevailing opinions, partly to his tendency to express the compensatory view, and partly to his continuing empiricism, which was constantly admitting new data. Indeed, van der Post (1975) reported:

> [Jung] was to confess that he never clearly understood what caused the severest forms of this particular sickness of spirit [schizophrenia]. In one of the last utterances just before he died,

he suggested that there could be pathological forms of schizophrenia that might have a physical origin in some undiscovered mutation in the chromosomes and genes of the individual. This demonstrated conclusively, I would have thought, that dedicated as he was to psychology and the world within he had never been fanatically dedicated, and that he had always remained open to the claims and validity of the physical and the external as well. Yet he stood firm and proved in his practice that many more cases than were imagined, condemned as incurable forms of this disturbance, could be made whole again by applied analytical psychology. (p. 134)

Since Jung's death, the evidence for a genetic component in schizophrenia has become increasingly convincing. Indeed, Jung seemed to be groping toward the conclusion that is now current among many psychologists and psychiatrists who are students of behavior genetics, that a genetic component is a necessary but not sufficient basis for schizophrenia.

Manic-Depressive Psychosis

In most of Jung's comments on psychosis he seemed to be referring specifically to schizophrenia. He mentioned manic-depressive psychosis, however, and described it partially in terms of function type:

You occasionally find that in the manic phase one function prevails and in the depressive phase another function prevails. For instance, people who are lively, sanguine, nice and kind in the manic phase, and do not think very much, suddenly become very thoughtful when the depression comes on, and then they have obsessive thoughts and vice versa. I know several cases of intellectuals who have a manic-depressive disposition. In the manic phase they think freely, they are productive and very clear and very abstract. Then the depressive phase comes on, and they have obsessive feelings; they are obsessed by terrible moods, just moods, not thoughts. (CW18, par. 61)

Treatment of Neurosis and Psychosis

Jung wrote little on the treatment of neurosis and psychosis as such. He seemed to consider psychotherapy to be the treatment of choice for neurosis, including neurotic depression. He maintained also that schizophrenia often can be treated psychologically. Perry (1974) described a process by which a schizophrenic person's mental imagery can be used as the basis of a reorganization of the person's personality. This process is dependent upon a psychotherapeutic milieu that is far more complete than the usual psychiatric hospital or clinic. (Perry's work bears considerable resemblance to that of R. D. Laing, but the two innovators developed their approaches independently.)

Inasmuch as Jung's writings on psychopathology predated the discoveries of the current pharmacopeia, he did not comment on the efficacy of psychoactive drugs. Some of his students, however, (e.g., Hillman, 1964; Perry, 1976) have expressed the view that drugs suppress the symptoms (the visible psychotic contents) and thus prevent the self-regulation of the psyche, which might have occurred if those contents had been assimilated. Most Jungians seem to share this view and hold that it is better to avoid the use of drugs if at all possible.

Psychosomatic Disorders

Psychopathology seems to play a role in those organic physical disorders which have been designated "psychosomatic." (They must be distinguished from conversion hysteria, in which the symptom has no organic component.) Jung said of these disorders only that "the patient's psychology plays the essential part" (CW11, par. 15). Meier (1963) suggested an integration of the often-divergent opinions supporting either physical or psychological treatment. He presented the view that the connection between body and psyche is not a matter of cause and effect but, rather, "the psycho-physical functioning should be interpreted synchronistically" (p. 113). That is, psychic disorder and physical disorder sometimes reflect the same archetypal base, although neither can be said to cause the other. Meier's statement seems to support the usual Jungian approach of treating the person psychologically, as much as possible, but turning to medical treatment for conditions that are not amenable to psychotherapy. Consequently, Jungian analysts refer a client for medical evaluation to determine the cause of a symptom, chronic headaches, for example. With some assurance that the symptom is not dangerous, the analyst can work with the client to decide whether to use symptom-relieving medication.

Part IV

Individuation

12

Human Development from Birth to Old Age

Changes throughout the life span are included in the purview of Jungian psychology. This scope reflects a different view from that of many psychologists; evidently because they were influenced by Freudian thinking, their writings on infants, children, and adolescents have given to the term *developmental psychology* the connotation of birth through childhood or adolescence. Indeed, Jung's major developmental interests lay in the growth process of later adulthood—after age thirty-five or forty—which he called "the second half of life." The culmination of this developmental process is individuation, one of Jung's unique contributions to the psychology of mental health.

Infancy and Childhood

Assuming that his readers were familiar with Freud's work, Jung wrote relatively little on infancy and childhood. Even in his later years, he seemed to accept many of Freud's ideas and, hence, tended to state only his departures from them: for example, his reservations on the theory of infantile sexuality. To Jung, infantile sexuality was embryonic and "polyvalent" rather than the "polymorphous-perverse disposition" expounded by Freud.

Jung acknowledged that sexual interest produces psychic conflicts in children. He insisted, however, that the children's objective is the resolution of these conflicts rather than the immediate sexual goals of adult sexuality. Infantile sexuality usually "strives . . . far more toward the development of thinking" (CW17, p. 4)—concept building—to solve the psychic conflicts.

In 1913, the year that he broke with Freud, Jung published "The Theory of Psychoanalysis" (CW4, Part II) in which he modified Freud's sexuality theory by dividing human life into only three phases:

> The first phase embraces the first years of life; I call this period the *presexual stage*. It corresponds to the caterpillar stage of butterflies, and is characterized almost exclusively by the function of nutrition and growth.
>
> The second phase embraces the later years of childhood up to puberty, and might be called the *prepubertal stage*. Germination of sexuality takes place at this period.
>
> The third phase is the adult period from puberty on, and may be called the period of *maturity*. (CW4, pars. 263–65)

Much of Jung's work that is devoted to infancy and childhood is found in *The Development of Personality* (CW17). There he discussed the developmental process in relation to education (in school and elsewhere), the significance of the unconscious in the development of the child, and childhood psychopathology. In addition, Jung devoted considerable time to the interpretation of children's dreams that were brought by parents and childhood dreams that were remembered by his adult patients (see especially CW17 and CD36, 38, and 40). Through these interpretations and other clinical material, he contributed to our understanding of children and of the childlike qualities in adults. Jung's concepts are augmented in this chapter, even more than in most other chapters, by some ideas from his students that seem to be derived directly from Jung's.

The Infant and the Archetypal World

For the first year or two of postnatal life, in Jung's conception of development, the child is completely enveloped in the collective unconscious. In this state there is no "demonstrable ego-consciousness, for which reason the earliest years leave hardly any traces in the memory" (CW8, par. 668).

During this period the infant is likely to experience archetypal contents primarily in terms of parental images. Attachment to the actual parents is necessary for the child to relinquish his or her link to the archetypal parents. Jung saw this transition as happening gradually. When development is healthy, parents cease, over time, to seem godlike to the growing child. When development is sufficiently troubled or a parent is lost by death or desertion, the child does not become separated from the archetypal image and, hence, does not come to see the parents and other persons as finite beings. Thus, the child may carry pathological fears. The growing literature in "object relations" reflects the seemingly endless possibilities and problems arising out of the various kinds of parent-child interaction.

Through the early years until about age five, the child, in fantasy, maintains contact with the archetypal world. According to Wickes (1966), the child is likely to create an imaginary playmate-companion, who is "called into existence because of a psychological need" (p. 165). Wickes, whose book was published first in 1927, saw these imaginary companions as normal and constructive, although, at that time, they were generally considered to be dangerously removed from reality. A group of child psychologists who worked long after Wickes wrote her book supported her view. According to Pines (1978), Caldeira, D. Singer, and Jerome Singer found that a large proportion of the three- and four-year-old children they observed had imaginary playmates. The children were 141 participants in New Haven, Connecticut, nursery schools and day-care centers. The investigators observed, tested, and interviewed the children and asked their parents to fill out detailed questionnaires. The children's reports indicated that 65 percent had imaginary companions; the parents', that 55 percent of the children had such companions. "Furthermore, the children who had imaginary companions differed sharply from the rest: they were less aggressive and more cooperative; they smiled more, they showed a greater ability to concentrate; they were seldom bored; and their language was richer and more advanced, especially among the boys" (p. 38).

Development of the Ego

Among Jungians, the most detailed descriptions of the maturation processes of the first year of life have been provided by M. Fordham (1964) and other neo-Jungians of the British group of Jungian analysts. They incorporate much of the theory of Melanie Klein, a Viennese, self-taught student of psychoanalysis, who moved to England in 1926 and there founded what became known as the British school of psychoanalysis. Klein departed somewhat from Freudian theory, especially in her "more exclusive emphasis upon the earlier (pregenital) modes of infantile sexuality and the death instinct (aggression)" (Munroe, 1957, p. 211).

Following Klein, the neo-Jungians hypothesized that in the first year of life the Self "de-integrates" into fragments and some of them form the ego. Ego formation begins with the discrepancy between the infant's bodily needs and the environment. When the infant's needs are not met completely, he or she starts to perceive a separation from the nurturing (mother) figure; the infant's fingers and toes are part of him or her but the mother's breast is separate from the child. Somewhat later, the child learns to distinguish the mother figure from other persons. As the ego separates from the original state of unconscious identity with the mother, "ego fragments then form a more coherent and organized island around which a vast sea of personal and collective unconscious material exists" (Maduro and Wheelwright, 1977, p. 92).

Thus, the Self is the precursor of the ego and, according to Gerhard Adler (1951), the director of its development. One evidence of the existence of the Self, as in any psychic entity, is that it is projected. Von Franz (1972) saw the child's doll, teddy bear, or, Americans might add, "security blanket," as projections of the Self.

Origin of Consciousness

Perhaps unique to Jung's view of the development of the ego is the concept of the origin of consciousness in the process of "separating the opposites." By this he seemed to mean that it is necessary for people to come to understand that life is not a perfect unity. Rather, it is fraught with tension and conflict that result from the fact of "opposites," for example, light and dark, "I and thou," good and evil.

The biblical story of the Garden of Eden is a mythological image of the dawn of consciousness. The origin of consciousness is depicted in the eating of the fruit of the Tree of the Knowledge of Good and Evil; after eating the fruit, the eyes of the first man and woman were opened and they discovered that they were naked, that is, they became aware of themselves as separate, vulnerable human beings. This awareness was and is the beginning of consciousness. At the same time, as the serpent predicted, they became "like God, knowing good and evil" (Genesis 3:5). They became conscious adults, knowing, and suffering, the opposites of good and evil.

Matriarchal and Patriarchal Stages

As the ego gathers strength, it becomes increasingly separate from the archetypal world. Neumann (1973) saw the child's "true birth" as occurring at the end of the first year (of postnatal life), which culminates in the formation of an integral ego. The child emerges from the original state—the *"uroboric"* state of oneness—and enters the *matriarchal* stage in which the child lives "in a situation of identity with the Good Mother [archetype] and has the power to assimilate negative experience up to a certain point, or to abreact it" (p. 56). When the negative experience is too powerful to assimilate or abreact, however, "the Terrible Mother is constellated for the child and there is a disturbance in the unfolding . . . of the child's relatedness to its body, its Self, and the thou in all its aspects" (pp. 55–56).

Sometime between three and five years of age, Jung found, the first phase in the development of the ego has been accomplished so that "the profound darkness of the early infantile amnesia, or discontinuity of consciousness, begins to be illuminated by the sporadic continuity of memory" (CW4, par. 266). One evidence of this accomplishment is that the child ceases to refer to himself or herself in the third person and begins to use first-person pronouns.

The ego, in Jung's conception, probably continues to develop throughout life, that is, long after the age (about six years) at which Freud considered the personality to be basically set. Nevertheless, it is from the early years through young adulthood that a person achieves the firm establishment of the ego in relation to the environment. From the emergence of the ego out of the collective unconscious during early childhood until middle age, the ego is largely oblivious to the Self.

In his view of early development, Jung seems never to have agreed with Freud regarding the general applicability of the Oedipus and Electra complexes: the child's attachment to the parent of the opposite sex and the desire to get rid of the parent of the same sex. For Jung, the relation with the mother was primary for both sexes. He took the position that Freud had erroneously translated into genital sexuality the child's yearning for a return to the original oneness with the mother, that is, to become a part of her body again. In Freud's conception, the male's desire takes the form of a fantasy of coitus with the mother (one must wonder, of course, how a very young child conceptualizes coitus!) and the girl's "penis envy," if it exists, as a desire for the equipment that permits coitus with the mother. (Alfred Adler hypothesized a "masculine protest," that is, the female's envy of the male's preferred status in the family and in the world. This view seems sound and compatible with Jung's view.)

Jung did not deal with the question of how or when a child shifts some of his or her attachment from the mother to the father. Neumann (1973) hypothesized, however, that this new stage, which he called the *patriarchal stage*, begins when the child emerges from the primal relationship in which the mother archetype is dominant to literal and symbolic weaning when the father archetype becomes dominant. The shift is marked by increasing independence and by growing awareness of the world outside the family. A negative relation to the father can hamper these developments.

Adolescence and Young Adulthood

Neumann (1973) identified only three stages of childhood (uroboric, matriarchal, and patriarchal); Edinger (1968), however, conceptualized a fourth stage, the *integrative:*

> This is a decisive step in psychological integration that amounts to a reconciliation of opposites: masculine and feminine, law and love, conscious and unconscious, spirit and nature. In individual development of the youth, this phase corresponds to the emerging capacity to relate to girls during puberty, which is subsequently followed by love for a particular woman and eventually marriage. (p. 16)

Although Neumann dated "true birth" at about one year after biological birth, Jung identified a "psychic birth," which occurs at puberty with the "conscious differentiation from the parents . . . [and] the eruption of sexuality" (*CW8*, par. 756). He did not indicate how conscious differentiation from the parents occurs. Perhaps this process did not appear as difficult to him as it does to many Americans, or it may have been subsumed in the assertion of the ego, which he mentioned in connection with "the eruption of sexuality":

> The physiological change is attended by a psychic revolution. For the various bodily manifestations give such an emphasis to the ego that it often asserts itself without stint or moderation. This is sometimes called the "unbearable age." (*CW8*, par. 756)

The "unbearable age"—adolescence—might be more bearable, in the view of many Jungians, for both the young and other persons, if the culture provided an adequate initiation, comparable to the rituals of many preliterate societies. To be sure, young people who have reached sexual maturity are considered, in preliterate societies, to be closer to adulthood than they are in Western culture.

At one time religious ceremonies, such as Christian confirmation and Jewish bar mitzvah and bas mitzvah, provided maturational milestones for many young people. These ceremonies, although they are still observed by members of organized religions, seem to carry less transitional significance than they once did, even for the young people who are so recognized. Educational and personal milestones, such as obtaining a driver's license, graduating from high school, or leaving home for college or work, are far more effective initiation processes for many youth. For some, initiation comes only with marriage, thus putting an additional burden on that relationship. The lack of transitional ceremony remains, however, and may account for some of the enthusiasm of many young people for entering religious cults or joining their peers in the use of mind-altering drugs. A Jungian analyst, Mahdi (1976), has been experimenting with the application of the American Indian "vision quest" as a potentially valid initiation process for Swiss and non-Indian American young people. Although different Indian tribes proceed variously, the basic themes are solitude in the wilderness, prayer, fasting, focus on dreams, and openness to whatever happens. Mahdi has found that such a confrontation with oneself, without the use of drugs, meets the needs of some contemporary young people for an experience of initiation.

Jung hypothesized that a large degree of one-sidedness in attitude (introversion-extraversion—IE) and function (thinking-feeling and sensation-intuition) type is characteristic of most young people. This one-sidedness occurs because, in order to get along in the world, the young person must have the ego strength that comes with excelling in one or two functions. Thus, the young person expends a great deal of energy on his or her dominant attitude and function and gives only a minimum to the non-dominant.

Some Jungians have hypothesized that cultural demands make it difficult for introverted young persons to develop the attitude that is "naturally" dominant, however. For many Americans especially, a large degree of extraversion is necessary to meet the demands of the culture. Despite the reasonableness of this hypothesis, it has not been borne out empirically, that is, younger people were not found to be more extraverted, older people more introverted.

The study with the most representative sample was conducted by Bloch (1978). The 558 subjects were between the ages of seventeen and seventy-five, with the same proportions of men to women, blacks to whites, and white-collar to blue-collar to service workers, as are found in the general population. The subjects were selected from twenty-one locations in New Jersey and Mississippi. According to scores on the Myers-Briggs Type Indicator (MBTI), there was no significant difference in the IE dimension on the basis of age.

Schaefer's study (see Chapter 4) included an analysis according to age. Contrary to Jungian theory, she found a slight decrease in introversion between the subjects aged thirty-five or less and those over thirty-five. On the Gray-Wheelwrights Test (GWT) the proportions were 40% (thirty-five and under) versus 31% (over thirty-five), a nonsignificant difference. On the MBTI the difference was statistically significant at the .05 level, 41% as compared with 24%. However, Schaefer's data were gathered from people who had registered for a course in Jungian psychology. Consequently, the IE proportions she reported may be applicable only to younger and older people who are interested in Jung's ideas and not to the general populace.

Gray (1947) obtained results that seemed to support the theory of a decrease in extraversion with age. His one thousand subjects were accumulated in a series of studies that he conducted in the process of developing the GWT. Their ages ranged from ten to eighty and they were evenly divided between the sexes. "The persons observed were unselected, the questionnaire being offered wherever opportunity was found" (p. 274). Gray presented the data only in graphic form but it appears that the average extraversion score decreased from about 50 at age twenty to about 43 at age seventy, at the .004 level of confidence. Although the sample was large it was not selected randomly; thus, the results must be regarded with caution.

In a study conducted in Switzerland (Baumann, Angst, Henne, and Muser; 1975), where the culture seems to demand less extraversion, even of its young people, more extraversion was found in the younger age groups than in the comparable subjects groups of some of the American studies. The 646 subjects were from various age groups and sociological backgrounds. The investigators did not state how the subjects were recruited, but the age group fifteen to thirty and persons with more schooling were "overrepresented" in the sample. On the IE dimension no significant difference was found between older and younger men but younger women (ages fifteen to thirty) were found to be significantly less introverted (average score 16.04) than women aged thirty-one to fifty (average score 19.22) at the .01 level of confidence.

Only one study (Bradway and Detloff, 1976) gives any longitudinal data relevant to changes in individuals from introversion to extraversion or vice versa. In 1974, the investigators obtained from a group of California analysts measures of attitude and function types by self-typing and the GWT. Sixteen of the respondents had provided the same measures in 1961. The typologies of these analysts were remarkably stable. By self-typing, all of the sixteen remained the same on the IE dimension over the thirteen-year period. According to their responses on the GWT, twelve of the sixteen (75%) remained the same on that dimension. On the sensation-intuition dimensions, 75% remained the same by self-typing and 88% by the GWT. On the thinking-feeling dimension, 69% and 88% remained the same by the self-typing and GWT measures, respectively. (The investigators considered the GWT not refined enough for changes in individuals' raw scores to be significant.) Thus, even when the same individuals are studied longitudinally, there is little evidence of any marked change with age in attitude or function type.

Thus, Jung's hypothesis that some of the problems of youth stem from the culture's demand for extraverted adaptation is still open to question. He saw the basis of other youthful problems in an erroneous assessment of the world:

> In the period of youth . . . the demands of life . . . put an end to the dream of childhood. If the individual is sufficiently well prepared, the transition to a profession or career can take place smoothly. But if he clings to illusions that are contrary to reality, then problems will surely arise. No one can take the step into life without making certain assumptions, and occasionally these assumptions are false—that is, they do not fit the conditions into which one is thrown. Often it is a question of exaggerated expectations, underestimation of difficulties, unjustified optimism, or a negative attitude. . . . [However, Jung went on, problems may also arise from] inner psychic difficulties, . . . the disturbance of psychic equilibrium caused by the sexual instinct . . . [or] the feeling of inferiority which springs from an unbearable sensitivity. These inner conflicts may exist, even when adaptation to the outer world has been achieved without apparent effort. It even seems as if young people who had had a hard struggle for existence are spared inner problems, while those who [have had no difficulty adapting] run into problems of sex or conflicts arising from a sense of inferiority. (CW8, pars. 761–62)

Middle Life

During the 1970s, an upsurge of public interest centered on the "midlife crisis." To many women the idea of the crisis did not come as a surprise. Many of them, however, began to discuss with men what women had long discussed with each other: the physical and emotional concomitants of menopause. For most men, the crisis seemed to be a new idea but, in many instances, it was a relief to find a name for the psychic discomfort these men had experienced.

The midlife crisis appears to be synonymous with the beginning of what Jung called "the second half of life." He found that at around age thirty-five or forty a person is likely to find that youthful objectives have been met or given up and that old sources of a sense of meaning in life no longer serve. Physical energies wane. Fewer possibilities for achievements and other satisfactions are available. Thus, there is an inward turning of psychic energy and, for many people, an intensified concern with relationships, goals, meaning of life, and other ultimate concerns, which Jung called "religion." (With increasing longevity the midlife crisis may come five to fifteen years later, especially for women, but Jung's description of the experience is still valid.)

Levinson (1978), in his study of *The Seasons of a Man's Life*, found that, for males, "At around 40, a new period gets under way. . . . For the fifteen men in our sample who completed this period, the average age at termination was 45.5, the range 44 to 47" (p. 191). The task then becomes that of coming to terms with the past, preparing for the future, and "becoming one's own man." For women, the experience is somewhat different. Lips and Colwill (1978) found that "either sex can experience negative emotional reactions to the important changes in role that occur in later life. Women, however, have been taught to expect these changes and to label them as menopausal" (p. 100). For both sexes, the experience often is a trying one and can be the end of psychological growth, or a new beginning. After the midlife crisis, if psychological development continues or resumes, its requirements are different from those of youth. Jung seemed to think that the demands of life during and after this period require more introversion. The naturally extraverted person is likely to find this requirement difficult to meet. Although the natural introvert may feel relieved to be able to live the introverted side more fully than in the past, he or she may find a need to continue to work at developing the extraverted side. These problems of middle life can become an impetus to further psychological development. Some people find that they need a change in job or life style. Others may develop better by increased reflection, which can lead to new attitudes.

The studies reported in the preceding section show that there is no clear decrease in extraversion, hence no increase in introversion, between people aged under thirty or thirty-five and older people. However, some differences in function types emerged. Although Bloch (1978) found no significant differences on the basis of age for the thinking-feeling dimension, his data indicated a significant movement in the direction of sensation over intuition among older subjects. Gray (1947) found a decrease of intuition (agreeing with Bloch's increase in sensation) and a decrease of feeling function in older age groups. Schaefer's (1974) study obtained no significant differences in function type over age groups. The data of the Baumann study were not analyzed for the relation of function to age.

Thus, it is not at all clear that the demands on young people for developed extraversion and sensation are reversed in middle life to impel older people to develop introversion and intuition. A partially contradictory hypothesis may be sounder, however: that the *nondominant* attitude and functions increase in strength with age. This hypothesis has not been tested but should be. The research would require longitudinal studies of many individuals.

Old Age

Most personality theorists and researchers limit their discussion of the developmental process to childhood and adolescence or, at most, to the first half of life, that is, through young adulthood. Jung delineated three stages in the developmental process: (a) learning about a particular society and how to live in it; (b) establishing oneself in the society through work and personal relations, especially marriage; and (c) the age of acquiring wisdom. Thus, he was unusual in developing hypotheses about the second half of life and emphasizing it as a fruitful period for psychological development. Indeed, according to some of Jung's students, he often said, "The natural end of life is not senility but wisdom" (Ellenberger, 1970, p. 712).

Jung believed that psychological development can continue, no matter how old one is. This belief was reflected in his practice of accepting for psychotherapy persons approaching or past retirement age. (The practice is continued by current Jungian analysts.) Jung's view that development can continue throughout life is shared by Erikson (1963), who identified stages of psychosocial development and their corresponding tasks covering the entire life span: (a) infancy, basic trust versus basic mistrust; (b) early childhood, autonomy versus shame and doubt; (c) play age, initiative versus guilt; (d) school age, industry versus inferiority; (e) adolescence, identity versus role confusion; (f) young adulthood, intimacy versus isolation; (g) adulthood, generativity versus stagnation; and (h) old age, ego integrity versus despair. The first five stages are roughly equivalent to Freud's stages of libidinal development. The remaining three generally parallel Jung's concept of individuation.

The "conflict" of the last stage succinctly states Jung's concept of the developmental tasks of old age: the search for meaning and the movement toward wholeness. These tasks require a reflectiveness that would not serve a person's best interests earlier in life. Jung wrote, "For a young person it is almost a sin, or at least a danger, to be too preoccupied with himself; but for the aging person it is a duty and a necessity to devote serious attention to himself" (CW8, par. 785). Only through reflection can a person consolidate his or her life's experience and seek its meaning. This reflection is necessary so that ego demands can recede and the concerns of the Self can be given priority.

Attention to the tasks of old age seems to contribute to the individual's comfort and serenity. Although controlled studies are desirable, it is helpful to know that at least one analyst, Riklin (1970), reported from his clinical experience that he was "profoundly impressed by what freedom from anxiety and what an uncomplicated old age [he found] in people who [had] seriously concerned themselves, in any way at all, with the irrational and with the question of a life after death" (p. 10).

Life as a Whole

Throughout life there are backward as well as forward processes, tendencies to regress as well as to progress. For example, an individual who encounters a situation for which he or she has no precedent, is likely to regress to earlier patterns of behavior.

The tendency to childish behavior is always in tension with the tendency to become more mature.

Thus, childish behavior is a link to the childlike part of the psyche, the part that is in flux and thus capable of further growth. The individual must give attention to the "inner child" so that the growth potential can continue to influence the adult personality. Maturity tends to be more stable and, hence, less subject to a process of development. The later years, the period of retirement from active life or at least of decreased activity, provide a renewed opportunity for further growth through increased attention to inner experience and, through reflection, to the assimilation of the many events of the past.

13

Ways of Individuation

The calendar does not determine when a person stops developing psychologically. In fact, the developmental process continues throughout one's life, according to Jung. For many people the process merges, especially in the second half of life, with the individuation process. Individuation leads, by definition, toward wholeness—completeness and undividedness—of personality by integrating the conscious and unconscious parts of the personality. Individuation leads also to uniqueness, which results from differentiating oneself fully from other persons. Thus, Jung defined the term *individuation* differently from non-Jungian theorists. The latter usually apply the term *individuation* to the early childhood process of discovering that one is separate from one's parents, especially the mother figure. Jung called this process ego development (see Chapter 12).

Individuation does not mean individualism. Jung explained the differences:

Individualism means deliberately stressing and giving prominence to some supposed peculiarity, rather than to collective considerations and obligations. But individuation means precisely the better and more complete fulfillment of the collective [archetypal] qualities of the human being. (*CW7*, par. 267)

Individuation is a process rather than a state; it is never completed in a person's lifetime. The process may be more or less fulfilled, however, depending on one's circumstances, psychic constitution, willingness to struggle, and an "irrational factor," which Jung called "vocation"—being "called" to "obey one's own law" (*CW17*, par. 300). By an irrational factor Jung seemed to mean one that cannot be predicted from such known influences as heredity and early experiences.

Individuation is collective and universal and, at the same time, intensely individual. It is collective in that it draws on archetypal contents and integrates functions and faculties that are shared by all humans. It is universal in that it is possible, to some degree, for everyone. Indeed, Jung considered individuation to be a drive as compelling as those of hunger and sex. He wrote that "every life is the realization of a whole, that is, of a self; . . . this realization can also be called individuation" (*CW12*, par. 330). Despite its universality, the individuation process and its results are different, that is, individual, for each person.

Jung used the term *individuation process* for the first time in *Psychological Types* (*CW6*), originally published in 1921. The development of the concept reached its culmination in his last major work, *Mysterium Coniunctionis*, published in German in 1956 (in English in 1963). The idea was already present, however, in his doctoral dissertation, "On the Psychology and Phenomenology of the So-called Occult Phenomena" (*CW1*), first published in 1902. In that early work, based on his observations of a young mediumistic woman, Jung concluded that the "spirits" manifesting themselves during the séances represented the invasion of the medium's field of consciousness by autonomous "splinter personalities," which evidently were components of a more comprehensive personality hidden in her unconscious psyche. It became Jung's untiring scientific and psychotherapeutic endeavor to work out a methodological procedure that would bring such components to consciousness and integrate them with the ego in order to realize the "greater personality," which is potential in every individual (see *CW9-I*, Section VI, and the whole of *CW12*).

Elements of Individuation

Characteristic of individuation is the process of strengthening, differentiating, and assimilating—integrating—into consciousness the various nonego parts of the psyche: the shadow, the persona, the nondominant attitude and functions and the animus/anima. The order in which the process is carried out is an individual matter; indeed, work on one part of the psyche is unlikely to be completed before another is begun. Moreover, each element is changed by the others as they are worked on. A crucial aspect of integrating any part of the psyche to the whole is assimilating the complexes relating to that part.

Individuation is not solely an inner process, however; it is marked by an improved capacity for relationships with people who are the objects of one's positive and negative emotions. Whatever conflicts exist within one are mirrored by the conflicts between oneself and those with whom one associates and on whom one makes projections. For example, part of a man's individuation process is to "withdraw the projections" that he has made on the woman in his life; that is, he ceases to expect the woman to have all the "feminine" qualities (e.g., gentleness and receptivity) and comes to acknowledge and value such qualities in himself. In addition, he may be able to be more open and accepting with his wife or woman friend (see Chapter 15).

Reconciliation of Opposites

When the opposites have been separated (see Chapter 12) a dynamic state comes into being. For each quality that is realized or valued consciously by the ego there is a devalued and, hence, repressed opposite in the unconscious. Whenever the unconscious content begins to become conscious a state of tension results that is uncomfortable to the person. The discomfort impels a search for a resolution. A symbol may arise that transcends the opposites (see Chapter 9). In practical terms, this transcendent function modifies both members of the pair of opposites. For example, reliability in the ego may be opposed by unconscious playfulness, which bursts forth now and then. As the consistency becomes tempered with playfulness and the playfulness ceases to be totally erratic, the two traits coexist in the same person without undue stress. Then it can be said that these opposites have been reconciled.

Ego and Self

After the ego emerges out of the Self (see Chapter 12) the connection between the two is relatively tenuous during infancy and childhood; the ego moves away from the Self, so to speak, in order to establish itself in the world. In the second half of life, however, the ego may reestablish the connection by acknowledging the primacy of the Self. Von Franz (1964) saw a kind of "meandering pattern [in dream life] in which individual strands or tendencies become visible, then vanish, then return again. If one watches this meandering design over a long period of time, one can observe a sort of hidden regulating or directing tendency at work, creating a slow, imperceptible process of psychic growth—the process of individuation" (p. 161).

A strong ego is necessary for individuation. In retracing the path to the Self and, thus, to the collective unconscious, a weak ego risks being deluged with archetypal contents, as happens in psychosis. When the ego is strong, however, unconscious contents are assimilated into it and it becomes stronger.

Jung postulated that the Self guides the individuation process, shaping the relation of the various parts of the personality to each other. The process is not directly observable but one sometimes has a sense of glimpsing the essence of one's being—what one was "meant" to be. Thus, the process is that of discovering this essence and removing the obstacles to its unfolding and development.

Individuation in the Two Halves of Life

Individuation, whether achieved naturally or through psychotherapy, has two major phases, according to Jung, one in the first half of life and the other in the second. The first half of life, after the emergence of the ego, is governed by the expansion of experience and adaptation of the psyche to outer reality: becoming established in personal relationships, the world of work, and, for most people, family life. Jung seemed to assume that early development prior to the emergence of the ego is not included in individuation but some Jungians (e.g., M. Fordham, 1968) maintain that individuation begins in infancy and continues throughout life. The disparity of opinion may be due, in part, to differing definitions of terms. Maduro and Wheelwright (1977) discussed these definitions and described the distinction between the individuating processes of childhood and youth and the individuation of adulthood:

> Although individuating processes occur throughout infancy and childhood, a distinction is made between these and what might be called individuation proper in adulthood: a challenge typically encountered in middle age in relation to life crises. If accepted, individuation may proceed at an accelerated pace and lead to increased inner growth and transformation. This is an *active* life process in which arduous self-exploration and the scanning of inner resources take place. It is a period of creative introversion of libido in which what has heretofore remained unconscious seems to "push" forward or "press" toward greater self-realization as part of the psyche's natural tendency to achieve total integration. (p. 98)

Thus, the accomplishments of the tasks of youth are the prerequisites for psychic development during the second half of life.

The individuation that occurs in the period after age thirty-five or forty may begin with a "midlife crisis," (see Chapter 12) after which development can cease or take a new direction. With or without the recognizable experience of a midlife crisis, development in the second half of life is likely to be characterized by preoccupations with philosophical or spiritual questions (e.g., values, creative endeavors, and the search for life's meaning); these interests are in sharp contrast with the attention to the temporal goals (e.g., material possessions and status) of the first half of life. The second half of life culminates in the preparation for and acceptance of death. In his one essay that focuses specifically on death, "The Soul and Death" (*CW8*), Jung envisioned death as the goal of life, not just its conclusion. He described death as a state of rest (see Chapter 14) and a state of wholeness:

> [Death] is the great perfector, drawing his inexorable line under the balance sheet of human life. In him alone is wholeness—one

way or another—attained. Death is the end of the empirical man and the goal of the spiritual man. (*CW10*, par. 695)

The Experience of Individuation

The ritual of Coué, "Every day, in every way, I am getting better and better," does not describe the process of individuation. The process does not follow a straight line nor does it always lead onward and upward. It consists of progress and regress, flux and stagnation. Because the process includes the assimilation of negative as well as positive contents, it is impossible to say which way is up. Many people who work at the individuation process in psychotherapy find it helpful to see the process as a spiral in which the same problems and themes occur again and again under different conditions and at different "levels." Whether those levels are high or low is a matter of definition.

The process is less cognitive than emotional. It is likely to begin with psychic pain (e.g., depression, anxiety, resentment) which is severe enough to arouse a desire for change. The suffering continues when the change requires facing one's dark side. The prospect is a depressing one, but the depression and other suffering serve as the impetus for continuing the individuation process.

Sometimes the process seems to be all joy and light because it is an encounter with the Self in its positive aspect. This experience is ecstatic because one transcends the limits of the ego, but it is also dangerous because it is likely to lead to "inflation"—the prideful state that accompanies a loss of ego boundaries. (Mania, a form of psychosis, may be an extreme form of inflation.) Consequently, even the agreeable aspects of individuation are problematic; when there is some progress, the ego is tempted to take pride in it and thus to destroy much of the value of the forward movement.

The rigors of the individuation process are possible to endure because images of the Self are glimpsed occasionally. It is a fairly common experience for an image of the Self to appear, perhaps in a dream, early in the analytic process. This experience may make it possible for the person to persevere later, when it is difficult to see whence one has come and whither one is going.

Despite the difficulties to most of its pilgrims, the process seems to be worth the struggle. It carries high rewards: emotional growth, discovery of meaning in life, and occasionally enlightenment or victory over inner obstacles.

Images of the Individuation Process

For some people the individuation process works primarily through spontaneous inner images: dreams, fantasies, and sometimes visions. These images can contribute to individuation if the person pays attention to them, reflects on them, and interacts with them in "active imagination" (see Chapter 16). Through this process the unconscious components of the psyche, such as the shadow, can be experienced and perhaps assimilated.

A traditional image that is used often by Jungians to denote the individuation process is the night-sea journey and the closely related images of death and rebirth. Jacobi (1959) regarded any sinking into the unconscious, even in sleep, as a prototype of the night-sea journey and thus comparable to the journey of Jonah, the biblical figure who tried to escape from God, was thrown into the sea, and spent three days and three nights in the belly of a fish before he was vomited out. After this experience, Jonah was obedient to God's command. In psychological terms, his ego submitted to the Self.

Another image is that of death/rebirth, the prototype of which is the crucifixion and the resurrection of Jesus. The theme is apparently archetypal; it has appeared, also, in many pagan rites in which gods died and were reborn, sometimes as gods and sometimes in other guises.

Psychologically, the image of crucifixion followed by resurrection can be interpreted as a crucifixion of the ego so that the Self can reign. In the life of an individual, death and rebirth may be experienced through one fundamental crisis but it is more likely to be manifested in a series of small deaths and rebirths, for example, the experience of being fired from a job, followed by a change of attitude that makes possible better work in the next job.

Descriptions of Individuation

The individuation process can be described variously as (a) the development of the attitudes and functions, (b) making archetypal contents conscious, and (c) an alchemical process.

Attitudes and Functions

From about 1928 on, Jung spent much of his time amplifying the dynamics of the individuation process. The blueprint of that process had been laid, according to Meier (1971), in Jung's typology. Indeed, Jung's book *Psychological Types* (CW6) was subtitled *The Psychology of Individuation*. Accordingly, individuation proceeds from the development of one's superior attitude (extraversion or introversion) and one or two of the four functions (feeling, intuition, sensation, thinking) to the development of the inferior attitude and functions. Most people develop their first and second functions in the first half of life, the third much later, and the fourth, usually not at all. For example, an extraverted thinking type may have sensation as second function. Later, some introversion comes into consciousness along with intuition. It is rare for the inferior function—in this case, feeling—to be developed to any appreciable extent.

The development in the attitudes and functions is likely to be experienced by the individual as changing interests, appreciations, and skills. Because of these changes, the developmental process also may be experienced through difficulties in accomplishing tasks that were easy in the past and through new conflicts with other persons, perhaps in relationships which were previously harmonious.

There are no quantitative data to evaluate Meier's hypothesis. It could be a basis for studying individual cases, however. Indeed, Meier recommended that Jungian analysts give their clients the Gray-Wheelwrights Test at the beginning of treatment and again during therapy in order to ascertain changes in the client's pattern of attitudes and functions. Another test of Meier's hypothesis would be to study many individuals over time (longitudinally). Such instruments as the Personal Orientation Inventory (see later section) could be used in conjunction with the Jungian types tests to ascertain whether individuating persons experience shifts in the balance of their attitudes and functions.

Archetypal Contents

The second way of describing the individuation process is through experiences of archetypal contents. These contents are likely to include some or all of the elements listed earlier (shadow, persona, nondominant attitude and functions, and animus/anima), plus the Wise Old Man and/or Great Mother, and, ultimately, the Self. As each of these archetypal contents is encountered, consciousness is broadened and deepened, and the ego is placed in perspective, taking its rightful place as subordinate to the Self.

The experiences of archetypal contents often occur through dreams, but waking experiences can be archetypal also. For example, a young woman perceives an older woman as an all-nourishing Earth Mother (an aspect of the Great Mother archetype). Lengthy acquaintance reveals the older woman to be not always generous and available. The younger woman comes to the painful realization that the older woman is an ordinary human being with some of the desired qualities but just as many deficiencies. By withdrawing the projection, the younger woman has gained a deeper understanding of humanness and she has taken a step in the individuation process. If she can find in herself some of the qualities she sought in the older woman, a further step has been taken. Later she may seek the Great Mother in another older woman but her expectations are likely to be less urgent.

The psychological process of individuation has parallels in many myths and other stories. The myth of Heracles (Hercules), for example, depicts the hero accomplishing a series of exceedingly difficult tasks or labors. These can be seen as steps in the development of consciousness.

Bunyan's *Pilgrim's Progress* is another story that seems to be prototypical of the individuation process. Harding (1956) traced the parallels in the journey described by Bunyan. The image of one city (Destruction) is the initial condition of the traveler and the Celestial City—the New Jerusalem—is the goal. On the way the traveler encounters persons and experiences that are, in

Harding's view, "personifications or projections of something from within his own psyche" (p. 4).

Alchemy

Still another manner of describing individuation is as an alchemical process. Jung saw the concrete substances and processes of medieval alchemy as projections of psychic contents and processes (see CW12, CW13, CW14). Thus, alchemy's *prima materia* (initial matter), often feces or lead, is the image of the undeveloped psyche. The various stages of the alchemical process are projections of stages in psychic development during which the different elements of the psyche are made conscious and integrated. For example, the alchemical stage of *nigredo*, or blackness, corresponds to the confrontation with the shadow. The alchemical work parallels the life experiences that change the personality. The goal, wholeness, is analogous to the gold into which the *prima materia* is transmuted. Another image of the goal is the philosophers' stone, the stone of the wise, which was supposed to be incorruptible and eternal. Like wholeness, the gold or the philosophers' stone was never achieved.

Areas of Experience Conducive to Individuation

Certain areas of experience are especially conducive to the individuation process. Primary among these areas are the quest for an adequate religious perspective, personal relationships, and analytic therapy.

The religious quest, in Jung's view, is crucial to the individuation process because the Self is both the pattern for individuation and the image of God. Some of the central experiences of individuation, such as the night-sea journey or death and rebirth, are paradigms of religious experience. The ultimate integration of the personality can be described as wholeness, the result of individuation, or as union with God, the goal of the religious quest.

Personal relationships contribute to the individuation process because through them one encounters many unconscious facets of oneself in projected form. An important aspect of individuation is the integration into consciousness of as many of these facets as possible.

Analytic psychotherapy almost always contributes to individuation and often focuses heavily on it. Like other human relationships, the psychotherapeutic one works through integrating parts of the personality that are expressed in relation to the analyst and to other people. More directly, it seeks to bring consciousness and the unconscious into a harmonious relation, a process which is necessary for the attainment of wholeness.

The psychotherapeutic process often contributes best to individuation when it focuses on the client's dreams. Jung found that dreams often follow an arrangement or pattern that indicates the dreamer's particular path of individuation. (Waking fantasies often supplement the dreams.) Conscious attention in therapy to dreams and fantasies enhances the individuation process.

Quantitative Evidence of Individuation

As with many Jungian concepts, individuation has not been the focus of direct testing of hypotheses. Studies have been conducted, however, testing the concept of self-actualization, which is virtually synonymous with individuation. The similarity between the two concepts is evident from the description of Hall and Lindzey (1970), drawing on the works of the various theorists of self-actualization (Goldstein, 1963; Maslow, 1962; Rogers, 1959): "Self-actualization is . . . the organic principle by which the organism becomes more fully developed and more complete. . . . Although self-actualization is a universal phenomenon in nature, the specific ends towards which people strive vary from person to person" (p. 306). This definition is markedly similar to Jung's concept of individuation as development toward wholeness and differentiation of personality. Individuation and self-actualization have further similarity in that they tend to occur in the second half of life, but in some people the process (individuation or self-actualization) may begin in youth.

Evidence for the existence of self-actualization or individuation is presented in Maslow's (1954) early work. Through the empirical study of people whom he considered to be self-actualizing, Maslow identified fifteen characteristics of the self-actualized person: (a) accurate perception of reality and comfortable relations with it; (b) acceptance of self, others, and nature; (c) spontaneity; (d) problem centering (rather than ego centering); (e) detachment, the need for privacy; (f) autonomy (independence of culture and environment); (g) continued freshness of appreciation; (h) mystic experience (the "oceanic feeling"); (i) social interest (sympathy for humankind); (j) deep interpersonal relations; (k) democratic character structure; (l) discrimination between means and ends; (m) nonhostile sense of humor; (n) creativeness; (o) resistance to enculturation (pp. 203–28).

Because measurability is used often as a means of establishing the existence of a psychological construct (a characteristic that cannot be observed directly), Shostrom's (1964) Personal Orientation Inventory (POI) supports the concept of self-actualization by providing a means of measuring it.

The inventory consists of 150 two-choice comparative value judgments. Some of the items were selected from observed value judgments of both clinically healthy and troubled patients; others were derived from the writings in humanistic, existential, and Gestalt therapy (e.g., Maslow, 1954; Perls, 1947, 1951; Shostrom, 1964). Test scores are based on such categories as "Support Ratio: Other/Inner—measures whether reactivity orientation is basically toward others or self" (p. 209). One item so scored is, "I do what others expect of me" versus "I feel free to not do what others expect of me." After reliability coefficients of .91 and .93 were established by test-retest methods, the test was administered to 650 freshmen at Los Angeles State College, 150 patients in various stages of therapy, 75 members of the sensitivity-training program at UCLA, and 15 school psychologists in a group-training program in Orange County. The latter two groups were retested after courses of eleven and fifteen weeks duration. The test was also administered to 160 "normal" adults and two groups of "relatively self-actualized" and "relatively non-self-actualized" adults: the latter groups numbered 29 and 34 respectively. Persons in both groups were nominated by members of the Los Angeles Society of Clinical Psychologists and the Orange County Society of Clinical Psychologists. The test was found to discriminate between the self-actualized, normal, and non-self-actualized groups on eleven of the twelve dimensions measured.

Other investigators have identified self-actualization or individuation independently, albeit under different names. Loevinger and Wessler (1970) concluded that the sixth and highest stage of "ego development" is the "integrated stage," which the investigators described as including "existential humor and a feeling for paradox, respect for others' autonomy, search for self-fulfillment, value for justice and idealism, opposition to prejudice, coping with inner conflict, reconciliation of role conflicts, appreciation of sex in the context of mutuality, and reconciliation to one's destiny" (pp. 106–7). Thus, this stage is markedly similar to Maslow's concept of self-actualization and Jung's concept of individuation.

Like Maslow, Loevinger and Wessler (1970) developed their concept empirically. They used a sentence completion test "to identify qualitative differences in the successive stages of ego development" (p. 15). At various stages of the construction of their manual for scoring ego development they administered the test to a total of 1,765 subjects. The subjects were all female, of varied ages, marital status, occupations, and educational levels. The responses were submitted to four trained and four self-trained raters for rating. Interrater reliabilities ranged from .83 to .94. Ego development, including the integrated stage, proved to be measurable, hence, another empirical support for the concept of individuation.

Self-Actualization and Neuroticism

Knapp (1965) used Shostrom's POI and the Eysenck Personality Inventory to examine the relations between the constructs of "self-actualization" and "neuroticism." The subjects were 136 students at a liberal arts college. The differences between the "high" neurotic group and the "low" neurotic group on all scales of the POI were statistically significant $(p > .05)$. Thus, self-actualization seems to be correlated with low neuroticism and, presumably, with mental health.

Individuation as a Drive

Goldstein (1963) supported Jung's view of individuation as a drive when he stated that self-actualization is a drive, the goal of which is "not a discharge of tension" (p. 197). Maslow's (1954) research provided the supportive empirical evidence: In self-actualized people, he perceived growth-motivation as well as the better established motivations based on physiological needs. (Motivation is approximately the equivalent of drive.) Maslow found, further, that this broader spectrum of motivations produced an "unpredictability" because the self-actualized person's behavior is unique and devoted to the realization of individual goals. This unpredictability contrasts with the predictable, physiological, drive-oriented behavior of non-self-actualized persons. Thus, non-Jungian psychologists have confirmed Jung's view that self-actualization—individuation—is an essential motivation, not just "frosting on the cake."

Individuation and Typology

Tuttle (1973) studied the achievement of self-actualization, and hence, individuation, through differentiation and integration of Jung's four functions. The subjects were 233 graduate students in counseling psychology, school psychology, and clinical psychology programs at three California state universities. The students were given the Styles of Living Preference Scale (a test of self-actualization), the Detloff Psychological Types Questionnaire, and the Barron Ego Strength Scale. Tuttle found that self-actualization increased with the number of functions (sensation, intuition, feeling, thinking) found to be highly developed. This result supports Jung's hypothesis that individuation occurs, in part, through the development of an increased number of functions—the nondominant added to the dominant.

Concluding Note

It has been said that Jung's entire personality theory could be subsumed under the topic of individuation. There is enough truth in that statement that I gave some consideration to making the discussion of individuation the second chapter in this book. Individuation is a process, however, not a description of the totality of the psyche. Consequently, the discussion on individuation culminates the discussion of the components and dynamics of the psyche.

14

Religion

To understand Jung's statements on religion, it is important to distinguish between ideas about religion—that is, theology—and experiences that are religious in nature. To Jung, theology was speculation, whereas religious experiences were indisputable psychic facts. Such experiences, he found, come in different forms and include dreams, visions, and encounters with life crises, such as illness, loss, and conflict. His views on religion were influenced heavily by what the youthful Jung perceived as the sterility of his pastor-father's dogmatic theology, a sterility which led Jung's father to the loss of his belief (see MDR). As a result, Jung began to reject religious dogma in favor of experience.

Dogma versus Experience

The distinction between dogma and experience is paralleled by the distinction between the transcendent God hypothesized by theologians and the God image that is present in the psyche.

The latter can be known by direct inner experience, whereas the transcendent God must be accepted on faith and cannot be known empirically (i.e., experientially). Jung insisted that he was not commenting on the question of whether there is a God "out there" but merely reporting his clinical observations that each person has an inner image of God.

In addition to differentiating the transcendent God from the God image in the psyche, Jung distinguished the creeds and activities of churches from religion. He defined religion in accordance with the origin of the word *religio*: "a careful consideration and observation of . . . such factors in [man's] world as he has found powerful, dangerous, or helpful enough to be taken into careful consideration, or grand, beautiful, and meaningful enough to be devoutly worshipped and loved" (CW11, par. 8). These factors are aptly described as the *numinosum*, a "dynamic agency or effect . . . [that] seizes and controls the human subject. . . . [It] is an experience of the subject independent of his will" (CW11, par. 6). The *numinosum*, which can be defined also as "that which surpasses comprehension or understanding" (*Random House Dictionary of the English Language*, 1967), is probably what Maslow (1962) identified in his concept of "peak experience."

The religious attitude, then, following Jung's thought, is generated when the ego comes to know that it is not all-powerful, that life is ultimately beyond the control of the ego or a collection of egos, and must be accepted as it is. This attitude does not produce resignation and despair. Rather, it makes possible active participation in life by freeing energy that might have been wasted in battling against reality.

An important aspect of religion and mental health, according to Jung, is a sense of meaning in life. Indeed, Frankl (1963) developed a theory of neurosis and psychotherapeutic method— logotherapy—around the discovery of meaning. Frankl had spent three years in Auschwitz and other Nazi prisons; out of his suffering and the suffering of his fellow prisoners, and from his observations of the various responses, he concluded that prisoners who continue to find meaning in life are more likely to survive and, hence, that humans have a "will-to-meaning." Logotherapy (from *logos*, the Greek word for "meaning") wrote Frankl, "regards its assignment as that of assisting the patient to find meaning in his life" (p.163). Despite Frankl's expressly stating that "there cannot exist in any man any such thing as . . . a *religious drive*, in the same manner as we speak of man's being determined by basic instincts" (p. 158), his findings support Jung's view that people have a basic need for a sense of meaning in life. Frankl did not seem to acknowledge the similarity of his ideas to Jung's, although the similarity seems evident.

Unlike Freud, who considered religion to be an illusion—an idea determined by wishful thinking—Jung maintained that religion is so essential to human life and mental health that neglect of the religious need is the primary cause of neurosis in the second half of life. He wrote:

> Among all my patients in the second half of life—that is to say, over thirty-five—there has not been one whose problem was not that of finding a religious outlook on life. It is safe to say that every one of them fell ill because he had lost what the living religions of every age have given to their followers, and none of them has really been healed who did not regain his religious outlook. (CW11, par. 509)

Consequently, Jung hypothesized that the need for religion is an instinct. His view is supported by archaeological findings indicating that as long ago as Paleolithic times humans had religious beliefs and practices. According to current cultural anthropologists, all peoples have had or have some form of what theologians call "ultimate concern," and virtually all peoples hold some kind of supernatural beliefs.

In dreams and other unconscious contents, Jung found additional evidence for the religious instinct. For example, he recounted the dream of a patient who had a very strong attachment to him:

> Her father (who in reality was of small stature) was standing with her on a hill that was covered with wheat-fields. She was quite tiny beside him, and he seemed to her like a giant. He lifted her up from the ground and held her in his arms, like a little child. The wind swept over the wheat-fields, and as the wheat swayed in the wind, he rocked her in his arms. (CW7, par. 211)

This and other dreams that she reported gave Jung the impression that the patient saw him as the supernatural father-lover. He began to wonder whether the patient "had still not understood the wholly fantastic character of her transference, or whether perhaps the unconscious could never be reached by understanding at all, but must blindly and idiotically pursue some nonsensical chimera" (CW7, par. 212). Then another possibility occurred to him: The unconscious might be reaching out toward a god. The "longing for a god [might] be a *passion* welling up from our darkest, instinctual nature, a passion unswayed by any outside influences, deeper and stronger perhaps than the love for a human person" (CW7, par. 214).

The new hypothesis, that the figure of the doctor represented a god, was not entirely acceptable to Jung's patient. Nevertheless, "there now occurred . . . a kind of subterranean undermining of the transference. Her relations with a certain friend deepened perceptibly, . . . so that when the time came for leaving [Jung] it was no catastrophe, but a perfectly reasonable parting" (CW7, par. 217).

Church Affiliation and Religion

Despite Jung's distinguishing between church and religion, he noted a relation between institutional affiliation and religious outlook. In 1935 he stated, "During the last thirty years I have not had more than about six practising Catholics among my patients. The vast majority were Protestants and Jews" (CW18, par. 370). Roman Catholics appeared not to need secular therapists because "the Catholic Church . . . with its rigorous system of confession and its director of conscience, is a therapeutic institution. I have had some patients who, after having had analysis with me, even joined the Catholic Church. . . . I think it is perfectly correct to make use of these psychotherapeutic institutions which history has given to us" (CW18, par. 370).

Jung based his conclusion regarding the attitudes of Protestants and Catholics toward their churches on more than his clinical experience. He tested empirically his impression that Catholics who were in spiritual distress tended to turn to the clergy, whereas Protestants in a similar situation were more likely to consult a doctor. In response to a question from the leaders of a Christian students' conference in 1931, Jung sent out a questionnaire, which was answered by Swiss, German, and French Protestants, and a few Roman Catholics. He found that 57% of the Protestants chose the doctor as compared with only 25% of the Catholics; correspondingly, only 8% of the Protestants chose the clergyman, whereas 58% of the Catholics did so, 35% of the Protestants and only 17% of the Catholics were undecided (CW11, par. 511). In my experience the proportion of Roman Catholics entering psychotherapy seems to be increasing. It may be that changes in the liturgy and the increasing secularization of life for many people, including Catholics, are bringing about such a change. Currently, full-time psychotherapists may be seeing relatively fewer Protestants and Jews because their own clergy are increasingly interested and trained in pastoral counseling. To my knowledge, no studies have been conducted on whether such changes are occurring.

While expressing regret that he was not "sufficiently medieval" to join "such a creed" as Catholicism (CW18, par. 370), Jung recognized the ritual of the Mass, or Eucharist (see CW11, Part III) as a means by which some people are able to experience the individuation process, at least in projected form:

> Christ, as the Original Man (Son of Man, second Adam, . . .), represents a totality which surpasses and includes the ordinary man, and which corresponds to the total personality that transcends consciousness. We have called this personality the "self." . . . The mystery of the Eucharist transforms the soul of the empirical man, who is only a part of himself, into his totality, symbolically expressed by Christ. In this sense, therefore, we can speak of the Mass as the rite of the individuation process. (CW11, par. 414)

Although many Protestant churches celebrate Holy Communion, which is based on the Mass, the psychological effect on the worshiper is evidently not the same; much of the power seems to have been lost. The power, Jung deduced, is in the belief, which most Catholics hold, in transubstantiation, the mystery of the transformation of the bread and wine into the body and blood of Christ. In contrast, many Protestants view the bread and wine as representing, rather than becoming, the body and blood of Christ; to them, the statement, "This is my body" (Luke 22:19), is a metaphor. (A third position, held by many Lutherans, is that of consubstantiation: the belief that the body and blood of Christ coexist in and with the bread and wine. This position is probably closer to that of the Roman Catholics than of other Protestants.)

There may be a disadvantage in the Roman Catholic position, however. Jung found that the dogma tends to become a defense against the religious experience that is available through a direct encounter with the unconscious. For some Roman Catholics, of course, the Mass itself is a direct religious experience.

The absence of religious experience through the churches appeared to Jung to be synonymous with the loss of vitality in their traditonal symbolism, for example, the Trinity and the Communion. Indeed, these images and practices no longer function as true symbols for many people. Another development since Jung's time is the marked increase in charismatic groups, such as Jesus sects and faith-healing groups. These groups seem to attest to Jung's view of the perceived sterility of the established churches, but they do not provide a viable alternative for all disenchanted church members.

Jung tried to overcome the gap between people and symbols by understanding the psychology of traditional Christianity. This was not an attempt, he insisted, to "psychologize" the dogma. Rather, symbols have an archetypal foundation "which can never be reduced to anything else" (CW11, par. 171). Evidence for the archetypal foundation of the Trinity, for example, is the appearance of triads in the mythologies of widely separated peoples, such as the Hindu triad of Brahma, Vishnu, and Shiva.

When people find that traditional religion is no longer a vital force in their lives they are likely to turn to other potential sources of meaning. They may extract what meaning they can from material possessions or ideologies, such as those of political movements. Perhaps the best sources of meaning are experiences of the Self because, according to Jung, these are religious experiences. From the fact that the Self is an archetype, some people have inferred that Jung considered God to be "only" an archetype. Jung objected strenuously to this interpretation; he maintained that an archetype is not so "only." Moreover, he pointed out that the Self is the God image, not the actual God. Jung's idea of the God image within the individual psyche has been considered heretical by many theologians but others, such as Paul Tillich, expressed views that were very similar to Jung's. Such "immanental" theologians posit a "God within" that bears a strong resemblance to Jung's God image.

Religion and Individuation

The importance of religion in Jung's system of psychology is reflected in his vision of the attainment of a religious attitude as essential to the individuation process. Indeed, individuation and a religious attitude are almost synonymous in that both require the ego to become subordinate to the Self.

Although religious forms are not the same as a religious attitude, they sometimes contribute to it. Jung rejected all doctrines, including those of Christianity, but the Christian imagery carried for him the central images of the individuation process. Thus, he saw Jesus as the prototype of the individuating person:

> This apparently unique life became a sacred symbol because it is the psychological prototype of the only meaningful life, that is, of a life that strives for the individual realization—absolute and unconditional—of its own particular law. (CW17, par. 310)

Just as Christian theologians often do, Jung seemed to see Christ as another order of being from Jesus: in psychological terms, an exemplification of the archetype of the Self. This conceptualization presented problems for Jung, however, in that Christianity presents Christ as all good. Jung wrote:

> From the psychological angle [Christ] corresponds to only one half of the archetype. The other half appears in the Antichrist. The latter is just as much a manifestation of the self, except that he consists of its dark aspect. Both are Christian symbols, and they have the same meaning as the image of the Savior crucified between two thieves. (CW9–II, par. 79)

Thus, for Jung, Christ becomes an adequate symbol of the Self only in combination with the Antichrist.

Another view of Christ as symbol of the Self is through the crucifixion and resurrection: Jesus, the individuating ego, is crucified on the opposites (the cross is an image of the tension of heaven and earth or vertical and horizontal) and resurrected into the totality of the psyche, the Self. A comparable experience may occur psychologically in the life of each human.

Virtually all humans puzzle over the meaning of death. Jung's view was that death is the end, in the sense of "goal," as well as the termination of life:

> We are so convinced that death is simply the end of a process that it does not ordinarily occur to us to conceive of death as a goal and a fulfillment. . . .
>
> Life is an energy-process. Like every energy-process, it is in principle irreversible and is therefore directed toward a goal. That goal is a state of rest. . . . With the attainment of maturity and at the zenith of biological existence, life's drive toward a goal in no

wise halts. With the same intensity and irresistibility with which it strove upward before middle age, life now descends; for the goal no longer lies on the summit, but in the valley where the ascent began. . . .

From the middle of life onward, only he remains vitally alive who is ready to *die with life*. . . . The negation of life's fulfillment is synonymous with the refusal to accept its ending. Both mean not wanting to live, and not wanting to live is identical with not wanting to die. Waxing and waning make one curve. (*CW8*, pars. 797–98, 80)

Jung's Views on Religion

The two aspects of religion, religious experiences and ideas about them, were kept separate by Jung in much of his work, but he seemed to bring them together in some statements he made a few years before his death. Widely known is his reply to a question in the 1959 television interview, *Face to Face* (produced by the British Broadcasting Company); the interviewer asked, "Do you now believe in God?" Jung replied, "Difficult to answer. I know. I don't need to believe. I know" (McGuire and Hull, 1977, p. 428). Many people have puzzled over Jung's statement. However, it seems to have been explained in an earlier (1955) interview. On that occasion Jung said, "All that I have learned has led me step by step to an unshakable conviction of the existence of God. I only believe in what I know. And that eliminates believing. Therefore I do not take His existence on belief—I *know* that He exists" (McGuire and Hull, 1977, p. 251).

Answer to Job

Despite his firm conviction that God exists, Jung struggled mightly to understand the nature of God. Out of this struggle came one of his most controversial books, *Answer to Job* (*CW11*, Part VI). Jung described it as

not a "scientific" book but a personal confrontation with the traditional Christian world view. . . . It echoes the reflections of a physical and theological layman, who had to find the answers to many questions on religious matters and was thus compelled to wrestle with the meaning of religious ideas from his particular,

non-confessional standpoint. In addition, the questions were motivated by contemporary events: falsehood, injustice, slavery, and
mass murder engulfed not only major parts of Europe but continue
to prevail in vast areas of the world. What has a benevolent and
almighty God to say to these problems? This desperate question,
asked a thousand times, is the concern of [Answer to Job]. (CW18,
par. 1498a)

Jung responded to the biblical story of Job with some unorthodox conclusions. The first is an answer to the age-old
theological problem: What is the source of evil? How can a God,
who is omnipotent and all-good, allow evil? Jung answered that
God has a dark side. The answer may be no better than those of
theologians, but it is no worse. This idea is of psychological importance because it makes clear the limitlessness of the archetypal shadow.

A second conclusion that Jung reached in Answer to Job is
that God had to become human in order to attain consciousness.
This idea seemed to arise out of Jung's struggle to understand
why God permitted Satan to do as he pleased with Job. Jung's
hypothesis, that prior to the incarnation in Jesus God was unconscious, is provocative.

The Trinity

Still another one of Jung's unorthodox conclusions is that
the Christian Trinity is incomplete; wholeness is a quaternity.
The fourth principle was posited variously by Jung as evil, the
earth, matter, the body, and the feminine. Jung seemed to see
these manifestations of the fourth as various ways of describing
concrete reality, which contrasts with the entirely spiritual (and
presumably male) Trinity. This view presents a problem, however, by assuming evidently, that matter is evil. Jung considered
such an assumption to be based on an overemphasis on spirit:
"In themselves, spirit and matter are neutral, . . . capable of
what man calls good or evil" (CW9-I, par. 197).

If the fourth principle is feminine and also evil, an additional problem arises, an anomaly which can be understood,
perhaps, as a perception of males confronted with the mystery of
the female. Jung was deeply concerned that the feminine principle be acknowledged as essential to wholeness. Consequently, he

welcomed the dogma of the Assumption of the Virgin (proclaimed by Pope Pius XII in 1950). Jung saw this dogma as adding "a fourth, feminine principle to the masculine Trinity. The result is a quaternity, which forms a real and not merely postulated symbol of totality" (CW13, par. 127).

Jung struggled further with the problem of evil in various essays (see especially CW10 and his correspondence with Victor White in Let 1 and 2). In such works, he rejected the idea that evil is only *privatio boni* (absence of good). Evil is a force in itself, he insisted; it is part of the collective shadow and empirically verifiable, as in the experience with Nazism in Germany.

It is no accident that the knowledge that good and evil are opposites (see Chapter 12) is a metaphor for the emergence of consciousness. A crucial factor in individuation is the encounter with the dark side of the personality and with the evil in the world. One of Jung's early experiences of psychological awakening was with such an encounter. Hannah (1974) recounted that Jung's fantasy experience, at about age eleven, of God dropping turds on Basel Cathedral, "had been the guiding line of his whole life"; in his struggle over this and other experiences he found "a way to live with the dark side of himself and with that of the Creator" (p. 31).

Conscience

A common error in speaking, writing, or typing is to substitute *conscious* for *conscience* or vice versa. The two words are related etymologically in the Latin word for "knowledge" (*conscious* translates as "sharing knowledge with"). Jung hypothesized a psychological relation between conscious and conscience. Jacobi (1976) clarified two kinds of conscience, one of which is similar to consciousness as Jung defined it:

> Now Jung has made an original and far-reaching contribution to the problem of conscience. He said that people basically have two kinds of conscience. One kind corresponds with the collective commands and prohibitions of the society we live in. If we disobey that, the bad conscience that results is from fear of being thought anti-social and from fear of punishment. But there is also a different sort of conscience, which operates individually in every

human being in accordance with the laws of creation. It is not always, though that also happens, in harmony with prescribed human laws. Sometimes there are collisions from which a serious struggle between the two kinds of conscience may arise. (p. 86)

The second, individual kind of conscience, evidently, is a sense of ethics. It is an important element in Jung's definition of consciousness—taking one's personal stance regardless of the prescriptions of society.

Sin

The adversary of conscience is known as sin. In an earlier work (Mattoon, 1965), I hypothesized originally that the Christian concept of sin is the equivalent of the psychological concept of the shadow and should be treated as such; that is, sin can be assimilated to the ego for the enhancement of consciousness. In order to support this hypothesis, however, it would have been necessary to explain away the Apostle Paul's admonition to repress the dark side (e.g., Romans 8:5–8). I was forced to conclude that the stage of development of consciousness was such in biblical times that it necessitated a rejection of the dark side in order to separate the opposites. Currently, however, in my view as in Jung's, the task of humans seems to be the reuniting of the opposites. Although "sin" and "shadow" are identical to some people, the designation of "shadow" implies the possibility of embracing the dark side for the sake of wholeness, while "sin" suggests rejection of the dark side in the pursuit of perfection.

Eastern Religions

Westerners' exposure to religions of the East was much less common in Jung's day than it is now. In his discussion of Eastern religions (CW11, Parts VII & VIII), Jung held that a Westerner cannot fully embrace an Eastern religion. This view has been challenged seriously by the large numbers of Americans and Europeans who have become devotees of Yoga, Zen Buddhism, and other Eastern religions. Nevertheless, Jung's view probably has some validity in that a Westerner's relation to an Eastern religion is much different from that of a person born into the

culture from which the religion stems. Jung seemed to feel that
the West could benefit substantially from encounters with the
East. He found, however, that abolition of the ego, which is a
goal of Eastern religions, is counterproductive for wholeness because then only the unconscious remains.

Jung's study of Eastern religion was probably most extensive
in relation to a major work of Chinese wisdom literature, the *I
Ching* (CW11, Part IX). He was interested in it as a basis for synchronistic phenomena, however, not as religion.

Empiricism and Religion

An empirical study relevant to the relation of Jungian
psychology and religion was conducted by Nightingale (1972).
He examined the relation between Jungian type and death concern and time perspective. The investigator used the Myers-
Briggs Type Indicator to select three males and three females for
each of the sixteen different types (all combinations of each of
the two attitudes with each of the four functions and judgment
or perception). Using the Personal Events Test, he assessed past
and future time perspective in the subjects, and with the
Templer's Death Anxiety Scale he assessed death concern. Subjects were asked, also, about their subjective life expectancy.
"The conclusions drawn were that a dominant Thinking process
acts to stabilize [minimize] variations in time perspective while a
dominant Feeling process acts to increase variation" (p. 3956).
The author acknowledged that the results could be due to a
sampling error so replication is necessary. Nightingale's study
provides, however, a sample of the empirical research that is
possible even in an abstract area of study such as religion.

Jung's ideas on religion, in my view, "tread the razor's edge"
between psychology and theology. He made impressive efforts,
with considerable success, to restrict his comments to observable
data and deductions from them. He did not always take into account, however, the variety of theological thinking that was
available; for example, the idea of the immanent God. Nevertheless, Jung's ideas on religion are valuable, especially because
he remains one of the few psychological theorists to have addressed the role of religion in the human psyche. The total body
of Jung's works on religion is enormous, probably because of his

personal interest and the close relation of the topic to the collective unconscious and individuation. Dry (1961), a critical writer on Jung, described him as a "pioneer" in that he "has been among the earliest psychologists to recognize the relevance of faith and religious practice to the needs and workings of the human psyche" (p. 209).

Part V

Applications

15

Relationships and Sexuality

Relationships provide the context in which psychological development occurs. To Jung, only in such relationships could the projection of unconscious contents (especially shadow and animus/anima) occur, and projection is usually necessary to integrate the contents. That is, discovering these psychic contents and reconciling them with each other are crucial to psychological growth.

The relating (eros) capacity has been confused often, among Jungians, with the feeling (evaluative) function. The distinction between the two requires clarification. In my view, the foundation of any relationship is valuing—appreciating—the other person. Thus, differentiated feeling contributes more to relating than do the other functions. Valuing and relating are not equivalent, however; valuing is directed by one person to the other, whereas relating is made up of complex interactions. Morever, as Hillman (1962) explained, feeling includes not only positive valuing but also evaluating, negatively as well as positively. Consequently, feeling can separate the evaluator from the other person and thus may not serve eros, which brings the two together.

Even though relationships (including sexual ones) are very important to the individuation process, the Jungian literature is relatively sparse on the subject. However, Jung made many relevant, though scattered, comments on relationships.

Effects of Early Experience

The bases for adult relationships seem to be laid in childhood, first in the child's experience with the nurturant and protective (mother) figure. In addition to food, physical warmth, and relief from pain, the infant needs physical contact with other people and emotional tenderness. However well-fed and cared for physically, a child who is neglected emotionally may die or become seriously retarded. No one person caring for an infant supplies all these needs perfectly, and the lack of fulfillment, as perceived by the child, gives rise to some of the problems of later life. Often, these problems are expressed in projections to friends, lovers, spouses, and/or children. The projection may take the form of seeking to be "mothered" by or to "mother" other adults. Men as well as women can seek to mother. Some people seek to be mothered by their children. Similarly, a disturbance in the relationship with the structuring (father) figure can leave an individual with a tendency to seek a strong authority or to act the father by behaving in an authoritarian manner.

The nurturing parent and the structuring parent, respectively, seem to have archetypal roots in what Jung called the "Mother archetype" and the "Father archetype." When archetypal forces are activated, they intensify human situations. The increased intensity can be positive or negative. It is positive if the person, now an adult, is able to make use of the inner resources that the archetypal forces provide (e.g., the "inner mother" finds ways of meeting one's needs). The negative side of this archetypal dimension is seeing other people as having the godlike power that, as a small child, one perceived in one's parents.

Ample clinical evidence documents the specific effects of early experience on later relationships. Freud hypothesized that males are more attached to their mothers, and females to their fathers; Jung's view seemed to be that a person of either sex can have either a positive or negative mother and/or father complex.

The truth may lie somewhere between Freud's and Jung's views. Aron and his associates (1974) reported their findings that both men and women tend to marry persons with whom they have relationships that are similar to those they had with their mothers. The subjects were a random sample. "During a period of one week, the experimenters approached couples waiting in line at the marriage license bureau of the Toronto City Hall. Members of each pair were requested to complete independently a one-page questionnaire and return it to the experimenter immediately upon completion. Subjects who refused, were illiterate, or did not speak English were excluded" (p. 18). The study population consisted of forty six males and fifty two females who had lived with both parents beyond the age of ten and who answered all the questions. In the questionnaire, each subject was asked to select the position on the four-point scale (Never; Once in a while; Often; Almost always) that best described his or her relationships with the father, mother, and future spouse on such items as, "We talk easily on any subject." The predicted similarity of relationships between male subject and mother and those between male subject and future wife was significant at only the .10 level of confidence; for females, the similarity of relationships with future husband and with mother was significant at the .05 level of confidence (although this similarity was not predicted).

Relatively little attention has been paid in analytic (Jungian and Freudian) circles to relations among siblings, except for the well-known rivalry. From clinical observations, however, it seems that relations with siblings have a profound influence on relations with adult peers—spouses, friends, and co-workers. This influence becomes evident in such behaviors as affectionateness, assertiveness, cooperativeness, and competitiveness.

Forming Relationships

Relationships begin, often, with mutual attraction, that is, positive projections that are experienced as liking. Without such projections, people are not sufficiently interested to spend time together, much less to bear the pain of working out the problems that arise in any lasting association.

Is it possible to discover why one person is attracted to

another? Anast (1966) sought to answer the question in relation to function types. His subjects were 111 female and 98 male introductory psychology students at Eastern Washington State College. They were classified for sensation-intuition and thinking-feeling on the Myers-Briggs Type Indicator (MBTI) and then were asked to rate their preferences for fictional and mass-media heroes and heroines according to four descriptors, each of which seems to be characteristic of one of the four Jungian type combinations: (a) practical-logical (sensation-thinking); (b) sociable-friendly (sensation-feeling); (c) intellectually brilliant (intuitive-thinking); and (d) witty (intuitive-feeling). These descriptions had been suggested to Anast by the MBTI manual. According to the results, persons of both sexes preferred their fictional heroes and heroines to be similar to themselves. Three categories (males' choice of heroines and females' choices of both heroes and heroines) were signficant at the .001 level; the fourth (males' choice of heroes) was significant at only the .10 level.

The use of the terms *hero* and *heroine* suggests attraction based on positive qualities. Jung hypothesized, however, that the attraction between persons may be based on imperfections:

> A human relationship is not based on differentiation and perfection, for these only emphasize the differences or call forth the exact opposite; it is based, rather, on imperfection, on what is weak, helpless and in need of support—the very ground and motive for dependence. The perfect have no need of others, but weakness has, for it seeks support and does not confront its partner with anything that might force him into an inferior position. (CW10, par. 579)

Beyond the initial attraction, development of a relationship requires the withdrawal of projections, that is, the modification of one's image of the other in the light of experience. This process has both positive and negative aspects. Some of what one finds in the other person is to one's liking, some of it not. If the disliked qualities are dominant, the association is likely to be severed. If there is more on the positive side, however, mutual affection and concern are strengthened. These attitudes can grow into a regard that deserves the name of love.

Withdrawal of projections depends on a degree of individual development. Perry's (1971) statement is apt: "Only when one's self-image has developed to a sufficient degree can one be in a position to perceive other people's selves as they actually are" (p. 302).

The development of relationships does not depend entirely on the withdrawal of projections, however. Relationships are enhanced, also, by awareness of one or both parties that some of their perceptions are partially projections. Such awareness produces a degree of humility that makes it easier for people to make emotional contact with each other.

Just as positive projections seem to contribute to the formation of relationships, negative projections probably are a hindrance. Indeed, Jung hypothesized a general tendency for a person of one attitude type to depreciate someone of the opposite type. This hypothesis was not borne out in a study by Taylor (1968), however. He gave the MBTI and a modified version of Ryans' Classroom Observation Record to 156 college juniors in six classes in human development. The six instructors of the classes were given only the MBTI. The MBTI of each student and teacher was scored for the four indices: extraversion-introversion, sensation-intuition, thinking-feeling, and judgment-perception. The Classroom Observation Record yielded a score that was the difference between the student's rating of the ideal teacher and the student's actual teacher; the estimated reliability coefficient for this instrument was .91 (based on the Hoyt estimate of reliability). When the difference scores between the student's and teacher's psychological types were correlated with the scores from the classroom observation record, the relationship was found not to be significant. Thus, students who were similar to their teachers in type were no more or less likely to respond positively to the teachers than were students who were different from their teachers.

The term *relationship* has been used thus far to mean any voluntary association between two persons. Jung made a distinction, however, between emotional bonds that are based largely on projection and what he considered to be a true or, in his term, *psychological* relationship. For him, the term denoted a "conscious" relationship; that is, one in which some of the projections have been withdrawn and there is mutual appreciation, understanding, and adaptation on the basis of each other's reality without either person's losing his or her own individuality. Jung pointed out the necessity of a high degree of consciousness in each person:

There is no such thing as a psychological relationship between two people who are in a state of unconsciousness. From the psychological point of view they would be wholly without relationship. From any other point of view, the physiological for example, they could be regarded as related, but one could not call their relationship psychological. It must be admitted that though such total unconsciousness as I have assumed does not occur, there is nevertheless a not inconsiderable degree of partial unconsciousness, and the psychological relationship is limited in the degree to which that unconsciousness exists. (CW17, par. 325)

Sometimes relationships are delayed or prevented by specific psychological problems. Von Franz (1970) found, for example, that the *puer aeternus* (see Chapter 5) has great difficulty in forming relations with women because of the strong attachment to his mother. He seeks in every woman the image of the mother: the perfect woman who will give everything to him and who is without shortcomings. Whenever he is fascinated by a woman he discovers that she is an ordinary human being and he turns away disappointed, only to project the mother image onto one woman after another.

Friendship

Different investigators have obtained similar but inconclusive results regarding the tendency of persons to select as friends individuals of the same type. On the basis of clinical data, Gray and Wheelwright (1945) found that pairs of friends tend to be similar to each other in psychological type. Osgood (1972), to test the relations of friends' Jungian personality types, recruited seventy-one volunteer subjects (forty-six females and twenty-five males), all twenty-four years old or older and all residents of their local communities for at least two years. Various occupations were represented among the subjects, with a leaning toward the professions. Two self-report instruments were obtained from each subject: the MBTI and Osgood's Friendship Bond Identification Form. The latter, a self-awareness, self-report instrument, which underwent four revisions, was developed specifically for the study. It was designed to provide subjects with a criterion for evaluating their friendships and a measure to determine which friendships were most meaningful.

The directions instructed respondents to list friends according to the criterion and then to evaluate and type each friendship. Three types of friendship bonds were described within the instrument: full friendship bonds, specialized friendship bonds, and potential friendship bonds. The two friends of each subject who were listed closest to the center of the full friendship bond category were given the MBTI. A profile similarity index was computed from the MBTI raw scores for each subject-friend pair and each pair composed of a subject with a randomly chosen person. Only a slight and insignificant difference in the direction of greater similarity between the psychological type profiles of subject-friend dyads was found. Thus, the Gray and Wheelwright clinical hypothesis was not supported.

From Jung's theory of types, one might assume that extraverts would tend to care more about maintaining friendships. Osgood tested this hypothesis, also, using the same seventy-one subjects who had participated in the preceding study. The total numbers of friendship bonds reported by each subject on the Osgood Friendship Bond Identification were classified into a frequency tabulation to determine differences in bonds. The results, which were statistically insignificant, indicated that introverts developed and cared about maintaining friendships just as much as extraverts did. Consequently, if introverts are less social, as is assumed often, it does not mean they have fewer total and close friendships.

Marriage

Relationships between men and women that lead to long-term commitments, including marriage, often begin with mutual animus-anima projections. If the relationship is to thrive, however, projections must give way to seeing and valuing the other person as he or she actually is and not as an embodiment of the partner's animus or anima; the "'other' person . . . has a whole universe of his or her own, a whole developmental process of his or her own" (Sandner, 1979, p. 19). As persons mature they discover how exaggerated and inconsistent are their expectations of their partners and they also begin to develop some of the desired qualities in themselves. Hence, they can relinquish some of the demands they have made on their partners. According to Wheelwright (1971), the necessity to withdraw projections is especially true in the second half of life when children have left home and husband and wife are left with only each other.

Jung made scattered comments on marriage and wrote one essay on the subject: "Marriage as a Psychological Relationship" (*CW17*). He hypothesized that marriage partners' early experiences, whether positive or negative, contribute to adjustments in the relationship:

> In most cases one [partner] will adapt to marriage more quickly than the other. The one who is grounded on a positive relationship to the parents will find little or no difficulty in adjusting to his or her partner, while the other may be hindered by a deep-seated unconscious tie to the parents. He will therefore achieve complete adaptation only later, and, because it is won with greater difficulty, it may even prove the more durable. (*CW17*, par. 331b)

A workable marriage, in Jung's view, can be based on the partners' differences in personality, differences that may favor each partner in a different area of life. The result is a "containment" of one partner in the other, Jung explained.

> There is always so much experience available that the simpler personality is surrounded, if not actually swamped, by it; he is swallowed up in his more complex partner and cannot see his way out. It is an almost regular occurrence for a woman to be wholly contained, spiritually, in her husband, and for a husband to be wholly contained, emotionally, in his wife. One could describe this as the problem of the "contained" and the "container." (*CW17*, par. 331c)

By "containment" Jung seemed to mean setting the tone of or even being dominant in a designated area of life. The term *spiritually*, as used by Jung, does not connote religion so much as *logos*, that is, structure, meaning, and the world of ideas. Such a view of man-woman relations reflects the prevailing attitude toward marriage during the first quarter of the twentieth century. Carl and Emma Jung probably had such a marriage in their early years but it changed enough, later, for them to share professional interests.

Who Marries Whom

At least three studies have been conducted to ascertain whether the "average" husband and wife tend to be similar or different. Using the Gray-Wheelwrights Test (GWT), Gray (1949) found that of 271 married couples, 15% were alike in attitude (introversion or extraversion) and both major functions (thinking or feeling and sensation or intuition); an additional 38% had two of the three alike (e.g., both introverts and both intuitives) and one different (e.g., one thinking, the other feeling). Thus, the split was nearly even: 53% of the couples were more alike than different and 47% were more different than alike. (The statistical significance of the results was not given.)

Williams (1971) used the MBTI for much the same purpose. The meaure has four dimensions: the three of the GWT plus judgment-perception. The investigator compared the proportion of married couples who have two or three MBTI preferences in common with the proportion that could be expected by chance. Chi-square analysis revealed that significantly fewer couples than expected shared only one preference (18% instead of 25%) and significantly more couples than expected shared four preferences (24% instead of 7%); thus, 58% shared two or three preferences.

A third study (Lewis, 1976) used the Holtzman Ink-Blot Test, which is scored for Jungian type characteristics. Lewis found that couples tend to be both introverted or both extraverted but that one member is likely to be stronger in the thinking and the other in the feeling function. He found no pattern between spouses in the perceptual functions.

Marital Adjustment

All three studies indicate a tendency for persons with a balance of similarities and differences to choose each other. With some similarities and some differences between persons in relationships, the commonalities presumably make communication possible and the disparities provide zest and interest: something to communicate about. Williams (1971) tried to test this hypothesis, in effect, by investigating the degree of marital adjustment in couples with various combinations of similar and different typologies. She recruited a sample of two hundred married couples through an advertisement in an unspecified publication for "happily married couples who are interested in information on marital enrichment," and administered to them the Locke-Wallace Short Marital Adjustment Test. She found no statistically significant relation between the number of type preferences shared and scores on the marital adjustment test. The trend, however, was in favor of the hypothesis. Couples sharing one, two, or three preferences tended to be more happily adjusted than couples at either extreme, that is, completely alike or completely dissimilar. Since the subdivisions were many for a sample of two hundred couples, a study using a larger sample might produce more conclusive results.

Another measure of marital adjustment is whether the couple stays married or gets divorced. The prognosis seems to be no different when husband and wife are similar in temperament from when they are dissimilar. Bradway and Detloff (1975) used the GWT to study twenty-eight divorced and seventy-two currently married couples (analysts and their spouses). The investigators wanted to ascertain whether husband and wife were the same or different in attitude (IE) and in the two dimensions of function (thinking-feeling and sensation-intuition). They found no significant differences on any of the dimensions independently or on the three taken together.

Marriage Problems

Many of the problems in marriage arise from the fact that the partners have differing temperaments, values, and backgrounds. Jung found that other problems can result from too much similarity. He wrote:

> I once had an "ideal-looking couple" who came to consult me. Something had gone wrong. When I looked at them I wondered what could have brought them to me. They appeared perfectly suited to one another in every way and, as I soon discovered, they were blessed with all the material things life could offer. But eventually I found the real trouble was that they were *too* well suited. This prevented any tension existing in ˑtheir intimate relations. They coincided so much that nothing happened—a situation as awkward as the opposite extreme of total incompatibility. (McGuire and Hull, 1977, p. 247)

The problems in marriage often appear to arise, in Jungian terms, in the actions of the woman's negative animus. When the husband's anima has created an unpleasant emotional climate and the wife attempts to adapt to an impossible situation, she is blamed when she fails. The old sex-role stereotypes assumed that women are primarily responsible for the health of marital relationships, but these stereotypes are giving way to some degree, to an awareness that both partners contribute to the emotional climate in the home.

The phenomenon of projection is important not only in dealing with problems within an intact marriage but, also, in separation or divorce. When one no longer lives with the partner on whom one has made a host of projections, they persist and are unchallenged by the partner's reality. For the sake of psychological development, therefore, it is essential to explore the nature of the projections as thoroughly as possible before a decision on divorce is made.

Some couples who are experiencing serious difficulties in their marriage find that their problems stem from their different ways of viewing the world, differences that are rooted in different attitude and function types. Often, such couples find that one of the Jungian types tests, administered in conjunction with marriage counseling, can provide information on the reasons for misunderstandings due to their different perceptions. Sometimes the couple, independently, can gain considerable insight from understanding that they are of different types by reading a relevant book or, again, by responding to one of the tests.

Much that is written and said about marriage seems to be predicated on the assumption that the goal is happiness. Guggenbühl-Craig (1977) disputed this view, maintaining that the goal is individuation. He seemed to mean that one must not ask the spouse to live up to one's expectations but, instead, should undertake to develop in oneself the qualities that one has desired in the spouse: such qualities as understanding, acceptance, strength, protectiveness, stability, and adventuresomeness.

It is worth considering that Guggenbühl-Craig may be right that happiness and well-being are no longer sufficient bases for marriage and that these values can be achieved better through other means. If marriage becomes one's path to individuation, however, one can expect to suffer before attaining the rewards.

Groups

Of the relatively little research that has tested Jungian hypotheses on relationships, nearly all applies to relationships within the family or one-to-one relationships outside the family. An exception is the study by Kilmann and Taylor (1974) in which they investigated the responses of persons with various attitude and function types (as measured by the MBTI) to a group situation—a T-group "laboratory." The subjects were ninety-two graduate students in business administration (eighty-five male and seven female); over a twelve-week semester they participated in groups of six to eight members. Group exercises helped the members to get acquainted, to practice giving feedback, and to develop cohesiveness and trust. The investigators hypothesized that persons with dominant extraversion, feeling, and intuition were more likely to accept the laboratory experience, whereas persons with dominant introversion, thinking, and sensation were more likely to reject the experience. Both hypotheses were confirmed at the .001 level of significance. In this situation, at least, group interpersonal relations seemed to be more congenial to extraverts with dominant feeling and intuition.

Conflict

A basic component in all human relations, whether one-to-one or in family and other groups, is conflict and the way it is handled. Kilmann and Thomas (1975) studied this component in the functioning of persons of various Jungian types. The MBTI was administered to eighty-six male students in a graduate course, Behavioral Science for Management. Shortly thereafter, the students completed a package of instruments, including three measures of conflict-handling modes (Hall Conflict Management Survey, Lawrence and Lorsch set of proverbs, and Thomas-Kilmann MODE instrument). There was no significant difference in conflict handling by persons with dominant sensation as compared with those with dominant intuition. The thinking-feeling dimension did reflect differences, however. Individuals who scored higher on feeling tended (.001, .01, and .05 levels of significance for the three measures) to be relatively less taking than giving. There was also a tendency (significant at the .05 level of confidence) for feeling persons to be less assertive and more cooperative. The most consistent and significant results on this dimension indicated that feeling persons tend to be more accommodating than thinking persons.

On the extraversion-introversion dimension the strongest and most consistent correlations indicated that extraverts were more likely to strive for integrative solutions. There was a lesser tendency for extraversion to be related to assertiveness and cooperativeness.

Sexuality

The specifically sexual aspect of relationships was discussed relatively little by Jung, probably because Freud gave so much attention to the subject and Jung assumed that his readers were familiar with Freud's work. An exception is "The Love Problem of the Student" (CW10), in which Jung discussed the sexual and other problems that arise between the sexes when marriage must be postponed, as it was in the 1920s for many young people, including many students, who were economically dependent. In this essay and other scattered comments, Jung indicated that he viewed sexuality as instinctive and therefore essential. He saw it, however, as having significance beyond the biological drive. For him, sexuality was psychological and even creative. He described it as

> a power which seeks expression and evidently may not be trifled with, and therefore cannot be made to fit in with our well-meaning moral laws. Sexuality is not mere instinctuality; it is an indisputably creative power that is not only the basic cause of our individual lives, but a very serious factor in our psychic life as well. (CW8, par. 107)

Although Jung developed no hypothesis linking any of his personality theories with sexual behavior, Eysenck (1971) did so with extraversion-introversion. He cited a study by two German researchers, Hans Giese and Gunter Schmidt (reference not given), and reported some results of his own. In the German study extraverts were found to have intercourse more frequently with more different partners and extraverted females to reach orgasm more readily. Eysenck's study distinguished between "orthodox permissive" and "orthodox Christian"; the results indicated that extraverts petted more and had more intercourse than introverts. He concluded:

> There are two nonpathological ways of sexual adjustment, the extraverted and introverted, that are opposed in a very meaningful

manner. The extravert endorses the orthodox permissive, promiscuous approach to sex, with frequent changes of sex partner and much healthy appetite for frequent sexual contacts. The introvert, on the other hand, endorses the orthodox Christian approach; he puts stress on virginity and fidelity, and downplays biological factors.

Taken to their extremes, these approaches become the libertine and the puritan, respectively, but if they are not taken to excess they are both probably viable modes of adjustment. (p. 51)

Homosexuality

Jung had little to say on the subject of homosexuality. However, he hypothesized that in a male homosexual the heterosexual libido is tied up with the mother so that sex cannot be experienced with a woman. In such men masculinity is underdeveloped, that is, only partially conscious, hence, it tends to be projected, and the object of the projection is another man (see CW7, pars. 167–83 and CW17, pars. 266–81). Kettner (1968) found that Jung's thesis of the homosexual's tie to the mother is supported by his exaggerated interest in the phallus, which was also an aspect of the Great Mother cults of antiquity. Guggenbühl-Craig (1960) stated that homosexuality, for some homosexuals, is an expression of narcissism.

Jung had even less to say about female homosexuality, but he seemed to assume that many female homosexuals seek the mother in the partner. In my experience, this assumption, like those regarding male homosexuals, seems to be warranted for some individuals but not for all.

Because Jungians have shown little empirical interest in homosexuality, attention must be given to current research from other sources. Jung's theoretical statements have begun to be modified by Guggenbühl-Craig (1960). Challenging the idea that homosexuality is a deviation, he stated that anything that helps to bring persons closer to each other is desirable.

Jung's unique contribution to our understanding of sexual experience, probably, was his understanding of its symbolic role. Sexual intercourse is a concrete experience that can serve as a supreme symbol of the union of opposites. The physical fertilization that may occur in the sex act can become a symbol of the mutual emotional and intellectual fertilization that characterizes an intimate relationship (see *CW14* and *CW16*, Part II, Section III).

Relationships and Individuation

There are many arenas for relationships, each with many opportunities and problems. A common factor is the possibility for enhancing the individuation process. To realize this possibility a relationship must be a truly psychological one, however. The role of any relationship in individuation is similar to the situation in marriage (see earlier section) except that nonmarital relationships often lack the intensity and the sexual component that accompany marriage, and other relationships are easier to terminate. Hence, they often have a lesser degree of motivation for individuation.

Moreover, individuation is not always enhanced by relationships. It can be impeded if one person's deficiencies produce persistent dependency on the other person to make up for them. Such dependency, which is based on projection, works against individuation by slowing the development of the weak side of one or both parties to the relationship.

Jungian theory sometimes seems to recommend the complete withdrawal of projections; the logical end result would be complete independence and, hence, the destruction of interdependence, which is necessary for relationships to exist. Jung seemed to be reassuring such people, however, when he wrote:

> Even if . . . projections [that substitute for a real psychological relationship] are analyzed back to their origins—and all projections can be dissolved and disposed of in this way—the patient's claim to human relationship still remains and should be conceded, for without a relationship of some kind he falls into a void. (*CW16*, par. 285)

16

Psychotherapy

Psychotherapy was the fertile field in which Jung's personality theory grew. Holding to an individualized theory of personality, he continually advanced the claim that he had no "method" of psychotherapy. "The real and effective treatment of neurosis is always individual, and for this reason the stubborn application of a particular theory or method must be characterized as basically wrong," he wrote (CW17, par. 203). This tailor-made approach was based on the premise that the goals of therapy are set by each client. The analyst is not a doctor who treats a patient but, rather, "a companion on the way." Each analyst brings to the work not a method, therefore, but an individual style, which is modified in response to each client and even to each session.

Although their differences in method are often subtle, "Jungian analysts are far from being narrow or constricted in their practice" (Bradway and Wheelwright, 1978, p. 223). Considerable variety was found among the 172 analysts from the United States, England, and Europe who responded to the investigators' questionnaire on their prevailing psychotherapeutic procedures, that is, those they used with more than 50% of their clients. The analysis of the responses showed that 91% of the analysts engage in analysis of dreams; 22%, self-revelation to patient (e.g., analyst's dreams and feelings); 21%, intense relationships with patients, and 15%, diaries or other written reports. The percentages total well over 100% because many respondents reported more than one method.

Some characteristics, which are common to virtually all Jungian analyses, reflect the premise that the aim of psychotherapy is personality development more than the cure of symptoms. In Jung's view, symptoms are an attempt at psychic self-regulation. Thus, the symptoms become part of the therapy in that they indicate what is needed for a more nearly whole personality. They may point to complexes, for example, which must be integrated in order for development to proceed. The relief of symptoms is not the primary goal of therapy but often is experienced as a by-product of development when complexes are integrated and psychic energy is released and redirected.

Although Jungian psychotherapy tends to be an inward-directed approach, it is conducted in the context of the patient's life in the world. Jung stated, "Try as we may to concentrate on the most personal of personal problems, our therapy nevertheless stands or falls with the question: What sort of world does our patient come from and to what sort of world has he to adapt himself?" (CW16, par. 212).

The goals of psychotherapy vary, of course, with the client, but, by definition, the goal of therapy is healing. Persons who have not experienced Jungian therapy sometimes say that it attempts to bring about healing by means of insight even though there is ample evidence, both clinical and quantitative, that insight is not highly effective in bringing about personality or behavior change. Fortunately, Jungian therapy does not rely on insight but, rather, it makes use of all available resources of the client's consciousness and unconscious and the psyches of both analyst and client to bring about changes in attitudes and emotional responses.

Terminology

The terms for the principals in psychotherapy reveal, to some extent, the conceptualizations of their roles. Traditionally, *psychotherapists* work with *patients* and *analysts* with *analy-sands*. The labels carry implications of inequality inasmuch as therapists and analysts are presumed to act and patients and analysands to be acted upon. In the Jungian analytic or thera-peutic process, however, the relation of the principals cannot be described by the traditional terms. No one acts on or is acted on; instead, the two principals relate to each other as co-workers in a process that affects both. Consequently, I use the term *client* much more often than *analysand* or *patient*. I still use *analyst* or *therapist* to characterize my role because either designation, when paired with *client*, loses some of its implication of power over another person.

Psychotherapy and Analysis

The question often asked is, What is the difference between psychotherapy and analysis? In the Jungian school there is no clear distinction, either in method or content. Various methods (e.g., dream analysis, emotional support, confrontation, plans for behavior changes) and contents (conscious and unconscious) are likely to characterize any series of sessions. In the view of many Jungians, analysis, more than therapy, deals with unconscious material, especially dreams and transference (see later section).

Whether the work with a particular client is therapeutic or analytical is a decision that is likely to be made by the client. Some clients' resistance to dealing with dreams and other un-conscious material is so strong that the analyst must accept the resistance as a fact and work only to strengthen the client's ego, not to facilitate enlarging it by the integration of unconscious contents. Other clients may be clearly willing and able to con-sider what the unconscious has to offer consciousness: examina-tion of conscious attitudes, modifying or changing them, and eventual transformation and reintegration of the personality.

Sometimes, however, the analyst must decide whether to press for attention to material from the unconscious. As a criterion for making this decision, Plaut (1964) recommended that the analyst assess whether "the ego is comparatively sound and has boundaries which are also permeable" (p. 332); that is, if the candidate for analysis has the requisite degree of emo-tional stability and flexibility. Such assessments can be made, however, without labeling the work with a specific client as analysis or therapy. Some analysts use the term *analytic therapy* to denote the entire range of their work.

Although analysts are the only officially designated Jungian psychotherapists, there are also some practicing counselors who are Jungian oriented. Such a counselor usually has some of the training that analysts undergo but lacks one or more basic requirements (see later section). Counselors' work is likely to differ from that of analysts in the degree to which unconscious material is emphasized in the therapeutic process. However, a client who has consulted both a Jungian analyst and a Jungian counselor may not be able to distinguish their ways of work. Indeed, an informal study in which I participated came to the conclusion that a Jungian counselor is likely to work in a way that is similar to an analyst's. This finding is true, especially when the counselor has undergone personal analysis and tends to apply the methods and insights that were learned in the process.

Differences from Freudian Analysis

The major difference between Freudian and Jungian analysis is in the relative emphasis on reductive (Freudian) and constructive (Jungian) attitudes and interpretations of dreams and symptoms. Reductive means, literally, "leading back" to the causes, the antecedent conditions out of which the symptoms or dreams arose. This approach seeks to challenge or to break down illusions. Traditional Freudian analysis is almost exclusively reductive.

The constructive approach strengthens what is healthy and worth preserving in the person. This approach encourages psychic growth, particularly in heretofore undeveloped capacities. Jungian analysis uses reduction appropriately, to uncover hidden motives and to integrate previously rejected parts of the personality, but it moves as soon as possible into the healing process of the constructive approach.

A readily observable difference between Jungian and Freudian analysis is the arrangement of the consulting room. Jungians prefer armchairs and face-to-face encounters, whereas many Freudians still ask patients to lie down on a couch while the analyst sits in an armchair out of view. The face-to-face setting produces an atmosphere of equality and more active involvement by the analyst, whose posture and facial expression can be seen by the analysand. In contrast, the couch generates infantile dependency in the patient and impersonality in the analyst. The client of a Jungian analyst is likely to experience some dependency on the analyst, especially early in the process, but the dependency is less pervasive than with Freudian analysts, and the Jungian analyst is rarely impersonal.

The primary method of traditional Freudian analysis is free association, which requires the patient to say everything that comes into his or her awareness. This method often leads to reexperiencing feelings from infancy and early childhood. Free association is used little in Jungian analysis. Instead, the client focuses more on current problems. The analyst helps to relate them to the past only when recalling the past is necessary to understand the present. The Jungian here-and-now approach tends to require a smaller number of sessions than does the free-association method used in Freudian analysis. Consequently, the frequency of Jungian sessions is usually once or twice a week, instead of the four or five times Freudians prefer. (Exceptional among Jungians are the analysts, most of them in London, who follow some of the neo-Freudian concepts of Melanie Klein, including more frequent sessions.) Jungian therapy plumbs the depths of the psyche by tapping the archetypal levels, often through dreams and their amplifications, rather than depending on frequency of sessions and digging into the past.

The problem of resistance arises whenever unconscious material is under consideration. *Resistance* may have any of a variety of meanings. Jung sometimes seemed to mean the client's reluctance to discuss a painful topic or, perhaps, even to admit that such a topic exists. In other contexts he seemed to use the term in the Freudian sense of the client's reluctance to accept the analyst's interpretation of a dream or behavior. Jung said that the resistance must be respected and not assaulted; Freudian analysts often attempt to "break down" the patient's resistance. There are at least three reasons for respecting the resistance: (a) The client is likely to be a better judge than the analyst of how much emotional pressure is tolerable; (b) the resistance may be a necessary ingredient in the client's developmental process; and (c) the resistance may be a correction by the client's unconscious of a faulty attitude held by the analyst. Jung's view seems consistent with his premise that the analyst should not set goals for the client.

Freudian analysts often require their analysands to refrain, during the course of analysis, from making major decisions, such as marrying or changing jobs. There is no such rule in Jungian analysis.

Varieties of Jungian Therapy

From his knowledge of the work of various groups of analysts, Gerhard Adler (1967) identified three major kinds of Jungian analytic therapy. In all three the procedure is dialectical, that is, a conversation is conducted in which the analyst is a fellow participant and affects and is affected by the client.

The first "orthodox" approach places the emphasis on archetypal interpretation and greater reliance on dreams than on transference. Analysts who use this approach give most of their attention to the constructive meaning of dreams and symptoms rather than to pathology.

The second, "neo-Jungian" approach, modifies Jung's concepts with an admixture of psychoanalytic concepts, especially those of Melanie Klein with her emphasis on the experiences of infancy. The focus in this approach is on the reductive interpretation of dreams and symptoms, hence, on pathology.

Analysts of a third, middle group make consistent use of Jung's concepts but accept modifications in the light of their own experiences with clients. This approach, which I share, is largely tailor-made to fit the individual analysand and uses both reductive and constructive attitudes and interpretations. The remaining discussion of psychotherapy is based on this middle approach.

Analyst and Analysand

Because the relation between analysand (client) and analyst is crucial to the therapeutic process, it is important to consider here the selection and training of analysts, the sort of person who can benefit from analysis, and what factors may enter into a client's choice of analyst.

The Analyst

Why does a person become an analyst? For me the reply is relatively simple: The Jungian approach had worked for me in my personal analysis, unlike the other therapeutic approaches I had experienced. I did not set out to be a psychotherapist but, while in the process of personal analysis, I became interested in the application of Jungian concepts to others and then to analysis as a profession. For Jungian analysts, especially those who entered training after the age of thirty-five, my experience is fairly typical. However, many Jungian analysts chose the profession of psychotherapist through a particular discipline (e.g., clinical psychology, social work, or psychiatry) and others became interested in Jung's ideas through theological or humanistic studies.

The idea that a prospective analyst must undergo a thorough personal analysis was originated by Jung. Freud subsequently followed his lead. Jung also insisted on the lifelong analysis of the analyst by dreams and other unconscious material and by consulting an analyst colleague from time to time. These measures are necessary because the analyst, like the client, is affected by their mutual work. Moreover, the analyst's psyche, rather than a method, is the operative factor in the work. Thus, as an analyst one must know one's "personal equation" and experience the encountering of the unconscious as preparation for accompanying another person in a comparable encounter.

In addition to extensive personal analysis, a prospective analyst must hold a graduate degree, which is delimited differently by various training institutes, and must undergo a thorough screening process. The analytic training includes, in addition to advanced study of the many areas of Jungian psychology presented in this book, work in several fields relevant to Jungian psychology, such as archetypal material (e.g., mythology, religions, and primitive practices). In addition, a candidate must be knowledgeable about psychopathology and non-Jungian schools of personality theory and psychotherapy. Finally, extensive clinical experience is required, including "control" work, that is, supervised work with clients. The details of the Jungian training program in Zurich, Switzerland, are presented in an earlier work (Mattoon, 1978).

Basic to the selection of prospective analysts is a large element of self-selection—an applicant's sense of vocation to become an analyst. Among Jungians, this self-selection has resulted, according to two studies, in a predominance of introverted and intuitive analysts. Plaut (1972) surveyed the members of the International Association for Analytical Psychology and senior trainees of its member groups. He received replies from 46% of a possible population of 378. Using self-typing, he found that 72% of the respondents considered themselves to be introverted and 81% considered intuition to be their primary or secondary function. Bradway and Wheelwright (1978) used both self-typing and the Gray-Wheelwrights Test (GWT) to obtain responses from 172 analysts in a study conducted at an international meeting of analysts: 63 from San Francisco, 29 from Los Angeles, 25 from York, 30 from London, and 25 from Europe. Most of the Continental participants were from Germany or Switzerland; the inclusion of other groups was limited by the fact that English and German were the only languages used in the test and questionnaire. Once again, the preponderance of analysts was found to be introverted (76% by self-typing, 83% by the GWT) and intuitive (76% and 70% respectively by self-typing and the GWT). In both studies, feeling and thinking were about 60% and 40% respectively, as primary or secondary functions. Compared to the general population figures of 45% to 55% introverts and 29% to 51% who preferred intuition over sensation (Gray and Wheelwright, 1946; Myers 1962; see Chapter 4), it seems clear that Jungian analysts are disproportionately introverted and intuitive.

A study by Meier and Wozny (1978) cast some doubt on the findings of Plaut and of Bradway and Wheelwright. Twenty-two Jungian analysts in Switzerland and Germany indicated what types they thought they were and, four months later, responded to the GWT. Only six of the analysts typed themselves in accordance with their types as indicated by the test. The investigators conjectured that "we could be dealing here with a discrepancy between what the individual analyst *actually* is (the Gray-Wheelwrights profile) and *what he would like to be*" (p. 228), that is, the self-typing. Because they did not specify the numbers of respondents who fell into each type category according to either method of assessment, their results cannot be compared directly with those of the Plaut and Bradway-Wheelwright studies.

Comparison between Jungian analysts and other therapists may be useful. Witzig (1978) found that 58% of 102 professional staff members of public mental health clinics in Oregon were of extraverted attitude and 44% were intuitive. If this population is representative of psychotherapists in general, it appears that non-Jungian therapists are different from Jungians in including more extraverts. Both Jungians and non-Jungians tend to be intuitive, but proportionately more Jungians are so.

The Analysand-Client

Any psychic problem, including the emotional component of a physical illness, that troubles a person can be the stimulus for undertaking Jungian analysis. Quenk (1978) hypothesized that persons of different attitude and function types are likely to enter analysis for different kinds of reasons; for example, the extravert, because difficulty with adapting to the inner world may result in the appearance of physical symptoms, and the introvert, because difficulty in adapting to the outer world makes such a person feel isolated.

Some non-Jungian therapists say that a "philosophical neurosis" (an intense concern with questions of life's meaning) is not an appropriate focus for psychotherapy. In light of Jung's view of the importance of religious problems in neurosis, especially for persons over thirty-five, it is not surprising that the focus of many Jungian analyses is specifically on the meaning of life and suffering. Indeed, consideration of meaning is often essential for healing.

There is no maximum age for entering Jungian analysis. In fact, the second half of life is, in general, the preferred time for working on the individuation process, which, for many clients, is the ultimate goal of analysis. The minimum age for a person entering Jungian analysis was not defined by Jung and often is determined by the particular analyst. For example, for me it is highly preferable that the client be old enough to be self-supporting, because a person who is still economically dependent is not as free to set goals and make choices. Other Jungian analysts, however, have found ways of working with adolescents and young children. The therapeutic approach varies, of course, with the age of the client.

Although no one is excluded categorically, certain personality factors may make an analysis optimally effective. Dicks-Mireaux (1964), for example, hypothesized that introverts may make better candidates for analysis than extraverts. On the premise that the analytic process is one of relearning, she surveyed the literature of learning theory as a source of understanding the psychotherapeutic process and concluded that

> Extraverts and introverts . . . respond differently to similar stimuli. Thus, each group might be expected to behave differently in analysis. . . .
>
> If, for example, one assumes that in analysis learning takes place (here learning is defined in the widest sense as the new adjustment to given stimuli) and that a certain amount of motivation is necessary . . . then to the extent that anxiety is used as a drive in analysis, the introvert will accept (or learn) an interpretation more quickly and at a lower level of anxiety than the extravert. Moreover, the introvert will retain the interpretation longer. (p. 124)

Dicks-Mireaux acknowledged, however, that the difference in prognosis between extraverts and introverts may mean, alternatively, that different techniques are needed for the two types of personality. It seems evident, also, that further research is necessary. Nevertheless, Dicks-Mireaux's work suggests the kind of research that is possible.

The Relation between Client and Analyst

The client's choice of analyst is important and must take a number of factors into consideration. The sex, attitude type, and function type of the analyst are important because different problems and possibilities are "constellated" in a particular client by each sex and type. Even more important is the potential quality of the relationship between analyst and client. An analyst who is right for one client may be wrong for another, and no one analyst can work effectively with every client. A truly therapeutic relationship begins with the right "chemistry," including mutual respect and liking, out of which can be forged a bond that is strong enough to withstand the difficulties of the analytic process.

The relationship is affected by the combination of typologies of the principals, but in a manner that cannot be predicted with any degree of accuracy. Similar typology between the two is likely to enhance the process of getting acquainted and feeling comfortable with each other. This combination is often less psychically stimulating, however. Opposite types stimulate and intrigue each other, but the client may be tempted to depend heavily on the analyst for strength in those areas in which the client is weak. It may be, as in other relationships, that the optimal combination is one dominant function in common, the other different. The effect of similarity or difference in attitude type is even more difficult to predict. It seems evident that prospective clients must base their judgments on their spontaneous responses to initial meetings with prospective analysts.

The Analytic Process

The nature of the analytic process is a topic of continuing discussion among Jungians, especially analysts. Is it medical, religious, educational, a combination of these, or something other? The controversy stems, partly, from the fact that Jung was a physician and, despite his challenge to the medical model on such issues as whether diagnosis is useful, he continued to describe analytic work in the terminology of the medical profession; for example, *doctor, psychotherapy,* and *healing.* Contemporary Jungians, however, increasingly seek to find a model for the analyst's work outside the metaphors of medicine. Thus, they speak of shamans, gurus, soul guides, and the like. Much as I respect and support these efforts, I find it important, also, to remember that the work is one of therapy that seeks to heal psychic wounds. At the same time a therapist must be aware of being a *wounded* healer—a person who has experienced psychic wounds.

Stages of Analysis

Whatever the philosophical basis, the analytic process can be described in general terms, at least. Gerhard Adler (1967) identified four stages of Jungian analysis, which do not necessarily occur in chronological order and are likely to be repeated for each problem area: (a) confession or *catharsis,* a process that occurs in all psychotherapy; (b) elucidation or *interpretation* (this stage is the major one in Freudian analysis); (c) *education,* that is, adaptation to social demands and needs (this stage is approximately equivalent to psychotherapeutic work based on Alfred Adler's theory; he considered the work to be reeducation); and (d) *transformation* or individuation, the stage in which the analysand discovers and develops his or her unique individual pattern of life; this stage is the most specifically Jungian.

The first three stages were generally considered by Jung to belong to therapy in the first half of life, when the client is still achieving adaptation to the environment and archetypal material usually does not play a large role in the therapy. When the tasks of youth and early adulthood have been accomplished, however, a Jungian analysis is likely to center increasingly on archetypal images and the search for meaning, so that the transcendent function is activated.

Diagnosis

The "medical model" of psychotherapy assumes that a diagnosis is necessary to prescribe treatment and carry it out. Jung challenged the importance of distinguishing specific categories of neurosis. However, he advised analysts to try to determine whether a client seemed to be psychotic (rather than neurotic) or in danger of psychosis, because if such danger existed, the unconscious should not be stimulated. Hillman (1964) took an even more negative view of diagnosis on the ground that knowledge *about* a person gets in the way *knowing* him or her.

Because *diagnosis* implies a medical model the better term to use probably is the one that is more common among psychologists, *assessment.* Even that concept is anathema to some Jungians because it seems to necessitate viewing the psyche from the outside. However, to other Jungians the concept is useful because assessment is a source of information. The only instruments of assessment that are related clearly to Jungian theory are interviews and the types tests, the Gray-Wheelwrights Test (GWT) and the Myers-Briggs Type Indicator (MBTI). Even these tests seem to be used relatively little by Jungian analysts in their practices. Of the 173 analysts who responded to Plaut's (1972) study, twenty-eight used the GWT and five used the MBTI; in addition, seven analysts used the Rorschach. In all, fourteen different tests were used by the respondents.

Transference and Countertransference

Transference literally means the client's transferring to the analyst feelings that were generated by experience with a past figure, usually a parent. Transference generally is considered to be a form of projection, although to some Jungians it cannot be so described. For example, Paulsen (1956) wrote that transference is "more than projection, being something archetypal, unconscious, and metaphorical" (p. 203), that is, transference arises out of archetypal contents as well as actual experiences. For example, a client who sees the analyst as a mother figure may attribute to her qualities which the client's mother did not have but which belong to the Mother archetype. Indeed, Jung's major work on transference (CW16, Part II, Section III) is concerned entirely with its archetypal dimensions. Although I agree that transference can be archetypal as well as personal, I believe that it still can be seen as a form of projection; both personal and archetypal contents can be projected.

The origins of transference are in the client's repressed "infantile wishes" but also in not-yet-realized psychic potentialities, which are rooted in the collective unconscious. Thus, Jungian analysts differ from most Freudian analysts in refusing to reduce transference feelings to merely the negative aspect of childishness. Jungians recognize that a child who is sometimes vulnerable and demanding at other times is curious and spontaneous. Thus, he or she has a potential for growth. A similar potential exists in adults and is the basis for healing. Moreover, as Jungian therapy progresses, transference is replaced increasingly by cooperation between analyst and client to distinguish projections from feelings toward actual people and to enable the client to integrate the contents that have been transferred.

Except for the analysts who have been influenced by Melanie Klein and other neo-Freudians, Jungians do not discuss transference a great deal; nevertheless, it plays a key role in most, if not all, analytic therapy. Indeed, the notion advocated by some schools of psychotherapy, that transference can be avoided, seems to be an illusion. The analyst must be constantly alert to the nature and intensity of the client's positive and negative transference feelings.

Not all feelings of a client toward an analyst are transferred from other relationships, according to Jung; some are simply the human responses of one person to another. It is important for the analyst and client to work together to distinguish such major categories of feelings.

The projections from client to analyst (transference) have a counterpart in projections from analyst to client (counter-transference). Countertransference is not the same as the analyst's basic liking for the patient and the perception that the client has potential for growth; these attitudes are necessary for healing and are not projections. Rather, countertransference is the projection of the analyst's complexes onto the client. For example, an analyst who has a complex about a frustrated desire to be an artist might become fascinated with a client's artistic achievements at the expense of the analytic process. In such a situation the analyst has an obligation to seek help from a colleague or, in extreme cases, to admit the problem to the client and perhaps offer to refer him or her to another analyst.

Countertransference, like transference, can be negative. For example, the analyst may be frustrated by the client's slowness to change and take the slowness as resistance to the analyst or to the process. Because the countertransference feelings stem from the analyst's complex, they must be subjected to scrutiny with the help of a colleague.

Whatever the emotional responses of the two parties to each other, they must be acknowledged in order for the analytic work to be productive. It is essential, also, for an analyst to pay attention to his or her own dreams and emotions and to recognize the analyst's influence on the client's psychological "climate." At the same time, analysts must insist that clients take responsibility for their own lives.

Other Expressions of the Unconscious

Probably even more important to the Jungian analytic process than transference is dream analysis, which is discussed extensively in the following chapter. Another source of unconscious material is a person's fantasies; Jung assumed that they reveal the unconscious in much the same way that dreams do. Also, behavior toward other people expresses the unconscious in that it reflects complexes and their projection. In addition, emotional responses give clues to the nature of projected complexes. Other events, such as accidents and errors, that "happen to" a person may be reflections of unconscious contents.

Some special methods of exploring unconscious material that are used in many Jungian analyses are the various techniques known as *active imagination*. The method resembles passive fantasy in that the contents arise out of the unconscious, but it differs from passive fantasy in that the ego initiates the process and participates actively. Initiating the process may consist of calling up an image that has appeared in a dream or in a previous "session" of active imagination; the ego then does more than observe the images or receive the thoughts: It enters into dialogue with the images from the unconscious.

The major purposes of active imagination are to give shape to complexes and their accompanying emotions and to provide a channel for the ego to confront directly the contents arising out of the unconscious. Although Jung considered all psychotherapy to be a vehicle for the individuation process, he considered active imagination to be particularly effective. It is a difficult procedure, however, and becomes possible for many persons only after many months of analytic therapy. In addition to its usefulness in the later stages of therapy, it can be continued by the analysand when the sessions with the analyst have been discontinued.

Active imagination can be carried out verbally, nonverbally, or in combination. Traditional nonverbal methods include drawing, painting, and sculpting. Dancing has been used, but less frequently, perhaps because it provides no record that can be shared with the analyst and refresh the memory of the analysand.

An additional nonverbal method is sandplay. The client employs a sandbox (about 19 × 28 × 3 inches) and miniature figures of humans, animals, scenery, and objects to create a three-dimensional picture. Often, the scene is photographed for later discussion. Kalff (1974) adapted the method from Lowenfeld's (1935) "World Picture."

In the verbal method of active imagination the client conducts an imaginary conversation with a human or nonhuman figure from the unconscious, perhaps one suggested by a dream. For example, the client questions a shadow figure with whom he or she is angry, or a Great Mother or Wise Old Man from whom wisdom can be sought.

Nonverbal and verbal methods are combined when the analysand starts with a dream image or spontaneous fantasy, watches it develop, and converges with it. The experience is then recorded in words.

Whatever form of active imagination is used by a particular client, most Jungian analysts recommend a medium in which the client is not trained, so that the work can be spontaneous, free of the inhibitions that often result from training. Thus, a writer is advised to use a nonverbal method, a painter, a method other than painting. The choice of medium is one factor in circumventing the tendency of some clients to focus too much on the aesthetic quality of the images; von Franz (1975) warned, "Too one-sided an emphasis on the aesthetic quality of the images obstructs the realization of their *meaning* and should therefore be avoided." An accompanying danger is an "impatience to get to the meaning as quickly as possible." The problem can be resolved, however, "When the two concerns operate together rhythmically, then the transcendent function, which strives to unite conscious and unconscious, operates with greatest effect" (p. 112; the transcendent function is discussed in Chapter 9).

Jung advocated the use of active imagination, especially in the later stages of analysis, but he pointed out its pitfalls: "The procedure may not lead to any positive result, since it easily passes over into the so-called 'free association' of Freud, whereupon the patient gets caught in the sterile circle of his own complexes" (CW8, p. 68). In addition, the patient may experience only aesthetic appreciation of his images and fail to integrate them. A more serious danger is that too much unconscious material may surface and overwhelm the conscious mind. For most analysands, however, the method seems not to be dangerous as long as it is not overused. The analyst can prevent overuse by helping the client to seek the meanings of images as they arise, before doing further active imagination and, thus, inviting additional images.

Some writers have warned of a further danger if the analyst concentrates on images (of the client) to the exclusion of other expressions of the psyche. According to Dry (1961), "so attuned may the analyst become to affective life expressed in visual imagery, that he may be prone to underestimate affective life which flows through other channels" (p. 251).

Psychotherapy of Neurosis and Psychosis

If neurosis is the dissociation of the conscious and unconscious (see Chapter 11), the healing power of analytic therapy is the introduction of interaction between the two, according to Jung. The conscious attitude is important but it must be compensated, that is, supplemented and rounded out, by contents from the unconscious.

Interaction between conscious and unconscious presupposes strength in consciousness, that is, in the ego. Many persons in therapy, however, manifest a weakness of ego, often in the form of predominantly negative feelings about themselves. Such persons require help in strengthening their egos before extensive work with unconscious material can be undertaken.

Extreme ego-weakness is characteristic of psychosis or the threat of psychosis; its presence may require the analyst to refrain from attending to unconscious material. In such cases, Jung recommended giving the client as much psychological knowledge as possible.

Perry (1974) developed a method of treating young schizophrenics during their first psychotic episodes. In a protected residential setting, he and his associates sought to accompany clients through the episodes, without the use of drugs or electroshock treatments, helping them to confront, assimilate, and use creatively the archetypal content that was disrupting their lives. Similar methods have been developed independently and used by non-Jungian therapists (e.g., R. D. Laing). Ellenberger (1970) stated, "Jung did a great deal to further the psychotherapy of schizophrenia, and he anticipated the research of contemporary existential analysts in their attempts to understand and make intelligible the subjective experience of schizophrenics" (p. 732).

Psychotherapy with Children

Jung's major observation on the subject of psychotherapy with children was that because nearly all the difficulties of children result from parental problems, the children should be treated through the treatment of their parents. He discussed children's dreams at length in some of his seminars but the dreams were those brought by parents of the dreamers or remembered by adults from their childhoods. Jung saw the educational process as providing children with direct help (CW17, Chapter III). Some Jungian analysts, however, work with children, often in conjunction with a colleague who is working with one or both parents (see M. Fordham, 1970).

Perhaps even more than in therapy with adults, Jungians emphasize synthetic-constructive processes over causality in child therapy. As in other schools of psychotherapy, play techniques are used in Jungian therapy with children. A few analysts work with children by including them in therapy with family groupings.

Analytic Therapy with Groups, Couples, Families

Groups

Through his contact with "Roland H.," which was described in his letter to "Bill W." (Let 2, pp. 623–25), Jung was instrumental in the founding of Alcoholics Anonymous, a highly effective form of group psychotherapy. Nevertheless, he expressed considerable doubt about group therapy and did not use it. Most Jungian analysts have followed his lead. Quenk (1978) saw this view as an introverted type bias.

Whitmont (1974) sought to adapt group therapy to an introverted point of view. He considered this form of therapy essential for adequate analysis because the individuation process must include becoming conscious of what and how one projects on a variety of persons, not just on the analyst. Brookes (1974) took a similar stand in finding that the group setting is a corrective for the isolation of the individual consultation hour. Illing (1957) took the view that the projections within the group have archetypal bases: "The average group has a 'secret' repertoire of roles, such as the 'wise old man' or the 'clown' or the 'mother' or [characters in] a fairy tale" (p. 393).

Thus, group therapy is often a useful adjunct to individual analysis. In my view, however, the group experience is not needed by all persons who seek Jungian analysis. Some clients make excellent use of the one-to-one therapeutic relationship and deal adequately through it with the many projections they make on a variety of persons in their lives.

Couples and Families

Jungians have not written about couple therapy and seem to engage in it little. Some Jungian-oriented counselors, however, have used the types tests (Gray-Wheelwrights Test and Myers-Briggs Type Indicator) to help couples to become aware that what appears to be obstinacy or hostility in one person may be a different way of viewing and dealing with the world. Quenk (1978), in his discussion of psychological types in relation to the various aspects of the analytic process, included marital therapy. He wrote, "Marital therapy permits one to view the types *in situ,* so to speak. Here the type of the therapist can have a direct influence on the course of therapy, as a function of the type mix of the couple" (p. 40). Quenk suggested that the analyst can help the husband and wife to understand each other's languages. If they are of different types, however, there is a danger that the analyst will communicate, subtly and perhaps unconsciously, an affinity with the partner who is more like the therapist.

The reluctance of Jungian analysts to engage in couple and family therapy arises, in part, from unfamiliarity with these methods and their possibilities for enhancing the individuation process. Hogle (1974) discussed his experiences in discovering these possibilities and learning the methods. He concluded, "If I had it to do over again, I would recommend from the outset extended couple or family therapy for about one-fifth of the individual patients I have ever treated" (p. 174). The proportion is not so large in my experience, although I have referred a number of couples for marital therapy, but I share Hogle's conviction that it is important to be open to the need for such treatments. In some instances, it is wise for the Jungian analyst to continue individual therapy and refer the couple or family to a therapist who specializes in the desired methods.

Despite the paucity of writings in the realms of group and family therapy, these treatments are being used, or referrals for them are being made, by some Jungian analysts. In the study by Bradway and Wheelwright (1978), 66 percent of the 172 responding analysts said they used group therapy or had referred at least one client for it; 73 percent did the same with family therapy. The investigators found that extraverts and intuitives make more frequent use of such variations in therapy than do introverts and sensates.

Selection of Treatment Mode

Jungians sometimes say that Jung incorporated such a broad range of treatment modalities that the Jungian approach can be adapted to virtually any client. There is a great deal of truth in this claim but it is important for any therapist to be open to the possibility that another therapist's approach would be more appropriate for a client.

Klopfer and Spiegelman (1965) provided a possible framework for the selection of treatment mode by describing various schools of psychotherapy in terms of Jung's attitude types. They found four major approaches that can be identified by combinations of the two variables: extraversion or introversion in the therapist, and extraversion or introversion in the client. According to these investigators, directive therapy (e.g., Thorne, 1961) is an extraverted approach to the outer reality of the client; nondirective therapy (e.g., Rogers, 1961) is an introverted approach to the outer reality of the client; Freud's approach is an extraverted one to the inner reality of the client; and Jung's is an introverted approach to the inner reality of the client.

Similarly, Witzig (1978) found Jung's function typology to be a useful tool for recommending to a client which treatment modality might be most effective for him or her. He was able to classify psychotherapies according to the dominant function required for its use:

> Thinking = *Informational/Cognitive:* Includes psychoanalytic, rational-emotive, educational, and transactional approaches to psychotherapy. [The leader of the rational-emotive school, Albert Ellis, explained the part thinking plays: "Man can live the most self-fulfilling, creative, and emotionally satisfying life by intelligently organizing and disciplining his thinking" (Ellis, 1974, p. 13).]

Intuition = *Symbolic/Intuitive:* Includes those approaches to psychotherapy which emphasize phantasy, meditation, brain-storming, or any other technique that attempts to transcend the rules of reason or sensory input. . . . Jungian psychotherapy is . . . included in this category [in that] the ultimate healing factor was perceived by Jung as an irrational, transcendent symbol.

Sensation = *Sensory/Experiential:* Includes most occupational, Gestalt, bio-energetic, and behavior modification therapies. These approaches . . . regard psychological health or growth as being dependent upon awareness of raw sense data.

Feeling = *Confrontation/Conative:* Includes encounter and T-group modalities, classical supportive-ventilative procedures, and the client-centered approaches of Carl Rogers. . . . [These therapies] make a conscious effort to face the meaning of one's own affect or emotion as distinct from what one thinks "should" be their [sic] response in these matters. (pp. 321–22)

Witzig pointed out, "Clinical experience demonstrates over and over again that highly motivated clients are often not helped even though they have the best of intentions and have the services of well-qualified psychotherapists" (p. 323). He hypothesized that a "considerable part of this therapeutic failure is due to the mismatch of the patient's dominant function with the orientation emphasised in the psychotherapy in each case" (p. 324).

To test his hypothesis, Witzig asked clinicians to assign each of four hypothetical cases to any one of the four categories of therapy that he had linked to the four function types. The four cases also conformed to the four function types by descriptions taken from the items in the Myers-Briggs Type Indicator. (The questionnaire did not mention Jung, psychological types, or the labels of the types.) The clinicians were asked, in addition, to indicate which of the type descriptions applied to themselves, rank-ordered best to worst; this procedure gave an indication of each clinician's function type.

In the assignment of clients to treatment modality, the factor of client's function type was significant for thinking (43 percent to the informational/cognitive mode) and intuitive (42 percent to the symbolic/intuitive mode) types but not in the assignment of sensation and feeling types. The clinician's function type was not significantly related to the assignment of clients to treatment modalities.

Witzig's hypothesis, that therapeutic failure is due to the

mismatch of the patient's dominant function with the orientation of the therapy, does not take into account Jung's premise that psychological development depends on strengthening the less dominant functions. Nevertheless, Witzig gathered useful information regarding clinicians' views on their uses of treatment modalities. Additional studies are needed to determine the effectiveness of the treatment after clients have been matched to treatments.

17

Dreams

Openness to the unconscious is the key to Jungian psycho-therapy, and Jung derived much of his understanding of the un-conscious from extensive study of his own and patients' dreams. For him psychotherapy was almost synonymous with dream analysis. Although Jung did not agree with Freud that the dream was the royal road to the unconscious (he held that the complex was that road), he considered dreams to be of central importance for the study of the psyche.

Jung developed his theory of dream interpretation over a lifetime. He was constantly testing, modifying, elaborating, and illustrating it. Consequently, statements on dream interpretation are found in nearly all his writings, whether publicly or privately published. He never considered his formulations to be final and, therefore, he never formally organized his body of concepts. An earlier work (Mattoon, 1978) brought together and presented sys-tematically all of Jung's theory of dream interpretation. In this chapter only the major points are discussed.

Everyone dreams, several times a night, whether the dreams are remembered or not, and the dreams become progressively longer throughout the night. If we are deprived of the opportunity to dream, we dream more on subsequent nights or engage in dreamlike mental content during our waking states. Jung recognized the equivalence of such contents and dreams when he treated spontaneous fantasies and waking visions as interpretable in the same manner as dreams.

Sources of Dream Images

The images or elements of which dreams are composed come from a variety of sources. Some seem to arise out of environmental stimuli, such as a fly buzzing near the dreamer, or from physical stimuli, such as a stomachache. Dream images also arise from memories and experiences of the distant past, which are not readily available in the waking state: those from early childhood, perhaps, those that have been repressed, and some which were not repressed but were not sufficiently important to remember. Jung found that some dream images anticipate future psychic contents which never have been present in consciousness.

A major source of dream images is the everyday experiences of one's life. Jung said that a dog dreams of bones and human beings dream of things that are familiar to them, such as their work. Some dreams seem almost identical with waking events. In other dreams, the images are generated by subliminal perceptions acquired during the day or days preceding the dream. In addition, some dreams contain traumatic content: experiences so painful that they continue to be rehearsed mentally.

However, the source of a dream element is not significant, according to Jung. What matters is the particular image and the psychic meaning the image has for the dreamer.

Dream Language

Images are the language of dreams and its grammar is unlike that of waking thoughts. The language is likely to be figurative and often fantastic. A dream image may express a thought but rarely directly.

Because Freud pioneered psychological dream interpretations, some of his views are reflected in many of Jung's statements. However, Jung disagreed with Freud on critical issues: (a) whether dream language consists of manifest or latent dream content, and (b) the nature of dream symbols. Freud held that because the manifest content is a disguise it cannot be interpreted directly and the interpreter must look for the latent dream thought behind it, a thought which can be discovered only by unraveling what Freud called "the dream work"; that is, by bringing to light the process by which the manifest content was produced.

Jung disputed the necessity of "unraveling the dream work" and insisted that the dream is not a disguise but means what it says. He argued that the unconscious does not deliberately conceal its meaning any more than a cloud deliberately conceals the sky; if we can understand the conditions out of which the cloud arose and the cloud's function, its meaning becomes apparent. Understanding a dream requires a comparable process.

Despite this seemingly straightforward approach, Jung advocated a process he called "translating the dream language"; it is difficult to distinguish this process from that of looking for the latent content of a dream. The basic issue, in my view, is in Jung's and Freud's different views of the nature of symbols and, thus, of the symbolic function of dream images. Freud saw symbolic images as having fixed meanings; the dream image, for him, was the one-to-one representation (what Jung called a "sign") of unconscious conflict, usually sexual. Jung, on the other hand, considered dream images to be symbols in the sense of the best possible formulations for still unknown (unconscious) psychic facts. Consequently, a symbol in Jung's sense cannot be interpreted without amplification (see later section), including the dreamer's personal associations to the dream images.

The unconscious conflict that Freud sought in the latent content was based on *wish fulfillment:* a wish that was incompatible with conscious attitudes and, therefore, had been repressed. Jung agreed with the idea that the dream offers a point of view that is missing in consciousness but he envisioned the concept as the broader *compensation* (see later section) rather than the narrow interpretation of wish fullfillment.

Still another issue between Freud and Jung was that of the causal (reductive) as opposed to the constructive interpretation of dreams. Freud viewed dreams only causally, that is, he sought the causes out of which dreams arose. Thus, his interpretations reduced the meanings of dreams to those causes. Jung acknowledged that although a causal approach to interpretation sometimes is warranted, a dream often is constructive in that it does not relate to a cause but, instead, leads the dreamer toward a goal of realizing some hidden psychic potential.

On the issue of dream interpretion Jung's view seems to have prevailed. Dream theorists who are neo-Freudian or neither Freudian nor Jungian increasingly have come to adopt Jung's method of interpreting a dream in terms of the individual dreamer rather than according to a preordained theory. Even many otherwise orthodox Freudian analysts have adopted this view, often without knowing that it stems from Jung's work and not from Freud's.

The Structure of Dreams

Most dreams, according to Jung, have a discernible structure, which helps to analyze them. In brief, the structure (*CW8*, pars. 561–64) is as follows: The dream begins with the *exposition*. It consists of statements of place (e.g., "I was in a large building, like a hotel"), protagonists, and often the initial situation of the dreamer (e.g., "I was with a friend; we met Mrs. Y."), and possibly time (e.g., time of day, season of the year).

The second phase is the *development of the plot*. For example, "Mrs. Y seemed to be very excited and wanted to whisper something to me hurriedly, which my friend X was obviously not intended to hear." The situation described is becoming complicated and a definite tension is developing because one does not know what will happen.

The third phase brings the culmination or *peripeteia*. A decisive event occurs or a significant change takes place: "Mrs. Y turned deathly pale and fell to the ground."

The fourth and last phase is the *lysis*, the concluding situation that is the solution or result: "We thought Mrs. Y was dead, but it was evidently only a faint."

The structure is useful for revealing the relations among the dream images. It also helps to prevent the overlooking of details;

for instance, neglecting the setting of the dream while rushing on to consider what happened. In addition, attending to the structure of the dream makes it possible to ascertain if any part is missing. When there is no lysis, for example, the dream has no conclusion and special caution is necessary to interpret it.

The Dream Context

The first step in interpretation is to delineate the dream context. It consists of amplifications, both individual and archetypal, the circumstances of the dreamer (the situation), and the relation of this dream to others, that is, its part in the series of dreams.

Amplification

Amplification begins by gathering the dreamer's personal associations to the images in the dream. Initially, Jung used Freud's method of free association (the dreamer's mind wandering where it will) but he discarded it when he concluded that where the mind usually chooses to go is away from the dream. To be sure, free association to dream images usually leads to the complex but free association to any image or idea, no matter how random, also leads to the complex. Jung found that associations that contribute to interpreting a particular dream are those relating directly to the dream elements; these associations maximize the dream's revelation of what the unconscious is saying about the complex.

Thus, Jung advocated the use of "personal associations": experiences and facts that are directly related to the dream images. Such associations often are elicited by the analyst's asking the dreamer what a dream image brings to his or her mind, what role the image plays in the dreamer's life, or simply saying, "Tell me about the person (or other figure) in the dream." Occasionally, the analyst can remind the dreamer of facts, including feelings, that the dreamer has mentioned previously.

Some dreams arise from an archetypal level that is beyond the dreamer's personal experience. Such dreams often can be recognized by the fact that the dreamer has no personal association to the image, and even if he or she can dredge up an association, it may be remote from the dreamer's emotions. In such cases, an archetypal amplification is often relevant. For example, a man dreamed that he was on his way to an important meeting and looked back, perhaps at his home. He awoke, frightened. He had no associations to the dream image and no idea what he feared. The analyst thought first of the Greek myth of Orpheus: His wife, Eurydice, had died and was in the Underworld. Orpheus was given permission by the Underworld gods to take her back to earth on the sole condition that he would not turn to look at her during the journey. He looked back and Eurydice was returned to the Underworld forever. Another possible amplification is the biblical story of Lot's wife. When Lot and his family were escaping the destruction of Sodom and Gomorrah and were cautioned not to look back, his wife looked back and was turned into a pillar of salt. Both amplifications suggest that the reason for the dreamer's fear of looking back was the danger of some kind of catastrophe. (What in his life constituted "looking back" could be ascertained only by amplification of other images in the dream and by his conscious situation.)

Despite the vast amount of attention Jung gave to the study and amplification of archetypal images (see *CW9* through *CW18*), he warned that "the collective unconscious influences our dreams only occasionally" (*CW17*, par. 208). It is essential to valid dream interpretation, therefore, to explore thoroughly the personal associations. This exploration is necessary even when archetypal amplifications are applicable.

Although abundant clinical evidence indicates that some dream images arise out of an archetypal layer of the psyche, it is reassuring to know that quantitative evidence is available also. Kluger (1975) studied the dreams of 218 undergraduate and graduate students. Three classes of dreams were assessed by questionnaire: childhood, vivid (presumably more archetypal), and recent (presumably nonarchetypal) dreams. Each dream was rated on four criterion scales: (a) the presence or absence of a mythical parallel; (b) degree of affect; (c) degree of rationality; and (d) similarity to everyday life. Scoring reliability by two judges working independently was .94 to .97. Dreams reaching criterion scores on at least three of the four scales were judged to be archetypal. Childhood and vivid dream classes had significantly more archetypal dreams than the recent dream class. Kluger concluded that archetypal dreams do indeed exist as a measurable category, which is distinguishable from everyday dreams.

Interconnections

Amplifications often are numerous and not all are pertinent to the interpretation of a dream image. A choice of relevant amplifications must be made, largely on the basis of interconnections; that is, of the common factors or themes among the amplifications to the various dream elements. For example, a man's dream might depict three human figures: a young woman, a friend, and a minister. To the three figures he associates the facts of nearly having married the woman, the friend's impending divorce, and the minister's having performed the dreamer's wedding ceremony. Although he has other associations to all three figures, the common theme is marriage. In interpreting the dream, then, one would consider the possibility of problems in the man's marriage.

Conscious Situation

The dream context is not complete with only the amplifications, however extensive they may be, and their interconnections. Information is needed about the conscious situation of the dreamer: experiences of the day or two before the dream, especially those that aroused the dreamer's emotions; problems with which the dreamer has been occupied; and attitudes that relate to the amplifications and their interconnections.

A rather clear-cut example of the importance of the dreamer's conscious situation was given by Jung: A business man dreamed that his hands and forearms were covered with black dirt. The day before the dream, the man had been made what looked like a perfectly serious and honorable offer (he discovered later that he would have been involved in a disastrous fraud if he had accepted the offer). He could see no connection between this dream and the events of the preceding day because he was unable to admit to himself that the offer touched him on a vulnerable spot: his desire for a profitable business deal. Jung warned the dreamer of the danger the offer might represent. The man took precautions and saved himself from serious harm. Jung stated, "Had he examined the situation right at the beginning he would undoubtedly have had a bad conscience, for he would have understood that it was a 'dirty business'" (CW10, par. 826).

Dream Series

A dreamer's other dreams are also part of the dream context. A group of dreams that are related to each other by time or content is called a "dream series." Although the series in which the dream is embedded should always be considered, the series is especially useful when an individual dream is unintelligible. As one of a series it may take on meaning, just as in an anagram a group of letters becomes meaningful when it is rearranged to spell a word. Jung did not specify how many dreams formed a series but he mentioned numbers from ten to one hundred; he tended to assign to a series groups of successive dreams or all of one dreamer's dreams that had a specific common motif. To these categories may be added the dreams of a particular time period, perhaps a period of transition in the dreamer's life, such as a job change.

Two of the long series of the dreams of a young man exemplify a "mini-series" with a common motif. (Jung's book, *Psychology and Alchemy*, CW12, was based on the series.) The first dream is as follows: "The dreamer is at a social gathering. On leaving, he puts on a stranger's hat instead of his own" (CW12, par. 52). Jung was able to amplify this dream but not to interpret it until he came to a dream much farther along in the series: "An actor smashes his hat against the wall, where it looks like this" (a diagram of a circle with eight spokes and a solid black center; CW12, par. 254). Jung's interpretation was that the hat became a mandala, that is, a symbol of wholeness. The image indicated that the stranger's hat was the Self, which, while the dreamer was still playing a fictitious role, seemed like a stranger to him.

A special case of dream series is the recurring dream. The recurrence often seems to serve the purpose of emphasizing the dream's message. Jung found that a particular dream ceased to occur when it had been interpreted properly.

More common than the recurring dream is the recurring motif or theme, with changing details. By following such an image through several dreams, the interpreter may discover what change is occurring or is needed in the dreamer's life. Jung gave an example from his own experience. He had a series of dreams in which he would "discover" a part of his house that he had not known to exist. It contained interesting antique furniture and an old library whose books were unknown to him. In the last dream of the series he opened one of the books and found it to be full of "marvellous" symbolic pictures (CW18, par. 478). Later he discovered that these pictures were connected with alchemy. (The psychological significance of alchemy became one of Jung's major interests.) After this discovery, his dreams on the theme of the house and library stopped.

Tools and Criteria for Interpretation

Although Jung maintained that no one principle (e.g., Freud's wish fulfillment) is always applicable to the interpretation of dreams, some basic attitudes are necessary "tools" for valid dream interpretation. The first of these attitudes is that nothing can be assumed regarding the meaning of a dream. A corollary is that an interpretation should not yield what is expected; if it coincides with expectations, one should be suspicious.

The second attitude is that the dream is not a disguise (as Freud had it) but a set of psychic facts that are comparable to physiological facts. The interpreter must pay attention to all the facts and their interconnections in order to understand the dream.

To comprehend the psychic facts portrayed in the dream, the interpreter must approach it with all four functions. Intuition can suggest possibilities for interpretation but each possibility must be analyzed (with thinking), compared with the image-facts (with sensation), and evaluated (with feeling) for its relevance to the conscious situation of the dreamer.

The interpreter must keep in mind, also, that the dream belongs to the dreamer and the interpretation must accord with the dreamer's personality. Jung warned that it must not be assumed that the dreamer's psyche is like the interpreter's. In order to be valid, the dream interpretation must make sense to the dreamer. Thus, a cooperative effort is necessary between interpreter and dreamer.

One further attitude is required: the assumption that the dream does not tell the dreamer what to do. Some guidelines for action can be deduced, frequently, but mainly the dream shows the unconscious condition of the dreamer at the time of the dream and is not a prescription for action.

Objective/Subjective Characterization

The next step in ascertaining the dream's message is to characterize its images as objective or subjective. By *objective* Jung meant an interpretation that "equates the dream images with real objects." (The term is used in a different sense from the "objective" psyche mentioned in Chapter 3.) *Subjective* interpretation, on the other hand, is that "which refers every part of the dream and all the actors in it back to the dreamer himself" (*CW7*, par. 130). *Subjective* in this usage does not mean what is ordinarily meant by the word: insubstantial, personal, biased, one person's opinion; it means, rather, that "all the figures in the dream [are] personified features of the dreamer's [i.e., the subject's] own personality" (*CW8*, par. 509).

Jung offered guidelines for deciding which approach to use: (a) The objective level is more likely to be correct when one dreams of a person with whom the dreamer is connected by a vital interest. (b) If the dream is of a person who is not important to the dreamer in reality, then interpretation on the subjective level will be nearer the truth than an objective interpretation.

Jung tended to emphasize the subjective, perhaps to balance Freud's largely objective interpretations, but he warned that the subjective approach should not be overdone. If the dream elements are always interpreted subjectively, the dreamer will be disconnected from reality and, hence, become quite isolated. The objective approach should not be overdone, either; it can lead to avoidance of inner problems. Even when it is applicable, an objective interpretation must take into account the fact that the figure in the dream is the dreamer's image of the object, not the object itself.

Compensatory Function of Dreams

The keystone of Jung's theory of dream interpretation is generally considered to be the hypothesis that nearly all dreams are compensatory; they participate in the self-regulation of the psyche. With relatively few exceptions, dream interpretation answers the question: How does the dream compensate the conscious situation of the dreamer? Thus, the purpose of the dream is to reveal the *"actual situation in the unconscious"* (CW8, par. 505), to bring it into relation with consciousness and provide what is needed for psychic equilibrium and, ultimately, wholeness. The degree of disparity between the conscious situation and the message of the dream depends on the amount and nature of the dreamer's psychic one-sidedness.

Compensation is not simple opposition, however. A dream can compensate the conscious in modes ranging from confirmation to opposition. Although it is relatively rare for a dream to confirm the conscious situation completely, such dreams do occur. More often, confirmation seems to be evidenced by the lack of dreams commenting on the particular situation. Some dreams compensate the dreamer's conscious attitude by presenting it in exaggerated form; other dreams deviate only a little from the conscious situation and thus suggest but slight modification. Still others take a view that is generally opposite to consciousness; such dreams occur when the conscious attitude is inadequate or wrong.

Although virtually all dreams are compensatory, some compensate negatively, that is, *reductively*; others compensate positively, that is, *constructively* (see Chapter 16). Both kinds of compensation are purposive, or goal-oriented, in that they offer something that the dreamer needs for psychic balance.

To exemplify dreams requiring reductive interpretations, Jung chose those of a fifty-four-year-old widow who "had learnt nothing in the last forty years." He described her further as "a loyal widow [who had] clung to her marriage as best she could without her husband." Her dreams "had the character of snapshots: a gramophone playing a love song; herself as a young girl, just engaged; her husband as a doctor, and so on" (CW17, par. 185). Jung saw her dreams as expressing her "real intentions," what he called "instinctive facts," that is, she had repressed "disagreeable"—presumably sexual—thoughts. This repression produced a "psychic vacuum," which gradually became filled with the anxiety that led her to consult Jung. The reductive interpretation restores such unwelcome facts about the dreamer, facts that have been repressed.

Jung used the constructive method much more than the reductive. An example is the dream reported by an old general whom Jung met on a train. In the dream the general was asked for a definition of the beautiful; he was not able to answer, but a young major gave a very good answer. Jung asked what the young major looked like. The general replied that he looked like himself as a young officer. Jung said, "Well, then, it looks as if you had forgotten or lost something which you were still able to do when you were a young major." The general "thought for a while, and then he burst out, 'That's it, you've got it! When I was a young major I was interested in art. But later this interest got swamped by routine'" (CW17, par. 187). Jung's comment was a constructive interpretation, enlarging the dreamer's view of his own possibilities.

Both reductive and constructive approaches should be considered for each dream. If the constructive is overused, it can lead to an exaggeration of illusions. On the other hand, overemphasis on the reductive tends to disintegrate and even to destroy the dreamer's essential values. Sometimes both approaches can be used for the whole dream, or the reductive for some parts, the constructive for others.

The concept of the compensatory function means that consciousness and the unconscious form a totality. Neither is wiser than the other; thus, the dream cannot be treated as an infallible oracle. Jung stated:

> The recognition of the unconscious is not a Bolshevist experiment which puts the lowest on top and thus re-establishes the very situation it intended to correct. We must see to it that the values of the conscious personality remain intact, for unconscious compensation is only effective when it cooperates with an integral consciousness. Assimilation is never a question of this or that, but always of this *and* that. (CW16, par. 338)

Several attempts have been made to test experimentally the compensatory function of dreams but an adequate method has not yet been found. Hall and his co-workers (Hall and Domhoff, 1968; Hall and Lind, 1970; Hall and Nordby, 1972) used content analysis (developed by Hall and van de Castle, 1966) to study intensively the dreams of several individuals. If dreams are compensatory, they reasoned, dream behavior will contrast with waking behavior. The hypothesis seemed not to be confirmed. The data appeared to show, rather, that a person's dream behavior rarely differs substantially from his or her waking behavior.

Domino (1976) obtained similar results in a study of the dreams of sixty-two white, male college juniors and seniors. He selected randomly three dreams of each student. Each dream was rated by trained raters for various personality characteristics. Then the Edwards Personality Preference Schedule and the Adjective Check List were administered to each student. Domino found that "what occurs in dreams is not substantially different from what occurs in conscious thought" (p. 661).

Such evidence does not disconfirm the theory of compensation, in my view. Bell and Hall (1971) acknowledged the possibility of this view when they wrote: "Aggression in dreams tends to mirror aggression in waking life. Sometimes, however, aggressiveness in waking life does not manifest itself in overt behavior but expresses itself in private fantasy and thought" (p. 122). In addition, reflection of waking behavior is quite congenial with the compensatory function of dreams. Waking behavior is not always conscious, either in the sense of the dreamer's awareness of what he or she is doing or in the sense of the behavior's being under the individual's ego control. Moreover, compensation is a function rather than a type of content. Some dreams rehearse almost identically a situation in waking life. They may be compensatory nevertheless, in calling attention to that situation by selecting and/or changing details in the waking situation.

Beickel (1977) hypothesized that extraverts have more introverted dreams, introverts, more extraverted dreams. The subjects were twelve students in a graduate counseling psychology class in personality assessment. Six were extraverts and six were introverts, according to the Myers-Briggs Type Indicator (MBTI). The subjects kept dream records over a period of two and one-half months. Five measures were used to distinguish the dreams of extraverts from those of introverts: (a) intimacy scale; (b) social interaction scale; (c) emotion; (d) environmental press; and

(e) others/self. (No further information was given in dissertation abstracts on the criteria for distinguishing introverted from extraverted dream content.) Significant differences (p = .05) were detected between the groups on only one of the fifteen dimensions of the extraversion-introversion index. Analysis of within-group differences suggested that extraverts dreamed in an introverted manner on four of the fifteen dimensions, and introverts dreamed in an extraverted direction on only one of the fifteen dimensions. When a preference was found, both extraverts and introverts dreamed "introvertedly." The investigator found that the results of the study suggested the following conclusions: (a) Dreaming is an introverted process, subjective and personal in nature. (b) If, as Jung suggested, dreams function in a compensatory manner to balance the one-sidedness of the conscious attitude, the compensatory nature is of a different composition or scope than was identified in the study. It may be that Beickel's study revealed a predominance of subjective over objective dreams.

When Dallett (1973) tested the theory of compensation, she used hypotheses that were based on a more refined understanding of the theory than other experimenters had. She hypothesized that (a) dream sensory richness would increase following sensory monotony; (b) numbers of people and social interactions in dreams would increase following social isolation and decrease following social overload; (c) outdoor dream settings would increase following environmental confinement; (d) the extent of complementary dream responses to an environment would vary inversely with degree of expressed negative response to the environment; and (e) dream emotion would vary inversely with expressed negative emotion. Twenty subjects were exposed to eight hours each of sensory monotony, social isolation, and enforced social interaction, plus a control condition. Conditions were presented in randomized order at five-day intervals. Following each condition, two brief tests were given to assess expressed negative response to the envionments. Then subjects slept undisturbed in a homelike apartment and wrote their dreams in the morning. To provide a baseline, they had recorded their dreams at home for ten days prior to the experiment. At the end of their participation in the study they were given the MBTI. Dreams were scored blind; scores were adjusted for dream length and expressed as deviations from mean baseline scores. Analyses of variance failed to support any of the hypotheses for the subject group as a whole. When additional dream variables were included and data were analyzed separately for different personality types (MBTI), a provocative set of findings emerged:

1. For the subject group as a whole, sensory richness, number of people, social interactions, and outdoor settings in dreams did not differ among conditions, consistent with the experimenter's global impression that dreams following experimental conditions continued to deal primarily with enduring individual concerns already apparent in baseline dreams.

2. Selected cases in which "unusually high subject involvement" was known illustrated the compensatory dream function clearly. However, it was not always manifest as a simple complementary response to the environment.

3. Following monotony and isolation, the length of dream report increased. This finding approached significance for introverts but not extraverts and held for intuitive and sensation types but not for thinking and feeling types.

4. The group as a whole tended toward reduction in dream emotion following the social condition, a trend that emerged strongly in subsidiary analyses and held for extraverts but not introverts.

5. Subjects who responded to sensory monotony with extreme affect had more social interaction in their dreams after monotony than those who expressed moderate affect. Other conditions elicited only moderate expressed affect which was no different from the control condition.

6. Subjects whose first function was intuition decreased in dream sensory richness following monotony and increased richness following social overload.

7. Although they were infrequent compared to other themes, dream themes continuous with a condition increased following the appropriate condition, while themes complementing the condition did not. Condition-relevant themes and direct references to the experiment occurred in introverts' dreams but rarely in extraverts'.

8. During the baseline period when environment did not vary systematically, introverts had more outdoor settings in their dreams than extraverts had.

Because the findings were not predicted they are viewed tentatively pending replication. Simple and automatic complementary dream-content response to environment clearly does not occur although *amount* of dreaming may indeed be a complementary function of the sensory variety available in an environment. The concept of compensation must be distinguished from simple complementation (see Chapter 6). Coherent theoretical understanding of the results requires a return to the original complexity of the principle of compensation, which takes into account both the dreamer's personality and the importance of a particular situation to him or her. Indications are that *what* is compensated may be in part the dreamer's weakness in relation to a particular environment, if that environment is salient for the dreamer.

Noncompensatory Dreams

Not all dreams are compensatory. Noncompensatory dreams are classified as prospective, traumatic, extrasensory, or prophetic.

A dream correctly interpreted as prospective or anticipatory is capable of leading the conscious attitude in a different and better direction than it has been moving. Jung saw such a dream as arising not from some mystical or clairvoyant capacity of the dreamer but from the fusion of the dreamer's perceptions, thoughts, and feelings that consciousness has not registered. He maintained that prospective dreams "are merely an anticipatory combination of probabilities which may coincide with the actual behaviour of things but need not necessarily agree in every detail" (CW8, par. 493).

As an example of a dream that should be interpreted prospectively, Jung cited the dream of a young woman who had come to him after having seen another analyst. She had had the following dream at the beginning of treatment with the other analyst:

> I have to cross the frontier, but the night is pitch-black and I cannot find the customs-house. After a long search I see a tiny light far off in the distance, and assume that the frontier is over there. But

in order to get there, I have to pass through a valley and a dark wood in which I lose my way. Then I notice that someone is near me. Suddenly he clings to me like a madman and I awake in terror. (*CW16*, par. 308)

This treatment was broken off after a few weeks because the analyst unconsciously identified himself with the patient; the result was a complete loss of orientation for both. Jung did not interpret the dream but he indicated that it gave a clear picture of the situation that could have been expected to, and did, arise in the analysis with the other analyst.

Another kind of noncompensatory dream is the traumatic. In such a dream an actual experience of great emotional intensity is relived, for example, an automobile accident in which the dreamer had been injured seriously. Such a dream tends to recur until the emotion surrounding the traumatic event has been markedly diminished. These dreams cannot be interpreted because their significance is in the actual traumas.

Still another kind of noncompensatory dream conveys extrasensory perceptions (ESP). The dreams can be telepathic or clairvoyant, such as receiving a message or "seeing" an event at the same time or after the reported event occurs, or it can be precognitive (prophetic). Jung gave several examples of telepathic dreams; for example, a dream of a death shortly after the death occurred could be a telepathic message from someone who was with the person who died.

Dunne (1958) recounted a possibly clairvoyant dream:

I seemed to be standing on high ground—the upper slopes of some spur of a hill or mountain. . . . I recognized the place as an island . . . which was in imminent peril from a volcano. And, when I saw the vapour spouting from the ground, I gasped: "It's the island! Good Lord, the whole thing is going to *blow up!*" (p. 42)

The volcanic eruption was confirmed in a newspaper he received a few days later.

Jung gave only one example of a prophetic dream that conformed to his definition of agreement in every detail with actual subsequent events. The example seems rather trivial, unfortunately. A young man who was anticipating a trip to Spain dreamed of visiting an urban square and then he actually lived the experience on the trip.

A dream based on ESP often has a symbolic meaning that

can be interpreted but the extrasensory aspect of the dream can be verified only in the future. (See Chapter 10 for the relation of ESP dreams to synchronicity.)

Dreams and the Therapeutic Process

Although all dreams that occur while a person is in therapy are relevant to the treatment process, certain categories of dreams are especially so. One of these categories is that of "initial" dreams, those that occur when the dreamer enters therapy. Such a dream often gives a general description of the dreamer's psychological problem and some idea of the course of treatment. In a few instances, organic diagnoses can be made from the initial dream.

An analyst's own dreams are important for self-understanding in relation to his or her work and personal life. Jung claimed that he did not understand his own dreams any better than does someone who has no knowledge of dream interpretation. My experience is that there is an advantage to working on one's own dreams because more associations are at one's disposal. It seems likely, however, that if the dream touches an especially sensitive area of the interpreter's psyche, the world's greatest dream interpreter would not understand it.

Hypothesizing and Verifying the Interpretation

A dream interpretation is a psychological statement about the dreamer and his or her life situation. Discovering the meaning of a dream was likened by Jung to translating an unknown language. Each image in the dream is a "word" whose meaning can be discovered through the amplifications and their interconnections. Like a philologist, the dream interpreter examines the various ways in which the "word" is used in order to determine its meaning in the unknown language. When a possible translation has been found, it is tested against the dream facts.

The statement of the dream's meaning is treated like a hypothesis that must be verified and modified as necessary. Jung suggested a few criteria for verification. One criterion is the dreamer's response. If the interpretation seems to "click" with the dreamer, the interpretation is probably basically correct. However, the dreamer's nonacceptance of the interpretation does not mean, necessarily, that the interpretation is wrong; nonacceptance can be an indication that something does not fit or that the dreamer has not reached the point of being able to accept the interpretation.

Another criterion is what acts for the dreamer. A dream may act for the dreamer by producing a change of attitude. For example, the businessman's dream (that his hands were covered with black dirt) brought about a change in attitude. Prior to the dream he had been denying the dishonesty of the deal; after the dream, he was able to cease his denial.

Some dream interpretations are confirmed and more are corrected by subsequent dreams. For example, an analyst interpreted a woman's dream to mean that she should break off a certain relationship that meant a great deal to her; between that session and the next, she dreamed that she was having an abortion. The analyst understood the abortion to mean that an embryonic psychic content was being destroyed and promptly reconsidered the interpretation of the first dream.

Some dream interpretations are verified by subsequent events other than dreams. For example, a man with symptoms of mountain sickness dreamed of a train derailment. Jung interpreted the dream and the symptoms to mean that the man was moving ahead too fast and climbing too high. The dreamer continued to try to climb in his profession and, as Jung put it, "[went] to the dogs" (CW18, par. 201).

The effectiveness of dream analysis in psychotherapy has been tested only clinically, to my knowledge. The clinical evidence is extensive, however; it pervades a large portion of the Jungian literature. (For a complete dream interpretation following Jung's method, see Mattoon, 1978.)

Summary of Steps in Dream Interpretation

Although Jung never stated them systematically, a series of steps can be derived from his writings on dream analysis. It is often possible to arrive at a dream interpretation without following them but such an interpretation is likely to be distorted by not taking all the dream facts into account. The major steps in the Jungian approach to dream interpretation, then, are as follows:

1. State the dream text in terms of *structure,* and examine it for completeness.
2. Establish the *dream context,* the situational material in which the dream is embedded. The context is composed of:
   a. Amplifications of the dream images, which may include:
      (1) personal associations and/or
      (2) archetypal parallels;
   b. *Themes interconnecting* the amplifications;
   c. The immediate and long-term *conscious situation* of the dreamer; and
   d. The dream *series* in which the dream occurs.
3. Review the appropriate premises to bring to dream interpretation:
   a. Nothing can be assumed regarding the meaning of the dream or specific images;
   b. The dream is not a disguise but a set of psychic facts;
   c. The personality characteristics of the dream and the interpreter must be considered; and
   d. The dream probably does not tell the dreamer what to do.
4. Characterize the dream images as *objective or subjective.*
5. Consider the dream's *compensatory* function:
   a. Identify the problem or complex with which the dream is concerned;
   b. Ascertain the relevant conscious situation of the dreamer;
   c. Consider whether the dream images and the psychic development of the dreamer require a *reductive* or *constructive* characterization; and
   d. Consider whether the dream is noncompensatory: *prospective, traumatic, telepathic,* or *prophetic.*
6. Hypothesize an interpretation by translating the dream language in relation to the relevant conscious situation of the dreamer, test it against the dream facts, and modify the interpretation where necessary.
7. Verify the interpretation by the dreamer's immediate response or subsequent events.

18

Social and Political Issues

Humans are basically social beings, in Jung's view. Progoff (1973) interpreted this conception: "[Jung] derives the deeper levels of the unconscious not from individual experience, but from the great communal experiences of mankind, and he thus places social factors at the origin of the psyche" (p. 141). In this interpretation, social, or collective, factors seem to apply more to the unconscious than to consciousness. However, Homans (1979) saw Jung as a "social critic [who] interpreted the nature of modernity to his contemporaries" (p. 43).

> Modern man was characterized by a rigid persona that Jung associated with extraversion and excessive rationality. The cause of such rigidity was that modern man was separated from or alienated from his roots in the past. He had, in other words, lost touch with the archetypes of the collective unconscious, the source of all tradition. And the social consequences of a rigid persona were total and uncritical adaptation and submission to the roles and expectations dictated by the state. (p. 178)

Despite the confidence with which Progoff and Homans interpreted Jung's thoughts, Jung himself wrote relatively little about the application of his theories to particular social problems. He advocated "a society that can preserve its internal cohesion and collective values, while at the same time granting the individual the greatest possible freedom" (CW6, par. 758), but he did not specify how such a society can be achieved.

Some of Jung's comments on ethics, however, are as applicable to social and political issues as they are to personal life. These comments include his warning against the tendency of high-minded people to avoid facing the reality of evil, especially in themselves. He seemed to see this avoidance occurring by one of two devices: (a) the denial that evil exists or (b) projecting it onto other persons, classes, races, or nations. He pointed out that consistent use of either of these devices produces an attitude that one is all good. Jung called this attitude "addiction to idealism" and wrote, "Every form of addiction is bad, no matter whether the narcotic be alcohol or morphine or idealism" (MDR, p. 329). Beginning with such general statements, Jung's observations on social issues tended to focus on their psychological ramifications rather than on their moral and ethical implications.

Race

For Jung, a white person's disparaging attitude toward the darker races was a projection of the shadow. Just as an individual must recognize projections of the shadow to achieve greater consciousness, so, he held, must the culture as a whole. Recognition of such a projection is a first step toward withdrawing it.

Jung was right, no doubt, to place the responsibility for hostile interracial relations on the people who project their evil and inferior sides on other races but he neglected, at least in his writings, the historical, economic, and political forces that affect relations between the lighter- and darker-skinned races. These forces seem to account for much of the tension between races and, also, for the prejudices within groups of dark-skinned people who often give higher status to the lighter-skinned individuals among them. It may be that the problems began, milennia ago, with collective shadow projections, but the issue cannot be approached with that perspective alone.

War and the Crisis of Our Time

Hostility and aggression among nations, according to Jung, are manifestations of a deeper crisis, which he identified with a psychological and religious split within individual humans and between groups. His later observations often reflected what appeared, in the late 1940s and 1950s, to be the major danger of the time: the threat of a Third World War between the free and communist blocs of nations. In 1934 Jung described the time as one "of dissociation and sickness. . . . The word 'crisis,' so often heard, is a medical expression which always tells us that the sickness has reached a dangerous climax" (CW10, par. 290); this statement applied equally well to the state of the world following World War II.

The Undiscovered Self (CW10, Part IV) was written about a decade after the end of World War II. It reflected Jung's increasing concern with the "mass-mindedness" or mass "possession" he had seen in Nazism (see Chapter 1) and now saw in Soviet Communism. The gulf between the blocs of nations is a religious problem because it is rooted in the split in the individual soul, a split that is the result of identification with the good and rejection of the shadow. Mass-mindedness is equally a religious problem because "it is possible to have an attitude to the external conditions of life only when there is a point of reference outside them. Religion gives, or claims to give, such a standpoint, thereby enabling the individual to exercise his judgment and his power of decision" (CW10, par. 506). Thus, the best defense against the power of the sovereign state is a higher authority that transcends the claim of each state to the absolute loyalty of each of its citizens or subjects. The higher authority may be perceived as God or the image of God—the Self.

Mass-mindedness can be diminished and war prevented if enough individuals can bear the tension of the opposites in their own natures. This statement of Jung's has been repeated many times and seems to be the prevailing view among Jungians. It is a surprising statement, however, in that it is based on belief, not on evidence, and Jung rejected belief as an inadequate substitute for experience. When he rejected belief, to be sure, he was contrasting it with inner religious experience. The same principle applies, in my view, to beliefs about outer experience, such as international conflict.

Moreover, it seems increasingly evident that individual psychological development is no match for the forces and institutionalized structures with which twentieth-century people must deal. (Perhaps improved communications have made this perception clearer, rather than that the problem is any different from what it was in earlier eras.) These forces and structures have a life of their own that is unlikely to be affected by the state of individuals' psyches. Even people in high positions have limited power over the course of major events such as wars.

Perhaps the view that Jung espoused seemed tenable to people who viewed World War II and its aftermath from the relatively safe vantage point of the "island" of Switzerland. It might even be acceptable to those Americans who were relatively untouched by the vicious irrationality of the war. But Jung's view on this subject seems not to take into account some of his own insights regarding the motivating force of the power drive; when a nation or its leaders become possessed by the desire for power, forces of collective evil, in such forms as violence and cruelty, result. These forces are beyond the direct or indirect control of any collection of individuals, no matter how well integrated each personality is.

The Feminist Movement

The current feminist movement (previously known as women's liberation and sometimes now as the women's movement) has special significance in Jungian psychology because of the movement's relation to female psychology, to which Jungian theory has made an important contribution, and because of its potential role in the development of consciousness. When the movement was gaining momentum during the late 1960s, it appeared to many Jungians to express identification with the animus; participants in the movement at that time were described as "strident" and "aggressive," and were accused of being unconcerned about how their actions were affecting other people, especially their families.

The movement was and is an understandable and, in my view, necessary response to the fact that many women (in American and Western European culture, at least) have been victims of the "feminine mystique," a cultural brainwashing that convinced them that they should limit their lives to marrying early, bearing and rearing several children, and devoting themselves to homemaking. Thus they overidentified with the traditional female role and suffered from the "problem that has no name" (Friedan, 1963). Their suffering was aggravated by the fact that they considered other women to be competitors for the attentions of men; consequently, women who assented to the feminine mystique were isolated from other women.

Some of the women who knew they had choices (i.e., did not assent to the feminine mystique) knew themselves to be more fortunate than virtuous and sympathized with their sisters who did assent. Others felt their escape to be due to their own efforts and depreciated the importance of the feminist movement.

The impact of the feminist movement has made it possible for many women to become aware of their options. Thus, many more are pursuing higher education, remaining single or marrying in their late twenties or later, and making conscious choices regarding the bearing or adopting of children. They value themselves as women and, eschewing much of the competition for male attention, are finding depth and joy in friendships with other women.

As in all advances in consciousness, old problems are superseded by new ones. Perhaps most common is the stress that is inherent in the multiplicity of choices. In addition, relationships between women and men are more difficult because new ways of being together must be found. Competition with other women has moved out of the sexual arena and into the professional and political worlds.

Nevertheless, the feminist movement has brought some valuable changes in cultural attitudes. There is fairly general agreement that the desirability of the economic and legal goals of the women's movement (equal pay for equal work, and the same legal rights as men) is self-evident. (Even many of the people who have opposed the Equal Rights Amendment do not admit to opposing equal legal rights for women; they argue that the amendment is not necessary because women already have equal rights before the law.) The psychological significance of the movement is not as obvious. It certainly shares the danger inherent in any collective phenomenon, that persons will be swept along with group enthusiasms and not develop their individual values. Some women focus on their anger at men, the "oppressors," to the exclusion of positive concerns. At its best, however, the feminist movement has contributed to cultural changes, which affect individuals psychologically.

A change that has been vitally needed is a greater valuing of the feminine principle. Our culture has tended to judge everyone, women and men alike, by the degree to which they conform to "masculine" values: assertiveness, competitiveness, objectivity, and strength. It also has seemed to require of females many of the "feminine" values: relatedness, softness, receptivity, gentleness, even passivity and weakness. Thus, women have been caught in an often paralyzing double bind. They had to be "masculine" to be successful in the world but "feminine" to be acceptable in personal relations, especially with men. (Men faced their own difficulty, the necessity of being always masculine, which has meant not showing emotion or vulnerability.) The feminist movement has helped to open the way to the psychological development of persons of both sexes. Both women and men are freer to develop as much femininity and as much masculinity as is of value to each person.

A further contribution of the movement to psychological development is its help to women who once lived entirely in the feminine side of their natures. For them, the conscious development of the animus is essential to emotional health. Many women are realizing for the first time that they can make independent decisions and take initiative toward their own well-being. In these ways, at least, they are finding a more conscious relationship to the animus. Where "stridency" exists, it may be an indication that the negative animus is still ascendant and the positive animus not yet fully developed.

The feminist movement seems to have had a profound impact on men as well as women. Nearly every man is being pressed to reassess his conception of being a man. Thus, many men as well as women are discovering that a man can take care of children and a woman can be a business executive without upsetting the balance of nature. Such an awareness seems true to a basic Jungian assumption that each individual must find her or his own combination of femininity and masculinity in attitudes and behavior.

Some participants in the feminist movement have felt that some of Jung's ideas have delayed change. They see many of his ideas on the psychology of women as culturally conditioned by the sexism that was even more prevalent in his lifetime than it is now. Although many of Jung's pre-1960 concepts are inadequate for the 1980s, they were advanced ideas when they were proposed and have contributed to the cultural changes that culminated in the feminist movement. Specifically, Jung stated repeatedly his thesis that the feminine principle (which is now espoused by feminists) has been depreciated historically and, hence, currently is needed more than the masculine. He gave content to the equality of women by valuing their feminine traits and, at the same time, honoring their development of masculine (animus) qualities. Similarly, in this theory of the anima, Jung advocated less machismo in men by urging that they develop their feminine side.

Politics

Although all the topics mentioned in this chapter have implications for political decisions, the arena of governmental and institutional politics is distinguishable as an area of psychological concern. As I have indicated elsewhere (Mattoon, 1978b), Jungians engage little in the discussion of politics and seem to participate in it even less.

This apparent lack of interest seems inconsistent with the fact that politics has to do with the use of power, and Jung considered the desire for power to be instinctual. If an instinct is not made conscious and channeled into constructive expression, it is almost certain to be repressed. Repressed contents tend to burst forth in destructive form. A repressed desire for power may express itself in a grab for the control of a person or a group, solely for the satisfaction of having power. The social consequences of this repression can be seen in organizations, such as church bodies and Jungian groups, which may explicitly disavow concern with power; the consequent unacknowledged hostilities, however, often prevent the resolution of policy issues. The consequences to the individual of such repression include destructive personal relations and a blocking of the individuation process. The resulting psychic poison can be avoided by open acknowledgment of the power instinct and by expressing it in consciously recognized political channels.

Political expression is important on a larger scale as a contribution to the potential wholeness of disadvantaged people whose primary concerns are economic and even physical survival. The needs of these people can be met only through political decisions, national and international. Once again, the inward orientation of Jungian psychology does not address these needs. Spiegelman (1969) observed, "the real psychotherapeutic needs of the masses will be met by meaningful and therapeutic changes in the culture" (p. 48). Such changes are slow but they often begin with political decisions.

In addition to its instinctual (power) reality, each political issue, like each individual complex, has an archetypal core. Often one side of the controversy in dealing with poverty, for example, is the maintenance of structure, order, and the principle of economic "rationality" that government spending must not exceed income. The other side of the controversy is the attitude of nurturing and caring for the weak and helpless. Thus, the issue may be between serving the Father archetype, characterized by structure, and serving the Mother archetype, characterized by nurturance.

That introverts and extraverts are likely to have different points of view on political issues was hypothesized by Jarrett (1979). For example, "The virtues of 'freedom' and 'equality' seem to compete in history for predominance among ideals. Probably the introvert tends to be drawn to freedom, at least if it is taken to mean 'left alone,' not being put upon by laws and other requirements. . . . On the other hand, the extravert immediately points to a thousand ways that people will suffer unless the government and the law make explicit provision to insure fairness" (p. 55).

Whatever the archetypal and/or typological bases for political points of view, political expression already is part of every life, consciously or unconsciously. Supposed nonparticipation means leaving decisions to others and thus enabling them to misuse power and, often, to perpetrate evil. The unwillingness to confront evil is inconsistent with psychological development. Despite having little to say on the topic, Jung seemed to support my view of the importance of politics with his statement, "As the individual is not just a single, separate being, but by his very existence presupposes a collective relationship, it follows that the process of individuation must lead to more intense and broader collective relationships and not to isolation" (CW6, par. 758).

Further Exploration of Social Issues

The relative paucity of commentary on social and political issues suggests that the imaginations of Jungians have not been captured by these realms; interest has remained focused on the inward aspect of the individual psyche. And yet there are many parallels between the phenomena of the individual psyche and the sociopolitical realm. These parallels are written into our language. *Depression:* Do you think first of an emotional state or an economic condition? Whichever occurs to you first, the other probably follows close behind. *Inflation:* Psychological or economic? *Integration:* Psychological or sociopolitical? All are conditions of the individual psyche and, also, of the body politic. The significance of these parallels is not clear but may be evidence of a unity of individual and collective experience.

Part VI

Expanding Analytical Psychology

19

Research

The further development of Analytical Psychology, like every field of inquiry, depends on continuing research. *Research* has a variety of meanings, depending upon the people and the situations concerned. Jung used the word often to mean the comparative study of symbols. Such study qualifies, beyond doubt, as research: "diligent and systematic inquiry or investigation into a subject in order to discover or revise facts, theories, applications, etc." (*Random House Dictionary of the English Language*, unabridged edition, 1967). Many Jungians practice this kind of research as a scholarly pursuit, and virtually every Jungian analyst practices it in relation to the amplification of dream images and other aspects of psychotherapeutic work.

The question remains, however, how much research on Jungian psychology is possible in the sense of generating and testing hypotheses on the nature of the psyche. That Analytical Psychology is amenable to such research is clear: Jung generated many testable hypotheses, some of which have been tested already; quantitative studies are included in the relevant chapters of this book and further investigations are suggested.

(Some of the studies discussed were conducted with hypotheses that were derived from theory that is not specifically Jungian.)

Empirical and Experimental Research

In the effort to achieve recognition for psychology as a science comparable to physics, some nineteenth-century psychologists adopted the research methods of classical physics as the model: the positing of hypotheses, controlled testing in replicable experiments, and statistical analysis. Insofar as psychologists have been able to follow this model, their methods are *experimental*; they exclude work, such as Jung's, that does not use the methods of "controlled" manipulation of variables.

This view does not take into account the fact that research can be scientific if it uses *empirical* methods such as observation, classification, correlation, and comparison (including historical). Indeed, in some natural sciences (e.g., astronomy and zoology), observation, classification, and comparison are the major methods of advancing knowledge. Because there is little or no opportunity for laboratory manipulation (especially not in astronomy) hypotheses are tested by predictions. Nevertheless, no one disputes the scientific nature of astronomy.

Jung based his theories on clinical observations, a form of empirical data. Thus, his work was scientific even though most of it was not experimental. Indeed, he was not alone among psychologists in finding it necessary to eschew the manipulation of variables (experimentation) because it is often inhumane and because critical variables are difficult to isolate in the lives of humans. For example, the question of why some people become criminals can be studied only by "field observations" and correlational methods, not by controlled studies in which some people would be encouraged to become criminals, others not. It is equally difficult to investigate experimentally such Jungian hypotheses as the existence of archetypes, which cannot be manipulated or even observed directly.

Despite the limited opportunities, Jung engaged in some experimental work, especially in connection with the Word Association Test (see Chapter 7). By this work, he contributed significantly to scientific confirmation of the existence of the unconscious.

That Jung and others have not used the experimental method more is due, in part, to the limitations of the method. Its strict use requires the posing of research questions in terms that can be answered by experimentation. A statement attributed to R. B. Cattell humorously pointed out this limitation: "To the great clinicians, the experimental psychologist must have seemed like a drunkard who knows that his lost wrist watch is out in the alley but searches for it in the house because there is more light inside."

The limitations of the experimental method are matched, of course, by the limitations of clinical research, which Jung used extensively. Nearly any possible psychological hypothesis can be demonstrated by some clinical datum. Thus, contradictory theories have been developed, all based on clinical data. Nevertheless, clinically based studies are possible. If many clinical data are used, the method becomes comparable to the observation, classification, and comparison methods of natural sciences.

Prediction

A frequent objection, by academic psychologists, to Jung's (and Freud's) form of empiricism is that the theory explains phenomena after the fact and cannot be used to predict an outcome. H. J. Eysenck (1953) argued:

> The psychoanalysts . . . make use of concepts such as "reaction formation," which allow a person who theoretically should show behaviour pattern A to react away from this pattern to such an extent that he shows instead the opposite pattern. . . . Jung makes use of a similar mechanism by stating that persons who are outwardly introverted are unconsciously extraverted, while those who are outwardly extraverted are unconsciously introverted—thus making it possible to "explain" any type of conduct simply by referring it either to the conscious or to the unconscious portion of the patient's personality. (pp. 234–35)

A similar point was made by one of Jung's students. Bennet (1962) pointed out that the concept of the collective unconscious can be used as a satisfactory explanation for certain psychological facts but that applying it is not the same as proving it. In order to claim proof the phenomena must be "checked and observed by others and found to possess an unchanging and predictable order" (p. 98).

Although both Eysenck and Bennet argued for the experimental method in psychology, other theorists have pointed out its limitations. Bakan (1967), a leading thinker on research method, pointed out that "Brentano (1874), at the time of the founding of modern experimental psychology, argued that psychology should be empirical rather than experimental; that the experiment was too far removed from experience to be able to tell us much that was significant" (p. xii). Bakan went on to suggest:

> The experimental may *sometimes* stand in the way of the empirical. . . . Most experimentation in the field of psychology falls considerably short of being able to be considered really empirical. Consider the ideal of the "well-designed experiment." The usual meaning of "well-designed" is that the outcomes of the experiment have been completely anticipated, and that one will not allow the experience of conducting the experiment to lead one to consider alternatives outside of the ones already thought of beforehand. . . . Good research into the unknown cannot be well designed, in the usual sense of the term. Truly good research means that one allows the investigation to be guided by the experiences of the investigation. (pp. xiii–xiv)

It seems evident that useful and valid research must take into account both empiricism and experimentation. Empiricism is necessary for the generation of hypotheses that are close to the reality of psychological phenomena; experimentation is desirable, when possible, for testing those hypotheses.

Hypothesis Developing and Hypothesis Testing

The difficulty of proof or confirmation as an indication that Jung's theory was not sufficiently scientific is based on the assumption that hypothesis testing is all there is of scientific research. Jung's critics overlook the fact that hypothesis developing is also part of scientific method. Philosopher Hans Reichenbach (1938) called hypothesis development the "context of discovery" and hypothesis testing the "context of justification."

Jung contributed significantly to the context of justification but he was a genius at the context of discovery.

Jung as Scientific Pioneer

Jung was a pioneer in the range of subject matter that he brought under scientific investigation, for example, occult phenomena. Because his research led him into areas that were considered by many psychologists to be outside the realm of science, he was ahead of the philosophical climate of his time. Jung maintained that any product of the psyche, whether observable behavior or subjective phenomenon, such as a dream, is the rightful object of scientific investigation. It is the method, not the subject matter, which is or is not scientific.

Bakan (1967) gave implicit support to Jung's range of subject matter by acknowledging that psychology is not the only science to have a problem with its subject matter:

> Every science has its ultimate mystery. In biology, the ultimate mystery is life; in physics, it is the nature of light; in chemistry, the nature of matter. No biologist would maintain that it would be necessary for him to define life before he could go on to investigate biological phenomena. In psychology, of course, the ultimate mystery is the mind. (p. 44)

Vincent Brome (1978) took a different view from Bakan's when he criticized Jung as scientist at the same time that he criticized conventional science:

> Jung dealt with a different kind of evidence from that available to the hard sciences but he seemed desperately anxious to equate the two in an effort to acquire the bedrock reality of scientific fact. It was a mistaken undertaking. Until we know the precise *physical* nature of these millions of cells which make up the human brain any form of psychological investigation cannot satisfy the requirements of science, but since the verification principle itself is now in question and Popper's "falsifiability" widely accepted, the constructs of science are equally suspect. (p. 240)

Academic psychologists have come to accept Jung's point of view to some degree, however. Even B. F. Skinner, probably the leading contemporary proponent of behaviorism (the view that psychology should be limited to the study of observable behavior) admitted that "events taking place within the skin of the organism must be considered, not as psychological mediators of behavior, but as part of behavior itself" (1964, p. 84).

By recognizing that "every psychology—[his] own included—has the character of a subjective confession" (CW4, par. 774), Jung anticipated the awareness of "experimenter bias," an awareness that has become quite widespread among psychologists, even those who strive hardest to design and conduct studies that are controlled in order to eliminate influences that arise out of the experimenter's subjectivity.

Experimenter bias is akin to the "personal equation" that was discovered in the early nineteenth century. It was noted first by astronomers who had difficulty in estimating to a fraction of a second the observation of the transit of a star. When they made comparisons they found variations, from one astronomer to another, which they attributed to differences in mental processes, that is, to the effect of the personal equation in the observation of data.

At long last, psychologists have become aware that experimenter bias influences the results of research. It seems obvious that such bias can be communicated inadvertently to human subjects. Rosenthal (1976) found that bias in the form of experimenter expectations can influence even research with animals. In one study (Rosenthal and Fode, 1963), for example, student experimenters were told that their rat-subjects were either maze-bright or maze-dull. Performance of the animals that were run by experimenters who believed them to be bright was significantly better, at the .01 level of confidence.

Such an influence of experimenter bias on animals which, presumably, cannot be influenced verbally, makes unconscious and even conscious influences on humans seem quite likely. Although there are ways of controlling for experimenter bias (e.g., "double-blind" methods), it is likely that the bias cannot be eliminated completely. It seems surprising that psychologists have been so slow to recognize experimenter bias, inasmuch as the phenomenon occurs, according to Wolfgang Pauli and other physicists, even in the science of microphysics.

Variations in Research Method

In addition to recognizing the values of both empirical and experimental research, Jungians can expand their horizons by using existing methods and helping to develop new ones. Granted that many Jungians shun methods that deal with parts of persons rather than wholes, nevertheless statistical methods can be applied to the investigation of many hypotheses. Meier, one of Jung's students and his successor at the Federal Institute of Technology in Zurich, advocated the increased use of statistical methods in Jungian research. He insisted that "academic psychologists are right in wanting things shown to them statistically; and it is we Jungians who have the *onus* of showing them that our ideas stand their tests. Only in this way can the unconscious be re-introduced into a scientific discussion" (1971, p. 284). Meier did not consider his view to diverge completely from Jung's, however, because Jung used statistics in his work on the Word Association Test (*CW2*) and in his study on synchronicity (*CW8*).

One statistical method that is geared particularly to the study of individual personality is content analysis. Calvin Hall used content analysis of dream series for both the assessment of personality at a particular time and the tracing of personality change in the dreams of the writer Franz Kafka (Hall and Lind, 1970), a convicted child molester (Bell and Hall, 1971), and Freud and Jung (Hall and Domhoff, 1968). In all cases the investigators validated their assessments by means of other kinds of evidence regarding the individuals studied: objective observations of the behavior and various personality tests. Researchers on Jungian hypotheses, too, could adopt such a combination of methods.

Allport (1965) also used content analysis to study a single case. Examining a series of 301 letters written by a woman between the ages of fifty-eight and seventy, Allport showed in her accounts of her life experiences understandings that expressed different psychological theories: existential, Jungian, and learning.

A variety of methods for studying a single case was presented in *N = 1: Experimental Studies of Single Cases* (Davidson and Costello, 1969). In the chapter "Experimental Method in the Psychological Description of the Individual Psychiatric Patient," a method was presented for testing an individual's behavior "by predicting from such a theory how his behavior will vary from one circumstance to another" (Shapiro, 1969, p. 12). Another method was presented in the chapter "Statistical Inference and the Single Case." A given treatment of a particular patient was alternated with a placebo until a sufficiently large number of observations had been obtained to achieve statistical significance (Chassan, 1969, p. 36).

How much are rejections by psychologists of Jung's theories reflections of outdated approaches to psychology? Two interpreters of the counterculture of the 1960s and 1970s seemed to think that the answer is "a great deal":

> Jung belongs to the present because he refused to be limited by the fads of the past. Victorian science and rationalized religion provided for the mechanistic age a series of reciprocal explanations of life. . . .
>
> By refusing to man the bulwark, Jung freed himself to go beyond technical rationality into the next batch of questions. He treated myths as serious evidence and he sought coherence in the archetypes that recur in many societies. . . . His respect for subjective experience led him to formulate theories that now seem to be promising ground for psychological experiments. . . .
>
> So Jung knew the counterculture long before there was one. In the present mode of cognitive promiscuity, one person after another gets hold of dream analysis, or myths, or some other shred only to find that Jung has given it a context. "It's like landing on a strange road," one young admirer says, "and finding that Jung drew the whole map." (Keen and Harris, 1972, p. 64)

Despite all the controversy about the nature of research and Jung's role in science, it is evident that he contributed greatly both to thought about research and actual investigation. He enlarged the range of subject matter that is the province of scientific investigation; he challenged the assumption that a psychologist is *ipso facto* an objective, detached observer; and he pioneered research methods that can be applied increasingly to the inward-directed subject matter that composes much of depth psychology.

Comprehensive English-Language Bibliography of Jungian Psychology

(Arranged by Chapter Topic*)

Published Works of C. G. Jung

(Some sections of various volumes of the *Collected Works* have been published in special editions. These books are not listed here.)

(CW) *Collected Works of C. G. Jung* (H. Read, M. Fordham, G. Adler, and W. McGuire, eds.; except where indicated, R. F. C. Hull, trans.). Princeton: Princeton University Press (originally published by Pantheon). Bollingen Series 20.

Vol. 1. *Psychiatric studies* (2nd ed.), 1957.

Vol. 2. *Experimental researches* (L. Stein with D. Riviere, trans.), 1973.

Vol. 3. *The psychogenesis of mental disease*, 1960.

Vol. 4. *Freud and psychoanalysis*, 1961.

Vol. 5. *Symbols of transformation* (2nd ed.), 1956.

Vol. 6. *Psychological types* (H. G. Baynes, trans.; revised by R. F. C. Hull), 1971.

Vol. 7. *Two essays on analytical psychology* (2nd ed. rev. & augmented), 1966.

*Except for Jung's works. For topics in them, see CW contents and indices.

**indicates book recommended for further study on the topic.

(CW)   Vol. 8. *The structure and dynamics of the psyche* (2nd ed.), 1960.
Vol. 9 (Part I). *The archetypes and the collective unconscious* (2nd ed.), 1959.
Vol. 9 (Part II). *Aion: Researches into the phenomenology of the Self* (2nd ed.), 1959.
Vol. 10. *Civilization in transition* (2nd ed.), 1964.
Vol. 11. *Psychology and religion: West and east* (2nd ed.), 1958.
Vol. 12. *Psychology and alchemy* (2nd ed.), 1953.
Vol. 13. *Alchemical studies*, 1967.
Vol. 14. *Mysterium coniunctionis* (2nd ed.), 1963.
Vol. 15. *The spirit in man, art, and literature*, 1966.
Vol. 16. *The practice of psychotherapy* (2nd ed.), 1954.
Vol. 17. *The development of personality*, 1954.
Vol. 18. *The symbolic life: Miscellaneous writings*, 1976.
Vol. 19. *General bibliography of C. G. Jung's writings*, 1979.
Vol. 20. *General index to the Collected Works of C. G. Jung*, 1979.
Supplementary Vol. A. *The Zofingia Lectures*, 1983.

(DA)   *Dream analysis: Notes of the seminars given in 1928–1930* (W. McGuire, ed.). Princeton: Princeton University Press, 1984.

(FJ)   *The Freud/Jung letters* (W. McGuire, ed.). Princeton: Princeton University Press, 1974. Bollingen Series 94.

(Let 1 and 2) *C. G. Jung letters*, Vol. 1, 1906–1950; Vol. 2, 1951–1961 (G. Adler, ed. with A. Jaffé). Princeton: Princeton University Press, 1973, 1975. Bollingen Series 95.

(MDR) *Memories, dreams, reflections* (A. Jaffé, ed.). New York: Pantheon, 1963.

(MHS) *Man and his symbols* (C. G. Jung and M.-L. von Franz, eds.). Garden City, NY: Doubleday, 1964.

(VS)   *The Visions Seminars*, Vols. 1 and 2. Dallas, TX: Spring Publications, 1976.

Reference Works

Abstracts of the Collected Works of C. G. Jung (C. L. Rothgeb, et al., eds.). Rockville, MD: National Institute of Mental Health, 1978.
Catalogue of the Kristine Mann Library of the Analytical Psychology Club of New York, Inc. Boston: G. K. Hall, 1978.
Vincie, J. F. and Rathbauer-Vincie, M. *C. G. Jung and analytical psychology: A comprehensive bibliography*. New York: Garland, 1977.

Anthologies

** Campbell, J. (ed.). *The portable Jung* (R. F. C. Hull, trans.). New York: Viking, 1971.

de Laszlo, V. S. (ed.). *The basic writings of C. G. Jung.* New York: Modern Library, 1959.

de Laszlo, V. S. (ed.). *Psyche and symbol: A selection from the writings of C. G. Jung.* Garden City, NY: Doubleday (Anchor Books), 1958.

Jacobi, J. and Hull, R. F. C. (eds.). *C. G. Jung: Psychological reflections; a new anthology of his writings, 1905–1961.* Princeton: Princeton University Press, 1953, 1970. Bollingen Series 31.

Storr, A. (ed.). *The essential Jung.* Princeton: Princeton University Press, 1983.

Primers and General Introductions

Bennet, E. A. *What Jung really said.* New York: Schocken, 1983.

Evans, R. I. *Jung on elementary psychology.* London: Routledge & Kegan Paul, 1979.

** Fordham, F. *An introduction to Jung's psychology* (3rd rev. ed.). New York: Penguin, 1966.

Hall, C. S. and Nordby, V. J. *A primer of Jungian psychology.* New York: New American Library (A Mentor Book), 1973.

** Jacobi, J. *The psychology of C. G. Jung* (8th rev. ed.; R. Mannheim, trans.). New Haven: Yale University Press, 1973.

Laughlin, T. *Jungian psychology,* Vol. 1, *An introduction to the psychology of C. G. Jung.* Los Angeles: Panarion Press, 1984.

** Whitmont, E. C. *The symbolic quest: Basic concepts of analytical psychology.* New York: Putnam (for the C. G. Jung Foundation for Analytical Psychology), 1969.

Winski, N. *Understanding Jung.* Los Angeles: Sherbourne Press, 1971.

Chapter 1: Introduction: The Development of Analytical Psychology

Biographical and Critical

** Bennet, E. A. *C. G. Jung.* New York: E. P. Dutton, 1962.

Bennet, E. A. *Meetings with Jung: Conversations recorded by E. A. Bennet during the years 1946–1961.* Privately printed, 1982.

Brome, V. *Jung: Man and myth.* New York: Atheneum, 1978.

Burnham, J. and McGuire, W. (eds.). *Jeliffe: American psychoanalyst and physician. His correspondence with Freud and Jung.* Chicago: University of Chicago Press, 1983.

Carotenuto, S. *A secret symmetry: Sabina Spielrein between Jung and Freud.* New York: Pantheon, 1982.

Dry, A. M. The psychology of Jung: A critical interpretation. London: Methuen, 1961 (New York: Wiley & Sons, 1962).

Edinger, E., et al. Nine memorial messages by Edinger, Harding, Mc-Cormick, Murray, Northrup, and Tillich. Dallas, TX: Spring Publications, 1983.

** Ellenberger, H. F. The discovery of the unconscious. New York: Basic Books, 1970, 1981.

** Frey-Rohn, L. From Freud to Jung: A comparative study of the psychology of the unconscious (F. E. Engreen and E. K. Engreen, trans.). New York: Putnam (for the C. G. Jung Foundation for Analytical Psychology), 1974.

Glover, E. Freud or Jung. New York: Norton, 1950.

** Hannah, B. Jung: His life and work. New York: Putnam (for the C. G. Jung Foundation for Analytical Psychology), 1976.

Hoeller, S. The gnostic Jung and the "seven sermons to the dead." Wheaton, IL: Theosophical Publishing House, 1982.

Hogenson, G. Jung's struggle with Freud. Notre Dame, IN: University of Notre Dame Press, 1983.

Homans, P. Jung in context: Modernity and the making of a psychology. Chicago: University of Chicago Press, 1979.

Jaffé, A. (ed.). C. G. Jung: Word and image. Princeton: Princeton University Press, 1979.

Jaffé, A. Jung's last years and other essays. Dallas, TX: Spring Publications, 1984.

Jensen, F. C. G. Jung, Emma Jung, and Toni Wolff: A collection of remembrances. Analytical Psychology Club of San Francisco, 1982.

Kaufmann, W. Discovering the mind, Vol. 3, Freud versus Adler and Jung. New York: McGraw-Hill, 1980.

McGuire, W. and Hull, R. F. C. (eds.). C. G. Jung speaking. Princeton, NJ: Princeton University Press, 1977.

Samuels, A. Jung and the post-Jungians. London: Routledge & Kegan Paul, 1985.

Serrano, Miguel. C. G. Jung and Hermann Hesse: A record of two friendships. New York: Schocken Books, 1966.

Steele, R. S. Freud and Jung: Conflicts of interpretation. London: Routledge & Kegan Paul, 1982.

Stern, P. J. C. G. Jung: The haunted prophet. New York: Braziller, 1976.

Storr, A. C. G. Jung. New York: Viking, 1973.

van der Post, L. Jung and the story of our time. New York: Pantheon, 1975.

** von Franz, M.-L. C. G. Jung: His myth in our time. New York: Putnam (for the C. G. Jung Foundation for Analytical Psychology), 1975.

Wehr, G. Portrait of Jung. (W. A. Hargreaves, trans.). New York: Herder & Herder, 1971.

Welch, J. *Spiritual pilgrims: Carl Jung and Teresa of Avila*. New York: Paulist Press, 1982.

Chapter 2: The Components of the Psyche

Adler, G. *Dynamics of the Self*. London: Coventure, 1979.
Cox, D. *Modern psychology: The teachings of Carl Gustav Jung*. New York: Barnes & Noble, 1968.
** Jacobi, J. *Masks of the soul* (Ean Begg, trans.). Grand Rapids, MI: Eerdmans Publishing, 1976.
Mambert, W. A. and Foster, B. F. *Exploring your unconscious mind*. New York: Cornerstone Library, 1977.
Miller, W. *Make friends with your shadow*. Minneapolis: Augsburg, 1981.
Wickes, F. G. *The inner world of man*. New York: Frederick Ungar, 1948.
(See also Primers and General Introductions.)

Chapter 3: The Collective Unconscious

Gordon, R. *Dying and creating*. New York: Academic Press, 1981.
Guggenbühl-Craig, A. (ed.). *The archetype*. (Proceedings of the 2nd International Congress for Analytical Psychology.) Basel and New York: Karger, 1962.
Hillman, J. *Archetypal psychology: A brief account*. Dallas, TX: Spring Publications, 1983.
** Hillman, J. *Facing the gods*. Dallas, TX: Spring Publications, 1980.
Hillman, J. *Inter Views: Conversations with Laura Pozzo on psychotherapy, biography, love, soul, dreams, work, imagination and the state of the culture*. New York: Harper & Row, 1984.
Jacobsohn, H., von Franz, M.-L, and Hurwitz, S. *Timeless documents of the soul*. Evanston: Northwestern University Press, 1968. Studies in Jungian Thought.
Jung, E. and von Franz, M.-L. *The Grail legend* (A. Dykes, trans.). Boston: Sigo Press, 1970, 1984.
Kugler, P. *The alchemy of discourse: An archetypal approach to language*. Lewisburg, PA: Bucknell University Press, 1982.
Luke, H. M. *The inner story: Myth and symbol in the Bible and literature*. New York: Crossroad, 1982.
** Martin, P. W. *Experiment in depth: A study of the work of Jung, Eliot, and Toynbee*. Darby, PA: Darby Books, 1955, 1982.
Miller, D. L. *The new polytheism: Rebirth of the gods and goddesses*. Dallas, TX: Spring Publications, 1981.

Neumann, E. *Art and the creative unconscious* (R. Mannheim, trans.). Princeton: Princeton University Press, 1971. Bollingen Series 61.

Neumann, E. *Creative man.* Princeton: Princeton University Press, 1979. Bollingen Series 61: 2.

Neumann, E. *The great mother: An analysis of the archetype* (R. Mannheim, trans.). Princeton: Princeton University Press, 1972. Bollingen Series 47.

Singer, J. *The unholy Bible.* New York: Putnam (for the C. G. Jung Foundation for Analytical Psychology), 1969.

** Stevens, A. *Archetypes: A natural history of the Self.* New York: William Morrow, 1982.

von Franz, M.-L. *Creation myths.* Dallas, TX: Spring Publications, 1972.

** von Franz, M.-L. *An introduction to the interpretation of fairy tales.* Dallas, TX: Spring Publications, 1970.

von Franz, M.-L. *Patterns of creativity mirrored in creation myths.* Dallas, TX: Spring Publications, 1972.

Willeford, W. *The fool and his scepter: A study in clowns and jesters and their audience.* Evanston, IL: Northwestern University Press, 1969.

Zolla, E., et al. *Archetypes: The persistence of unifying patterns.* New York: Harcourt Brace Jovanovich, 1982.

Chapter 4: Attitude and Function Types

Grant, W. *Behavior of MBTI types.* Gainesville, FL: Center for Applications of Psychological Type, 1977.

Keirsey, D. and Bates, M. *Please understand me: An essay on temperament styles.* Del Mar, CA: Promethean Books, 1978.

Lawrence, G. *People types and tiger stripes: A practical guide to learning styles.* Gainesville, FL: Center for Applications of Psychological Type, 1979.

** Myers, I. B. *Gifts differing.* Palo Alto, CA: Consulting Psychologists Press, 1980.

Reardon, A. *Personality and morality: A developmental approach.* Woolwich, ME: TBW Books, 1983.

Shapiro, K. J. and Alexander, I. E. *The experience of introversion: An integration of phenomenological, empirical, and Jungian approaches.* Durham, NC: Duke University Press, 1975.

van der Hoop, J. H. *Conscious orientation: A study of personality types in relation to neurosis and psychosis.* Darby, PA: Darby Books, 1979.

** von Franz, M.-L. and Hillman, J. *Lectures on Jung's typology.* Dallas, TX: Spring Publications, 1971.

Wheelwright, J. B. *Psychological types*. San Francisco: C. G. Jung Institute of San Francisco, 1973.

Chapter 5: Females and Males

Bolen, J. S. *Goddesses in everywoman: A new psychology of women.* San Francisco: Harper & Row, 1984.

Bradway, K. *Villa of mysteries: Pompeii initiation rites of women.* San Francisco: C. G. Jung Institute of San Francisco, 1982.

** de Castillejo, I. *Knowing woman: A feminine psychology.* New York: Harper & Row, 1973.

Dieckmann, U., Bradway, K., and Hill, G. *Male and female, feminine and masculine.* San Francisco: C. G. Jung Institute of San Francisco, 1974.

** Downing, C. *The goddess: Mythological images of the feminine.* New York: Crossroad, 1981.

Greene, T. A. *Modern man in search of manhood.* New York: Association Press, 1967.

Grinnell, R. *Alchemy in a modern woman: A study in the contrasexual archetype.* Dallas, TX: Spring Publications, 1973.

Hall, N. *The moon and the virgin: Reflections on the archetypal feminine.* New York: Harper & Row, 1980.

** Harding, M. E. *The way of all women: A psychological interpretation.* New York: Harper & Row, 1970, 1975.

Harding, M. E. *Woman's mysteries: Ancient and modern.* New York: Harper & Row, 1976.

Hillman, J., Murray, H. A., Moore, T., Baird, J., Cowan, T., and Severson, R. *Puer papers.* Dallas, TX: Spring Publications, 1979.

Johnson, R. A. *He! A contribution to understanding masculine psychology.* New York: Harper & Row, 1977.

Johnson, R. A. *She! A contribution to understanding feminine psychology.* New York: Harper & Row, 1977.

** Jung, E. *Animus and anima.* Dallas, TX: Spring Publications, 1957, 1969.

Leonard, L. S. *The wounded woman.* Boulder, CO: Shambala Publications, 1983.

Luke, H. M. *Woman, earth and spirit: The feminine in symbol and myth.* New York: Crossroad, 1981.

Mankowitz, A. *Change of life: A psychological study of dreams and the menopause.* Toronto: Inner City Books, 1984.

Neumann, E. *Amor and Psyche: The psychic development of the feminine* (R. Mannheim, trans.). Princeton: Princeton University Press, 1956. Bollingen Series 54.

Perera, S. *Descent to the goddess: A way of initiation for women.* Toronto: Inner City Books, 1981.

Scott-Maxwell, F. *Women and sometimes men.* New York: Knopf, 1957.

Sharp, D. *The secret raven: Conflict and transformation in the life of Kafka.* Toronto: Inner City Books, 1980.

Singer, J. *Androgyny: Toward a new theory of sexuality.* Garden City, NY: Doubleday, 1977.

Stroud, J. and Thomas, G. (eds.). *Images of the untouched.* Dallas, TX: Spring Publications, 1981.

Te Paske, B. *Rape and ritual: A psychological study.* Toronto: Inner City Books, 1982.

Ulanov, A. B. *The feminine in Jungian psychology and in Christian theology.* Evanston, IL: Northwestern University Press, 1971.

Ulanov, A. B. *Receiving woman: Studies in the psychology and theology of the feminine.* Philadelphia: Westminster Press, 1981.

Ulanov, B. and Ulanov, A. B. *Cinderella and her sisters: The envied and the envying.* Philadelphia: Westminster Press, 1983.

Vitale, A., et al. *Fathers and mothers.* Dallas, TX: Spring Publications, 1973.

von Franz, M.-L. *Problems of the feminine in fairy tales.* Dallas, TX: Spring Publications, 1972.

** von Franz, M.-L. *Puer aeternus* (2nd ed.). Boston: Sigo Press, 1981.

Wheelwright, J. *For women growing older: The animus.* Houston: C. G. Jung Educational Center of Houston, 1984.

Wheelwright, J. H. *Women and men.* San Francisco: C. G. Jung Institute of San Francisco, 1977.

Whitmont, E. *The return of the goddess.* New York: Crossroad, 1982.

Wolff, T. *Structural forms of the feminine psyche* (P. Watzalawik, trans.). Zurich: Students' Association, C. G. Jung Institute, 1956.

Chapter 6: Psychic Energy and Self-Regulation

** Harding, M. E. *Psychic energy: Its source and its transformation* (2nd ed.). Princeton: Princeton University Press, 1963. Bollingen Series 10.

Hillman, J. *Emotion: A comprehensive phenomenology of theories and their meaning for therapy.* London: Routledge & Kegan Paul, 1960.

Chapters 7 and 8: Complexes and Projection

Harding, M. E. *The 'I' and the 'not-I': A study in the development of consciousness.* Princeton: Princeton University Press, 1965. Bollingen Series 79.

** Jacobi, J. *Complex/archetype/symbol in the psychology of C. G. Jung* (R. Mannheim, trans.). Princeton: Princeton University Press, 1959.

von Franz, M.-L. *Projection and recollection in Jungian psychology.* LaSalle, IL: Open Court Publishing, 1980.

Chapter 9: Symbol

** Jung, C. G., von Franz, M.-L., Henderson, J. L., Jacobi, J., and Jaffé, A. *Man and his symbols.* Garden City, NY: Doubleday, 1964.

McCully, R. S. *Rorschach theory and symbolism: A Jungian approach to clinical material.* Baltimore, MD: Williams and Wilkins, 1971.

Philipson, M. *Outline of a Jungian aesthetics.* Evanston, IL: Northwestern University Press, 1963.

Trinick, J. *The fire-tried stone: An enquiry into the development of a symbol.* Marazion, Cornwall, England: Wordens of Cornwall, 1967.

von Franz, M.-L. *Alchemy: An introduction to the symbolism and the psychology.* Toronto: Inner City Books, 1980.

Chapter 10: Synchronicity

** Bolen, J. *The Tao of psychology: Synchronicity and the Self.* San Francisco: Harper & Row, 1979.

Crookall, R. *The Jung-Jaffé view of out-of-the-body experiences.* London: World Fellowship Press, 1970.

Fodor, N. *Freud, Jung, and occultism.* New Hyde Park, NY: University Books, 1971.

Greene, L. *The Jupiter–Saturn conferences.* Reno, NV: CRCS Publications, 1983.

Jaffé, A. *Apparitions: An archetypal approach to death dreams and ghosts.* Dallas, TX: Spring Publications, 1979. Jung Classics Series.

** Nichols, S. *Jung and tarot: An archetypal journey.* New York: Samuel Weiser, 1980.

Progoff, I. *Jung, synchronicity and human destiny: Noncausal dimensions of human experience.* New York: Julian, 1973.

von Franz, M.-L. *Number and time: Reflections leading toward a unification of depth psychology and physics.* Evanston, IL: Northwestern University Press, 1974. Studies in Jungian Thought.

** von Franz, M.-L. *On divination and synchronicity: The psychology of meaningful chance.* Toronto: Inner City Books, 1980.

von Franz, M.-L. *Time, rhythm and repose.* Magnolia, MA: Peter Smith, 1983.

Chapter 11: Psychopathology

Bauer, J. *Alcoholism and women: The background and the psychology*. Toronto: Inner City Books, 1982.

** Cowan, L. *Masochism: A Jungian view*. Dallas, TX: Spring Publications, 1982.

** Guggenbühl-Craig, A. *Eros on crutches: Reflections on amorality and psychopathy*. Dallas, TX: Spring Publications, 1980.

** Perry, J. W. *The far side of madness*. Englewood Cliffs, NJ: Prentice-Hall, 1974.

Perry, J. W. *The Self in psychotic process: Its symbolization in schizophrenia*. Berkeley: University of California Press, 1953.

Schwartz-Salant, N. *Narcissism and character transformation*. Toronto: Inner City Books, 1982.

** Woodman, M. *Addiction to perfection: The still unravished bride*. Toronto: Inner City Books, 1982.

Woodman, M. *The owl was a baker's daughter: Obesity, anorexia nervosa, and the repressed feminine*. Toronto: Inner City Books, 1980.

Ziegler, A. J. *Archetypal medicine*. Dallas, TX: Spring Publications, 1983.

Chapter 12: Human Development from Birth to Old Age

** Fordham, M. *Children as individuals*. New York: Putnam, 1944, 1969.

Fordham, M. *The Self and autism*. Orlando, FL: Academic Press, 1981.

Harding, M. E. *The parental image: Its injury and reconstruction*. New York: Putnam (for the C. G. Jung Foundation for Analytical Psychology), 1965.

Henderson, J. L. *Thresholds of initiation*. Middleton, CT: Wesleyan University Press, 1967.

Neumann, E. *The child: Structure and dynamics of the nascent personality* (R. Mannheim, trans.). Putnam (for the C. G. Jung Foundation for Analytical Psychology), 1973.

** Neumann, E. *The origins and history of consciousness* (rev. ed.; R. F. C. Hull, trans.). Princeton: Princeton University Press, 1964. Bollingen Series 42.

Staude, J. R. *The adult development of C. G. Jung*. London: Routledge & Kegan Paul, 1981.

** Stein, M. *In midlife: A Jungian perspective*. Dallas, TX: Spring Publications, 1984.

** Wickes, F. *The inner world of childhood* (rev. ed.). New York: Appleton-Century, 1966.

Chapter 13: Ways of Individuation

Adler, G. The living symbol: A case study in the process of individuation. New York: Pantheon, 1961. Bollingen Series 63.

Carotenuto, A. The vertical labyrinth: Individuation in Jungian psychology. Toronto: Inner City Books, 1985.

Hannah, B. Striving towards wholeness. New York: Putnam (for the New York Foundation for Analytical Psychology), 1971.

** Harding, M. E. Journey into Self. New York: Longman, 1956.

Henderson, J. L. and Oakes, M. The wisdom of the serpent: The myths of death, rebirth and resurrection. New York: Collier, 1963.

Herzog, E. Psyche and death: Myths and dreams in analytical psychology. New York: Putnam, 1967.

** Hillman, J. Re-visioning psychology. New York: Harper & Row, 1975.

Howes, E. and Moon, S. The choicemaker. Wheaton, IL: Theosophical Publishing House, 1977.

** Jacobi, J. The way of individuation. New York: New American Library, 1983.

Moon, S. Dreams of a woman: An analyst's inner journey. Boston: Sigo Press, 1983.

Moon, S. A magic dwells: A poetic and psychological study of the Navaho emergence myth. Middleton, CT: Wesleyan University Press, 1970.

Pelgrin, M. And a time to die. Boston: Sigo Press, 1976.

von Franz, M.-L. Alchemical active imagination. Dallas, TX: Spring Publications, 1979.

** von Franz, M.-L. Individuation in fairy tales. Dallas, TX: Spring Publications, 1977.

von Franz, M.-L. The psychological meaning of redemption motifs in fairy tales. Toronto: Inner City Books, 1980.

Wheelwright, J. H. The death of a woman. New York: St. Martin's, 1981.

Wickes, F. G. The inner world of choice. New York: Harper & Row, 1963, 1976.

Williams, D. Border crossings: Carlos Castaneda's path to knowledge. Toronto: Inner City Books, 1981.

Chapter 14: Religion

Brown, C. A. Jung's hermeneutic of doctrine. Chico, CA: Scholars Press, 1981.

Bryant, C. Jung and the Christian way. New York: Seabury, 1984.

Clift, W. B. Jung and Christianity: The challenge of reconciliation. New York: Crossroad, 1983.

Cox, D. *Jung and St. Paul: The doctrine of justification by faith and its relation to individuation.* New York: Association Press, 1959.

Curatorium, C. G. Jung Institute, Zurich (ed.). *Conscience.* Evanston, IL: Northwestern University Press, 1970. Studies in Jungian Thought.

Curatorium, C. G. Jung Institute, Zurich (ed.). *Evil.* Evanston, IL: Northwestern University Press, 1967. Studies in Jungian Thought.

Dourley, J. C. *G. Jung and Paul Tillich: The psyche as sacrament.* Toronto: Inner City Books, 1981.

Dourley, J. *The illness that we are: A Jungian critique of Christianity.* Toronto: Inner City Books, 1984.

Edinger, E. F. *The creation of consciousness: Jung's myth for modern man.* Toronto: Inner City Books, 1984.

** Edinger, E. F. *Ego and archetype: Individuation and the religious function of the psyche.* New York: Penguin, 1973.

Edinger, E. F. *Melville's Moby Dick: A Jungian commentary.* New York: New Directions, 1978.

Goldbrunner, J. *Individuation: A study of the depth psychology of Carl Gustav Jung.* Notre Dame, IN: University of Notre Dame Press, 1964.

Grant, H. and Thompson, M. M. *From image to likeness: A Jungian path in the gospel journey.* New York: Paulist Press, 1983.

Hanna, C. B. *The face of the deep: The religious ideas of C. G. Jung.* Philadelphia: Westminster, 1967.

Heisig, J. W. *Imago dei: A study of C. G. Jung's psychology of religion.* Lewiston, PA: Bucknell University Press, 1978.

** Hillman, J. *Insearch: Psychology and religion.* Dallas, TX: Spring Publications, 1983.

Hostie, R. *Religion and the psychology of C. G. Jung* (G. R. Lamb, trans.). London: Sheed & Ward, 1957.

** Jaffé, A. *The myth of meaning* (R. F. C. Hull, trans.). New York: Penguin, 1975.

Kelsey, M. T. *Christo-psychology.* New York: Crossroad, 1982.

Kluger, R. S. *Psyche and Bible.* Dallas, TX: Spring Publications, 1974.

Kluger, R. S. *Satan in the Old Testament.* Evanston, IL: Northwestern University Press, 1967. Studies in Jungian Thought.

** Meier, C. A. *Jung's Analytical Psychology and religion.* Carbondale, IL: Southern Illinois University Press, 1977.

Moreno, A. *Jung, gods, and modern man.* Notre Dame, IN: Notre Dame University Press, 1970.

Philp, H. L. *Jung and the problem of evil.* New York: R. M. McBride, 1959.

Rollins, W. G. *Jung and the Bible.* Atlanta: John Knox Press, 1983.

Sanford, J. A. *Evil: The shadow side of reality.* New York: Crossroad, 1981.

** Sanford, J. A. *The kingdom within: A study of the inner meaning of Jesus' sayings.* New York: Paulist Press, 1980.

Sanford, J. A. *The man who wrestled with God: Light from the Old Testament on the psychology of individuation.* King of Prussia, PA: Religious Publishing House, 1977.

Schaer, H. *Religion and the cure of souls in Jung's psychology* (R. F. C. Hull, trans.). New York: Pantheon, 1950. Bollingen Series 21.

Stein, M. *Jung's treatment of Christianity.* Wilmette, IL: Chiron Publications, 1985.

Ulanov, A. B. and Ulanov, B. *Religion and the unconscious.* Philadelphia: Westminster Press, 1975.

von der Heydt, V. *Prospects for the soul.* London: Dartman, Longman & Todd, 1976.

von Franz, M.-L. *The passion of Perpetua.* Dallas, TX: Spring Publications, 1979.

von Franz, M.-L. *Shadow and evil in fairy tales.* Dallas, TX: Spring Publications, 1974.

Westman, H. *The structure of biblical myths.* Dallas, TX: Spring Publications, 1983.

White, V. *God and the unconscious.* Dallas, TX: Spring Publications, 1982.

White, V. *Soul and psyche: An enquiry into the relationship of psychotherapy and religion.* London: Collins & Harvill, 1960.

Wiggins, J. B. (ed.). *Religion as story.* Dallas, TX: Spring Publications, 1980.

Zimmer, H. (J. Campbell, ed.). *The king and the corpse: Tales of the soul's conquest of evil.* Princeton: Princeton University Press, 1948.

Chapter 15: Relationships and Sexuality

** Bertine, E. *Human relationships: In the family, in friendship, in love.* New York: David McKay, 1958.

Greene, L. *Relating: An astrological guide to living with others on a small planet.* New York: Samuel Weiser, 1978, 1981.

** Guggenbühl-Craig, A. *Marriage: Dead or alive.* Dallas, TX: Spring Publications, 1977.

** Johnson, R. A. *We: Understanding the psychology of romantic love.* New York: Harper & Row, 1983.

Layard, J. *A Celtic quest: Sexuality and soul in individuation.* Dallas, TX: Spring Publications, 1975.

Sanford, J. A. *Between people: Communicating one to one.* New York: Paulist Press, 1982.

Stein, R. *Incest and human love: The betrayal of the soul in psychotherapy.* Dallas, TX: Spring Publications, 1974, 1984.

von Franz, M.-L. *A psychological interpretation of "The Golden Ass" of Apuleius.* Dallas, TX: Spring Publications, 1970.

Chapter 16: Psychotherapy

Adler, G. *Studies in analytical psychology.* New York: Putnam (for the C. G. Jung Foundation for Analytical Psychology), 1966.

Adler, G. (ed.). *Success and failure in analysis.* (Proceedings of the Fifth International Congress for Analytical Psychology.) New York: Putnam (for the C. G. Jung Foundation for Analytical Psychology), 1974.

Bach, S., et al. *Spontaneous images: Relationship between psyche and soma.* New York: Interbook, 1980.

Baker, I. (ed.). *Methods of treatment in analytical psychology.* (Proceedings of the Seventh International Congress for Analytical Psychology.) Fellbach, Germany: Verlag Adolf Bonz GmbH, 1980.

Barker, C. *Healing in depth* (H. I. Bach, ed.). London: Hodder & Stoughton, 1972.

Barton, A. *Three worlds of therapy: Freud, Jung and Rogers.* Palo Alto, CA: Mayfield Publishing, 1974.

Borenzweig, H. *Jung and social work.* Toronto: Inner City Books, 1984.

** Bradway, K., et al. *Sandplay studies: Origins, theory and practice.* Boston: Sigo Press, 1982.

Brand, R. *The experiment.* San Francisco: C. G. Jung Institute of San Francisco, 1981.

Christou, E. *The logos of the soul.* Dallas, TX: Spring Publications, 1963.

Fordham, M. *Jungian psychotherapy: A study in analytical psychology.* New York: Wiley-Interscience, 1978.

** Fordham, M., et al. (eds.). *Technique in Jungian analysis.* New York: Academic Press, 1974, 1981.

** Guggenbühl-Craig, A. *Power in the helping professions.* Dallas, TX: Spring Publications, 1971.

Hannah, B. *Encounters with the soul. Active imagination as developed by C. G. Jung.* Boston: Sigo Press, 1981.

Hillman, J. *Healing fiction.* Barrytown, NY: Station Hill Press, 1983.

** Hillman, J. *The myth of analysis: Three essays in archetypal psychology.* Evanston, IL: Northwestern University Press, 1972. Studies in Jungian Thought.

Hillman, J., et al. *Soul and money*. Dallas, TX: Spring Publications, 1982.

Hillman, J. *Suicide and the soul*. New York: Harper & Row, 1964.

Hochheimer, W. *The psychotherapy of C. G. Jung* (H. Nagel, trans.). New York: Putnam (for the C. G. Jung Foundation for Analytical Psychology), 1969.

** Jacoby, M. *The analytic encounter: Transference and human relationship*. Toronto: Inner City Books, 1984.

Kalff, D. M. *Sandplay: A psychotherapeutic approach to the psyche*. Boston: Sigo Press, 1980.

Lambert, K. *Analysis, repair and individuation*. New York: Academic Press, 1981.

Laughlin, T. *Jungian psychology, Vol. 2., Jungian theory and therapy*. Los Angeles: Panarion Press, 1982.

Lopez-Pedraza, R. *Hermes and his children*. Dallas, TX: Spring Publications, 1977.

Meier, C. A. *Ancient incubation and modern psychotherapy* (M. Curtis, trans.). Evanston, IL: Northwestern University Press, 1967. Studies in Jungian Thought.

Mindell, A. *Dreambody. The body's role in revealing the Self*. Boston: Sigo Press, 1982.

** Perry, J. W. *Roots of renewal in myth and madness*. San Francisco: Jossey-Bass, 1976.

Sandner, D. *Navaho symbols of healing*. New York: Harcourt Brace Jovanovich, 1979.

Singer, J. *The boundaries of the soul*. Garden City, NY: Doubleday, 1972.

Spiegelman, J. M. *The knight: The theory and method of Jung's active imagination technique*. Helena, MT: Falcon Press, 1982.

Spiegelman, J. M. *The tree: Tales in psycho-mythology*. Dallas, TX: Spring Publications, 1974, 1982.

** Stein, M. (ed.). *Jungian analysis*. La Salle, IL: Open Court Publishing, 1982.

Watkins, M. M. *Waking dreams*. Dallas, TX: Spring Publicatins, 1984.

Weaver, R. *The old wise woman*. New York: Putnam (for the C. G. Jung Foundation for Analytical Psychology), 1973.

Weinrib, E. *Images of the Self: The sandplay therapy process*. Boston: Sigo Press, 1983.

Wheelwright, J. B. (ed.). *The analytic process: Aims, analysis, training*. (Proceedings of the Fourth International Congress for Analytical Psychology.) New York: Putnam (for the C. G. Jung Foundation for Analytical Psychology), 1971.

Whitmont, E. C. *Psyche and substance: Essays on homeopathy in the light of Jungian psychology*. Richmond, CA: North Atlantic Books, 1980.

Young-Eisendrath, P. *Hags and heroes: A feminist approach to Jungian psychotherapy with couples.* Toronto: Inner City Books, 1984.

Chapter 17: Dreams

Clift, J. and Clift, W. *Symbols of transformation in dreams.* New York: Crossroad, 1984.

Hall, J. A. *Clinical uses of dreams: Jungian interpretations and enactments.* New York: Grune & Stratton, 1977.

Hall, J. A. *Jungian dream interpretation: A handbook of theory and practice.* Toronto: Inner City Books, 1983.

** Hillman, J. *The dream and the underworld.* New York: Harper & Row, 1979.

Kirsch, J. *The reluctant prophet: An exploration of prophecy and dreams.* Boston: Sigo Press, 1971, 1984.

Layard, J. W. *The lady of the hare, being a study in the healing power of dreams* (reprint of 1944 ed.). New York: AMS Press, nd.

** Mahoney, M. F. *The meaning in dreams and dreaming: The Jungian viewpoint.* New York: Citadel, 1966.

** Mattoon, M. A. *Understanding dreams.* Dallas, TX: Spring Publications, 1984.

Reid, C. H. *Dreams: Discovering your inner teacher.* Washington, DC: Winston Press, 1983.

Roscher, W. H. and Hillman, J. *Pan and the nightmare* (A. V. O'Brien, trans.). Dallas, TX: Spring Publications, 1972.

** Rossi, E. L. *Dreams and the growth of personality.* Elmsford, NY: Pergamon Press, 1972.

** Sanford, J. *Dreams: God's forgotten language.* New York: Crossroad, 1982.

Sanford, J. *Dreams and healing: A succinct and lively interpretation of dreams.* New York: Paulist Press, 1978.

Williams, S. K. *Jungian-Senoi dreamwork manual.* Berkeley, CA: Journey Press, 1980.

Zeller, M. *The dream—the vision of the night.* Boston: Sigo Press, 1975, 1983.

Chapter 18: Social and Political Issues

Baynes, H. G. *Germany possessed.* New York: AMS Press, 1941 (reprinted).

Henderson, J. L. *Cultural attitudes in psychological perspective.* Toronto: Inner City Books, 1984.

** Neumann, E. *Depth psychology and a new ethic* (E. Rolfe, trans.). New

York: Putnam (for the C. G. Jung Foundation for Analytical Psychology), 1969.
** Odajnyk, W. *Jung and politics: The political and social ideas of C. G. Jung.* New York: Harper & Row, 1976.
Progoff, I. *Jung's psychology and its social meaning.* Garden City, NY: Doubleday (Anchor Books), 1973.

Chapter 19: Research

** Cohen, E. D. *C. G. Jung and the scientific attitude.* Totowa, NJ: Littlefield, 1976.
Davis, R. M. (ed.). *Toward a discovery of the person.* Burbank, CA: Society for Personality Assessment, 1974.

Collections of Papers

Adler, G. (ed.). *Current trends in analytical psychology.* (Proceedings of the First International Congress for Analytical Psychology.) London: Tavistock, 1961.
Adler, G., Whitmont, E. C., and Neumann, E. *Dynamics of the psyche: Selections from past Springs.* New York: Analytical Psychology Club of New York, nd.
Beebe, J. (ed.). *Money, food, drink, and fashion and analytic training.* (Proceedings of the Eighth International Congress for Analytical Psychology.) Fellbach, Germany: Verlag Adolf Bonz GmbH, 1983.
** Berry, P. *Echo's subtle body: Contributions to an archetypal psychology.* Dallas, TX: Spring Publications, 1982.
Bertine, E. *Jung's contribution to our time.* New York: Putnam, 1967.
Carson, J. (ed.). *The arms of the windmill.* (A Festschrift for Werner Engel.) Privately printed, 1983.
** Fordham, M., et al. (eds.). *Analytical Psychology: A modern science.* Library of Analytical Psychology, Vol. 1. London: Heinemann, 1973.
Head, R., et al. (eds.). *A well of living waters.* (A Festschrift for Hilde Kirsch.) Los Angeles: C. G. Jung Institute of Los Angeles, 1977.
Hillman, J. *Loose ends: Primary papers in archetypal psychology.* Dallas, TX: Spring Publications, 1975.
Kirsch, H. (ed.). *The well-tended tree: Essays into the spirit of our time.* (A Festschrift for James Kirsch.) New York: Putnam (for the C. G. Jung Foundation for Analytical Psychology), 1971.
** Lockhart, R. A. *Words as eggs.* Dallas, TX: Spring Publications, 1983.
Tuby, M. (ed.). *In the wake of Jung.* London: Coventure, 1983.
Wheelwright, J. B. (ed.). *The reality of the psyche.* (Proceedings of the

Third International Congress for Analytical Psychology.) New York: Putnam (for the C. G. Jung Foundation for Analytical Psychology), 1968.
** Wheelwright, J. B. and Blodgett, A. H. *St. George and the dandelion: 40 years as a Jungian analyst.* San Francisco: C. G. Jung Institute of San Francisco, 1982.

Periodicals

Anima
    1053 Wilson Avenue
    Chambersburg, PA 17201
Chiron: A Review of Jungian Analysis
    400 Linden Avenue
    Wilmette, IL 60091
Guild Lectures
    The Guild of Pastoral Psychology
    9 Phoenix House, 5 Waverley Road
    London N8 9QU, England
Harvest
    60, Stanhope Gardens
    London SW7 5RF, England
Inward Light
    3518 Bradley Lane
    Washington, DC 20015
The Journal of Analytical Psychology
    30 Devonshire Place
    London W. 1, England
Psychological Perspectives
    595 East Colorado Blvd.
    Pasadena, CA 91101
Quadrant
    28 East 39 Street
    New York, NY 10016
The San Francisco Jung Institute Library Journal
    2040 Gough Street
    San Francisco, CA 94109
Spring
    Box 222069
    Dallas, TX 75222

References

Adler, G. Notes regarding the dynamics of the Self. *British Journal of Medical Psychology*, 1951, *24*(2), 97–106.

Adler, G. Methods of treatment in Analytical Psychology. In B. Benjamin (ed.), *Psychoanalytic techniques*. New York: Basic Books, 1967.

Adler, G. Aspects of Jung's personality and work. *Psychological Perspectives*, 1975, *6*(2), 11–21.

Allport, G. W. (ed.). *Letters from Jenny*. New York: Harcourt Brace Jovanovich, 1965.

Anast, P. Similarity between self and fictional character choice. *Psychological Record*, 1966, *16*(4), 535–39.

Arieti, S. *Interpretation of schizophrenia*. New York: Basic Books, 1974.

Aron, A. et al. Relationships with opposite-sexed parents and mate choice. *Human Relations*, 1974, *27*(1), 17–24.

Astrup, C., and Flekköy, K. Association experiments in psychiatric patients and normal controls. *Activitas Nervosa Superior*, 1968, *10*(4), 373–81.

Bachant, J. L. Processes of transformation in the structure of the ego during emotion within the theoretical framework of C. G. Jung

(Doctoral dissertation, New School for Social Research, 1972). *Dissertation Abstracts International, 34*(9–B), 4619 (University Microfilms No. 74–7153).

Bakan, D. *On method.* San Francisco: Jossey-Bass, 1967.

Ball, E. D., A factor analytic investigation of the personality typology of C. G. Jung (Doctoral dissertation, Pennsylvania State University, 1967). *Dissertation Abstracts International, 28*(10–B), 4277–8 (University Microfilms No. 68–3524).

Bash, K. W. Zur experimentellen Grundlegung der Jungschen Traumanalyse. *Schweizerische Zeitschrift für Psychologie und ihre Anwendungen,* 1952, 11(4), 282–95.

Bash, K. W., Mental health problems of aging and the aged from the viewpoint of analytical psychology. *Bulletin World Health Organization,* 1959, *21,* 563–68.

Bash, K. W., The soul image: Anima and animus as projected in the Rorschach Test. *Journal of Personality Assessment,* 1972, *36*(4), 340–48.

Baumann, U., Angst, J., Henne, A., and Muser, F. E. The Gray-Wheelwrights Test. *Diagnostic,* 1975, *21*(2), 66–83.

Beickel, S. L. *A study of relationship between Jung's typology and dreams* (Doctoral dissertation, University of Oregon, 1977). *Dissertation Abstracts International,* 1978, *39,* 352B–353B (University Microfilms No. 78–10, 188).

Bell, A. P., and Hall, C. S. *The personality of a child molester.* Chicago: Aldine-Atherton, 1971.

Bell, J. E. *Projective techniques.* New York: Longmans, Green, 1948.

Bennet, E. A. *C. G. Jung.* New York: E. P. Dutton, 1962.

Bixler, R. H. A comparison of the incidence of complex signs in association of normal subjects to the Jung word list and to self-selected words (Unpublished doctoral dissertation, Ohio State University, 1952).

Bloch, D. L. The developmental properties of Jungian psychological type as measured by the Myers-Briggs Type Indicator (Doctoral dissertation, Mississippi State University, 1978). *Dissertation Abstracts International,* 1429–A (University Microfilms No. 7814858).

Bodin, A. M. and Geer, J. H. Association responses of depressed and non-depressed patients to words of three hostility levels. *Journal of Personality,* 1965, *33*(3), 392–408.

Bolen, J. S. *The Tao of psychology.* San Francisco: Harper & Row, 1979.

Bolgar, H. Consistency of affect and symbolic expression: A comparison between dreams and Rorschach responses. *American Journal of Orthopsychiatry,* 1954, *24,* 538–45.

Box, R. E. Temperament and the interpretation of freedom: A study of some of the psychological determinants of philosophical thought (Doctoral dissertation, School of Theology at Claremont, 1966). *Dissertation Abstracts International*, 29, 362 (University Microfilms No. 68-9423).

Bradway, K. Jung's psychological types. *The Journal of Analytical Psychology*, 1964, 9(2), 129-35.

Bradway, K. Hestia and Athena in the analysis of women. *Inward Light*, 1978, 41(91), 28-42.

Bradway, K., and Detloff, W. Psychological types and their relationship to the practice of Analytical Psychology. *Professional Reports* (annual), C. G. Jung Institute of San Francisco, 1975, 29-53.

Bradway, K. and Detloff, W. Incidence of psychological types among Jungian analysts classified by self and by test. *Journal of Analytical Psychology*, 1976, 21(2), 134-46.

Bradway, K. and Wheelwright, J. B. The psychological type of the analyst and its relation to analytical practice. *Journal of Analytical Psychology*, 1978, 23(3), 211-25.

Brentano, F. *Psychologie vom empirischen Standpunkte.* Leipzig: Duncker & Humblot, 1874.

Brome, V. *Jung: Man and myth.* New York: Atheneum, 1978.

Brookes, C. E. The group as corrective for failure in analysis. In *Success and failure in analysis* (G. Adler, ed.). New York: Putnam (for the C. G. Jung Foundation for Analytical Psychology), 1974, 144-52.

Calvin, A., Hanley, C., Hoffman, F., and Clifford, L. An experimental investigation of the "pull" effect. *Journal of Social Psychology*, 1959, 49, 254-83 (cited in D. S. Holmes, Dimensions of projection, 1968).

Campbell, D., Miller, N., Lubstsky, J., and O'Connel, E. Varieties of projection in trait attribution. *Psychological Monographs*, 1964, 78 (15, Whole No. 529) (cited in D. S. Holmes, Dimensions of projection, 1968).

Campbell, J. (ed.). *The portable Jung* (R. F. C. Hull, trans.). New York: Viking, 1971.

Campbell, J. *Myths to live by.* New York: Viking, 1972.

Cannon, W. B. *The wisdom of the body.* New York: Norton, 1932.

Carlson, R., and Levy, N. Studies of Jungian typology: 1. Memory, social perception and social action. *Journal of Personality*, 1973, 41(4), 559-76.

Carrigan, P. Extraversion-introversion as a dimension of personality: A reappraisal. *Psychological Bulletin*, 1960, 57(5), 329-60.

Cattell, R. B. *Personality and motivation structure and measurement.* Yonkers, NY: World Book, 1957.

Cattell, R. B. and Warburton, F. W. A cross-cultural comparison of patterns of extraversion and anxiety. *British Journal of Psychology,* 1961, *52,* 3–15.

Center for Applications of Psychological Type. *Introduction to Type.* Gainesville, FL: Author, 1976.

Center for Applications of Psychological Type, *Preliminary Guidelines for MBTI Workshops.* Gainesville, FL: Author, 1979.

Cermák, M., and Dornic, S. An experimental research of emotional reactions of TB patients, *Studia Psychologica, Bratislava,* 1961, *3,* 195–210 (*Psychological Abstracts,* 1963, *37,* 7095).

Chassan, J. B. Statistical inference and the single case in clinical design. In P. O. Davidson and C. G. Costello (eds.), *N=1: Experimental studies of single cases.* New York: Van Nostrand Reinhold, 1969.

Child, C. M. *Physiological foundations of behavior.* New York: Henry Holt, 1924.

Chomsky, N. *Language and mind.* New York: Harcourt Brace Jovanovich, 1968.

Cook, D. A. Is Jung's typology true? A theoretical and experimental study of some assumptions implicit in a theory of personality types (Doctoral dissertation, Duke University, 1970). *Dissertation Abstracts International,* 1971, *31,* 2979B–2980B (University Microfilms No. 70–21,987).

Dallett, J. The effect of sensory and social variables on the recalled dream: Complementarity, continuity, and compensation (Doctoral dissertation, University of California, Los Angeles, 1973). *Dissertation Abstracts International, 34,* 5705–5706 (University Microfilms No. 74–11514).

Davidson, P. O. and Costello, C. G. *N=1: Experimental studies of single cases.* New York: Van Nostrand Reinhold, 1969.

Davis, M. *An investigation of the reliability and validity of the Gray-Wheelwrights Jungian Type Survey.* An unpublished M.A. paper presented to the faculty of the graduate school, University of Minnesota, October, 1978 (copies not available).

De Becker, R. *The understanding of dreams.* New York: Hawthorn, 1968.

de Laszlo, V. S. (ed.). *Psyche and symbol: A selection from the writings of C. G. Jung.* Garden City, NY: Doubleday (Anchor Books), 1958.

de Laszlo, V. S. (ed.). *The basic writings of C. G. Jung.* New York: Modern Library, 1959.

Detloff, W. K. Psychological type research. *Professional Reports* (annual), C. G. Jung Institute of San Francisco, 1966, 25–29.

Dicks-Mireaux, M. J. Extraversion-introversion in experimental psychology: Examples of experimental evidence and theoretical implications. *Journal of Analytical Psychology*, 1964, 9(2), 117–28.

Domino, G. Compensatory aspects of dreams: An empirical test of Jung's theory. *Journal of Personality and Social Psychology*, 1976, 34(4), 658–62.

Douglas, W. A wise man and a young science. *Contemporary Psychology*, May 1959, 4, 72–75.

Dry, A. M. *The psychology of Jung: A critical interpretation.* London: Methuen, 1961 (New York: Wiley, 1962).

Dunne, J. W. *An experiment with time* (3rd ed.). London: Faber & Faber, 1958.

Edinger, E. Symbols: The meaning of life. *Spring* (annual), 1962, 45–66.

Edinger, E. An outline of Analytical Psychology. *Quadrant*, Spring 1968, No. 1.

Edinger, E. Psychotherapy and alchemy. I. Introduction, II. Calcinatio. *Quadrant*, Summer 1978 (a), 11(1), 5–37.

Edinger, E. Psychotherapy and alchemy. III. Solutio. *Quadrant*, Winter 1978 (b), 11(2), 63–85.

Edinger, E. Psychotherapy and alchemy. IV. Coagulatio. *Quadrant*, Summer 1979, 12(1), 25–46.

Elkind, D. Freud, Jung and the collective unconscious. *The New York Times Magazine*, Oct. 4, 1970, pp. 23 et seq.

Ellenberger, H. F. *The discovery of the unconscious.* New York: Basic Books, 1970.

Ellis, A. *A guide to rational living.* Hollywood: Wilshire Books, 1974 (cited in J. S. Witzig, Jung's typology and the classification of the psychotherapies, 1978).

Engen, T., Levy, N., and Schlosberg, H. A new series of facial expressions. *The American Psychologist*, 1957, 12, 264–66.

Erikson, E. H. *Childhood and society* (2nd ed.). New York: Norton, 1963.

Eysenck, H. J. *Dimensions of personality.* London: Kegan Paul, Trench, Trubner, 1947.

Eysenck, H. J. *The scientific study of personality.* London: Routledge & Kegan Paul, 1952.

Eysenck, H. J. *Uses and abuses of psychology.* New York: Penguin, 1953.

Eysenck, H. J. The inheritance of extraversion-introversion. *Acta Psy-*

chologica, 1956, *12,* 95–110 (Reprinted in H. J. Eysenck, *On Extraversion,* 49–65).

Eysenck, H. J. *The structure of human personality.* London: Methuen, 1960.

Eysenck, H. J. and Eysenck, S. B. *Personality structure and measurement.* San Diego: Knapp, 1969.

Eysenck, H. J. Introverts, extraverts and sex. *Psychology Today,* 1971, 4(8), 48–51, 82.

Fehrenbach, P. Personality as a factor in reported post-retirement anxiety among professionals (Doctoral dissertation, Duke University, 1972). *Dissertation Abstracts International,* 34, 873B (University Microfilms No. 73–19,478).

Fehrenbach, P. Personal communication, July 1980.

Fischer, R. Cartography of inner space. In A. K. Siegel and L. J. West (eds.), *Hallucinations, behaviors, experience, and theory.* New York: Wiley, 1975.

Fodor, J. A., Garrett, F., and Brill, S. L. Pi ca pu: The perception of speech sounds by prelinguistic infants. *Perception and Psychophysics,* 1975, 18(2), 74–78.

Fordham, F. *An introduction to Jung's psychology* (3rd rev. ed.). New York: Penguin, 1966.

Fordham, M. *New developments in analytical psychology.* London: Routledge & Kegan Paul, 1957.

Fordham, M. An interpretation of Jung's thesis about synchronicity. *British Journal of Medical Psychology,* 1962, 35(2), 205–210.

Fordham, M. The theory of archetypes as applied to child development with particular reference to the Self. In A. Guggenbühl-Craig (ed.), *The Archetype.* Basel: S. Karger, 1964.

Fordham, M. Individuation in childhood. In J. B. Wheelwright (ed.), *Reality of the Psyche.* Putnam (for the C. G. Jung Foundation for Analytical Psychology), 1968.

Fordham, M. *Children as individuals.* New York: Putnam (for the C. G. Jung Foundation for Analytical Psychology), 1970 (originally published, 1944).

Frankl, V. E. *Man's search for meaning.* New York: Washington Square Press, 1963 (originally published, 1959).

Freeman, G. L. *The energetics of human behavior.* Ithaca, NY: Cornell University Press, 1948.

Freud, S. (standard edition). *The complete psychological works of Sigmund Freud* (J. Strachey, trans.). London: Hogarth Press, various dates.

Frey-Rohn, L. *From Freud to Jung* (Engreen, F. E. and Engreen, E. K., trans.). New York: Putnam (for the C. G. Jung Foundation for Analytical Psychology), 1974.

Frey-Wehrlin, C. T. Reflections on C. G. Jung's concept of synchronicity. *Journal of Analytical Psychology*, 1976, *21*(1), 37–49.

Friedan, B. *The feminine mystique*. New York: Dell, 1963.

Gale, A., Coles, M., and Blaydon, J. Extraversion-introversion and the EEG. *British Journal of Psychology*, 1969, *60*(2), 209–23.

Gardner, H. *The quest for mind: Piaget, Lévi-Strauss, and the structuralist movement*. New York: Random (Vintage Books), 1974.

Gardner, H. The lives of Alexander Luria. *Psychology Today*, June 1980, 84–96.

Goldbrunner, J. *Individuation*. Notre Dame, IN: University of Notre Dame Press, 1964.

Goldings, H. J. On the avowal and projection of happiness. *Journal of Personality*, 1954, *23*, 30–47 (cited in D. S. Holmes, Dimensions of projection, 1968).

Goldstein, K. *The organism: A holistic approach to biology derived from pathological data in man*. Boston: Beacon, 1963 (originally published in English, 1939).

Goleman, D. Split-brain psychology: Fad of the year. *Psychology Today*, 1977, *11*(5), 89–151.

Goodman, D. Learning from lobotomy. *Human Behavior*, Jan., 1978, 44.

Gorlow, L., Simonson, N. R., and Krauss, H. An empirical investigation of the Jungian typology. *British Journal of Social and Clinical Psychology*, 1966, *5*(2), 108–17.

Gottesman, I. Heritability of personality: A demonstration. *Psychological Monographs, General and Applied*, 1963, *77*(9), (whole).

Gray, H. Jung's psychological types in relation to occupation, race, body-build. *Stanford Medical Bulletin*, 1946, *4*(3–4), 100–103.

Gray, H. Psychological types and changes with age. *Journal of Clinical Psychology*, 1947, *3*(3), 273–77.

Gray, H. Jung's psychological types in men and women. *Stanford Medical Bulletin*, 1948, *6*(1), 29–36.

Gray, H. Psychological types in married people. *Journal of Social Psychology*, 1949, *29*, 189–200.

Gray, H. and Wheelwright, J. B. Jung's psychological types including the four functions. *Journal of General Psychology*, 1945, *33*, 265–84.

Gray, H. and Wheelwright, J. B. Jung's psychological types, their frequency of occurrence. *Journal of General Psychology*, 1946, *34*, 3–17.

Greene, T. A. *Modern man in search of manhood.* New York: Association Press, 1967.

Greenfield, M. Typologies of persisting and non-persisting Jewish clergymen. *Journal of Counseling Psychology,* 1969, 16(4), 368–72.

Guggenbühl-Craig, A. Psychopathology of sexual deviance. Lecture, C. G. Jung Institute, Zurich, Winter 1960 (MAM notes).

Guggenbühl-Craig, A. On hysteria. Lecture, C. G. Jung Institute, Zurich, Summer 1963 (MAM notes).

Guggenbühl-Craig, A. *Marriage: Dead or alive,* Dallas, TX: Spring Publications, 1977.

Hall, C. S. and Domhoff, B. The dreams of Freud and Jung. *Psychology Today,* 1968, 2(1), 42–45, 64–65.

Hall, C. S. and Lind, R. E. *Dreams, life, and literature: A study of Franz Kafka.* Chapel Hill, NC: University of North Carolina Press, 1970.

Hall, C. S. and Lindzey, G. *Theories of personality* (2nd ed.). New York: Wiley, 1970.

Hall, C. S. and Nordby, V. J. *The individual and his dreams.* New York: Signet, 1972.

Hall, C. S. and Nordby, V. J. *A primer of Jungian psychology.* New York: New American Library (A Mentor Book), 1973.

Hall, C. S. and van de Castle, R. L. *The content analysis of dreams.* New York: Appleton-Century Crofts, 1966.

Hannah, B. *Striving towards wholeness.* New York: Putnam (for the C. G. Jung Foundation for Analytical Psychology), 1971.

Hannah, B. Some glimpses of the individuation process in Jung himself. *Spring* (annual), 1974, 26–33.

Harding, M. E. *Journey into Self.* New York: Longman, 1956.

Harding, M. E. *The way of all women.* New York: Putnam (for the C. G. Jung Foundation for Analytical Psychology), 1970.

Harms, E. Carl Gustav Jung. *American Journal of Psychiatry,* Feb. 1962, 728–32.

Harrison, N. W. Validation of Jung's typological framework (Doctoral dissertation, University of Mississippi, 1976). *Dissertation Abstracts International,* 37(3-A) 1467 (University Microfilms No. 76–20, 525).

Hawkes, J. *History of mankind: Cultural and scientific development,* Vol. 1, Part 1: Prehistory. New York: New American Library (A Mentor Book), 1963.

Hayes, S. P., Jr. The predictive ability of voters. *Journal of Social Psychology,* 1936, 7, 183–91 (cited in D. S. Holmes, Dimensions of projection, 1968).

Henderson, J. L. The inferior function. In J. Aylward et al. (eds.), *Studien zur analytischen psychologie C. G. Jungs*, Vol. 1. Zurich: Rascher, 1955.

Hess, E. Imprinting in animals. *Scientific American*, March 1958.

Hill, D. O. Extraversion-introversion: An investigation of typological theory (Doctoral dissertation, Texas Tech University, 1970). *Dissertation Abstracts International*, 1970, *31*, 6257B (University Microfilms No. 71–9641).

Hillman, J. *Suicide and the soul*. New York: Harper & Row, 1964.

Hillman, J. Why "archetypal" psychology? *Spring* (annual), 1970, 212–18.

Hogle, G. H. Family therapy: When analysis fails. In G. Adler (ed.), *Success and failure in analysis*. New York: Putnam (for the C. G. Jung Foundation for Analytical Psychology), 1974.

Holmes, D. S. Dimensions of projection. *Psychological Bulletin*, 1968, 69(4), 248–68.

Homans, P. *Jung in context: Modernity and the making of a psychology*. Chicago: University of Chicago Press, 1979.

Honegger, B. *Spontaneous waking-state psi as inter-hemispheric verbal communication: Is there another system?* San Francisco: Washington Research Center, 1979.

Hornberger, R. The projective effects of fear and sexual arousal on the ratings of pictures. *Journal of Clinical Psychology*, 1960, *16*, 328–31 (cited in D. S. Holmes, Dimensions of projection, 1968).

Hough, G. Poetry and the anima. *Spring* (annual), 1973, 85–96.

Illing, H. A. Jung's theory of the group as a tool in therapy. *International Journal of Group Psycho-Therapy*, 1957, *7*, 392–97.

Jacobi, J. *Complex/archetype/symbol* (R. Mannheim, trans.). Princeton: Princeton University Press, 1959. Bollingen Series 57.

Jacobi, J. *The psychology of C. G. Jung* (6th rev. ed.; R. Mannheim, trans.). New Haven: Yale University Press, 1962.

Jacobi, J. *Masks of the soul* (Ean Begg, trans.). Grand Rapids, MI: Eerdmans Publishing, 1976.

Jacobi, J. and Hull, R. F. C. (eds.). *C. G. Jung: Psychological reflections*. Princeton: Princeton University Press, 1953, 1970. Bollingen Series 31.

Jaffé, A. *From the life and work of C. G. Jung*. New York: Harper & Row, 1971.

Jahoda, G. Jung's meaningful coincidences. *Philosophical Journal*, 1967, 4(1), 35–42.

Jarrett, J. L. Introversion, extraversion and ethical theory. *Psychological Perspectives*, 1979, *10*(1), 53–57.

Jones, E. The life and work of Sigmund Freud. Vol. 1, 1856–1900: The formative years and the great discoveries. New York: Basic Books, 1953.

Jones, J. Jungian psychology in anthropological perspective. Lectures, University of Minnesota, Winter 1979 (MAM notes).

Jung, E. Animus and anima. Dallas, TX: Spring Publications, 1957, 1969.

Kalff, D. M. Sandplay: Mirror of a child's psyche. San Francisco: Browser Press, 1971.

Kant, O. Dreams of schizophrenic patients. Journal of Nervous and Mental Disease, 1942, 95, 335–47.

Katz, D. and Allport, F. Students' attitudes. Syracuse: Craftsman Press, 1931 (cited in D. S. Holmes, Dimensions of projection, 1968).

Keen, S. and Harris, T. G. Jung passes the electric Kool-Aid acid test. Psychology Today, 1972, 6(7), 64.

Kettner, M. G. Some archetypal themes in homosexuality. Professional Reports, C. G. Jung Institute of San Francisco (annual), 1967, 33–58.

Kettner, M. G. Patterns of masculine identity. In J. B. Wheelwright (ed.), The reality of the psyche. New York: Putnam (for the C. G. Jung Foundation for Analytical Psychology), 1968.

Kilmann, R. H. and Taylor, V. Contingency approach to laboratory learning: Psychological types vs. experiential norms. Human Relations, 1974, 27(9), 819–909.

Kilmann, R. H. and Thomas, K. W. Interpersonal conflict-handling behavior as reflections of Jungian personality dimensions. Psychological Reports, 1975, 37(3, Pt. 1), 971–80.

Klopfer, B. and Spiegelman, J. Some dimensions of psychotherapy. In C. T. Frey-Wehrlin (ed.), Spectrum psychologiae: Eine Freundesgabe. Zurich: Rascher, 1965.

Kluger, H. Archetypal dreams and everyday dreams: A statistical investigation into Jung's theory of the collective unconscious. Israel Annals of Psychiatry and Related Disciplines, 1975, 13(1), 6–47.

Knapp, R. Relationship of a measure of self-actualization to neuroticism and extraversion. Journal of Consulting Psychology, 1965, 29(2), 168–72.

Kotschnig, E. P. Womanhood in myth and in life. Inward Light, 31, Fall-Winter 1968–69, 16–30; 32, Spring 1969, 5–23. Reprinted as pamphlet, 1976 and 1978.

Krimsky, M. L. The rebirth fantasy in catatonic schizophrenia and its implications (Doctoral dissertation, University of Oklahoma,

1960). *Dissertation Abstracts International, 21,* 367 (University Microfilms No. 60–2635).

Levinson, D. J. *The seasons of a man's life.* New York: Knopf, 1978.

Lévi-Strauss, C. *The scope of anthropology* (S. O. Paul and R. A. Paul, trans.). London: Cape, 1967 (cited in H. Gardner, *The quest for mind*).

Lewis, D. C. Jungian theory and marital attraction (Doctoral dissertation, University of Notre Dame, 1976). *Dissertation Abstracts International, 36*(4), 4165 (University Microfilms No. 76–2332).

Liberson, W. T. Relationships between EEG abnormality and the word association test after prefrontal lobotomy. *Electroencephalogram and Clinical Neurophysiology,* 1949, 1, 378.

Lips, H. M. and Colwill, N. L. *The psychology of sex differences.* Englewood Cliffs, NJ: Prentice-Hall, 1978.

Loevinger, J. and Wessler, R. Measuring ego development (Vol. 1). San Francisco: Jossey-Bass, 1970.

Loomis, M. and Singer, June. Testing the bipolar assumption in Jung's typology. *Journal of Analytical Psychology,* 1980, 25(4), 351–56.

Lovell, C. A study of the factor structure of thirteen personality variables. *Educational Psycho-Measurement,* 1945, 5, 335–50.

Lowenfeld, M. *Play in childhood.* New York: Wiley, 1967. (Previously published in London, 1935).

MacKinnon, D. W. Creativity and transliminal experience. *Journal of Creative Behavior,* 1971, 5(4), 227–41.

Maduro, R. J. and Wheelwright, J. B. Analytical psychology. In J. Corsini (ed.), *Current personality theories.* Itasca, IL: Peacock, 1977, 84–125.

Mahdi, L. *Contemporary aspects of the North-American Indian vision-quest.* Unpublished diploma thesis, C. G. Jung Institute, Zurich, 1976.

Maslow, A. H. *Motivation and personality.* New York: Harper, 1954.

Maslow, A. H. *Toward a psychology of being.* Princeton: Van Nostrand, 1962.

Masserman, J. H. *Principles of dynamic psychiatry.* Philadelphia: Saunders, 1946.

Mattoon, M. A. *The Christian concept of sin as an approach to the shadow.* Unpublished diploma thesis, C. G. Jung Institute, Zurich, 1965.

Mattoon, M. A. *Applied dream analysis: A Jungian approach.* Washington, DC: V. H. Winston, 1978. (a)

Mattoon, M. A. Politics and individuation. *Spring* (annual), 1978, 77–87. (b)

McCully, R. S. *Rorschach theory and symbolism.* Baltimore, MD: Williams & Wilkins, 1971.

McGuire, W. and Hull, R. F. C. C. G. *Jung speaking.* Princeton: Princeton University Press, 1977. Bollingen Series 97.

Meehl, P. Clinical psychology. Lectures, University of Minnesota, 1966 (MAM notes).

Meier, C. A. Psychosomatic medicine from the Jungian point of view. *Journal of Analytical Psychology,* 1963, 8(2), 103–121.

Meier, C. A. Psychological types and individuation: A plea for a more scientific approach in Jungian psychology. In J. B. Wheelwright (ed.), *The analytic process.* New York: Putnam (for the C. G. Jung Foundation for Analytical Psychology), 1971.

Meier, C. A. and Wozny, M. A. An empirical study of Jungian typology. *Journal of Analytical Psychology,* 1978, 23(3), 226–47.

Mendelsohn, G. A. The Myers-Briggs Type Indicator. In Buros, O.K., *Personality tests and reviews,* 1970, 1126–31.

Munroe, R. L. *Schools of psychoanalytic thought.* London: Hutchinson Medical Publications, 1957.

Murray, H. A. The effect of fear upon estimates of the maliciousness of other personalities. *Journal of Social Psychology,* 1933, 4, 310–39 (cited in D. S. Holmes, Dimensions of projection, 1968).

Murray, H. A. *Explorations in personality.* New York: Oxford University Press, 1938.

Murstein, B. I. Studies in projection: A critique. *Journal of Projective Techniques,* 1957, 21, 129–36 (cited in D. S. Holmes, Dimensions of projection, 1968).

Myers, I. B. *Manual: The Myers-Briggs Type Indicator.* Princeton: Educational Testing Service, 1962.

Myers, I. B. Introduction to type (2nd ed.). Gainesville, FL: Center for Applications of Psychological Type, 1976.

Neumann, E. *The origins and history of consciousness* (rev. ed.; R. F. C. Hull, trans.). New York: Pantheon, 1964. Bollingen Series 42.

Neumann, E. *The child.* New York: Putnam (for the C. G. Jung Foundation for Analytical Psychology), 1973.

Nightingale, J. A. The relationship of Jungian type to death concern and time perspective (Doctoral dissertation, University of South Carolina, 1973). *Dissertation Abstracts International,* 33, 3956B (University Microfilms No. 73–3600).

North, R. D., Jr. An analysis of the personality dimensions of introversion-extroversion. *Journal of Personality,* 1948, 17, 352–67.

Ogilvie, B. C. The sweet psychic jolt of danger. *Psychology Today,* 8(5), 94.

Osgood, J. A. The relations between friendship and bonds and Jung's psychological types (Doctoral dissertation, Arizona State University, 1972). *Dissertation Abstracts International,* 1972, *32,* 6625B–6626B (University Microfilms No. 72-16,284).

Palmiere, L. Intro-extra-version as an organizing principle in fantasy production. *Journal of Analytical Psychology,* 1972, *17*(2), 116-31.

Pardes, M. Eysenck's introversion-extraversion, boredom, and time estimation (Doctoral dissertation, Columbia University, 1965). *Dissertation Abstracts International,* 26, 3489 (University Microfilms No. 65-9170).

Paulsen, L. Transference and projection. *Journal of Analytical Psychology,* 1956, *1*(2), 203-16.

Peavy, R. V. A study of C. G. Jung's concept of intuitive perception and the intuitive type (Doctoral dissertation, University of Oregon, 1963). *Dissertation Abstracts International,* 24, 4551-2 (University Microfilms No. 64-4414).

Penfield, W. Memory mechanisms. *Archives of Neurology and Psychiatry,* 1952, *67,* 178-98.

Perls, F. *Ego, hunger, and aggression.* London: George Allen & Unwin, 1947.

Perls, F., Hefferline, R., and Goodman, P. *Gestalt therapy.* New York: Julian, 1951.

Perry, J. W. Emotions and object relations. In J. B. Wheelwright (ed.), *The analytic process: Aims, analysis, training.* New York: Putnam (for the C. G. Jung Foundation for Analytical Psychology), 1971.

Perry, J. W. *The far side of madness.* Englewood Cliffs, NJ: Prentice-Hall, 1974.

Perry, J. W. *Roots of renewal in myth and madness.* San Francisco: Jossey-Bass, 1976.

Piaget, J. *Structuralism.* New York: Basic Books, 1970.

Pines, M. Invisible playmates. *Psychology Today,* 1978, *12*(5), 38, 106.

Plaut, A. On some relations between psychotherapy and analysis. In A. Guggenbühl-Craig (ed.), *The archetype.* Basel: S. Karger, 1964.

Plaut, A. Analytical psychologists and psychological types: Comment on replies to a survey. *Journal of Analytical Psychology,* 1972, *17*(2), 137-51.

Priestley, J. B. Books in general. *The New Statesman and Nation,* Oct. 30, 1954, 541-42.

Progoff, I. *Jung's psychology and its social meaning.* Garden City, NY: Doubleday (Anchor Books), 1973.

Quenk, A. T. Psychological types: The auxiliary function and the analytic process. Unpublished diploma thesis, Inter-Regional Society of Jungian Analysts, 1978.

Reyburn, H. A. and Raath, M. J. Primary factors of personality. British Journal of Statistical Psychology, 1950, 3, 150–58.

Richek, H. G. Jung's typology and psychological adjustment in prospective teachers: A preliminary investigation. Alberta Journal of Educational Research, 1969, 15(4), 235–43.

Riklin, F. The crisis of middle life. Spring (annual), 1970, 6–14.

Rogers, C. R. A theory of therapy, personality, and interpersonal relationships, as developed in the client-centered framework. In S. Koch (ed.), Psychology: A study of a science (Vol. 3). New York: McGraw-Hill, 1959.

Rogers, C. On becoming a person: A therapist's view of psychotherapy. Boston: Houghton Mifflin, 1961 (cited in Klopfer & Spiegelman, Some dimensions of psychotherapy, 1965).

Rokeach, M. Studies in beauty: II. Some determiners of the perception of beauty in women. Journal of Social Psychology, 1945, 22, 155–69.

Rosenthal, R. Experimenter effects in behavioral science. New York: Irvington, 1976.

Rosenthal, R. and Fode, K. L. The effect of experimenter bias on the performance of the albino rat. Behavioral Science, 1963, 8(3), 183–89.

Ross, J. The relationship between a Jungian personality inventory and tests, ability, personality and interest. Australian Journal of Psychology, 1966, 18(1), 1–17.

Ross, J. The resources of binocular perception. Scientific American, March 1976, 234, 80–86.

Rossi, A. M. and Solomon, P. Notes on reactions of extroverts and introverts to sensory deprivation. Perceptual and Motor Skills, 1964, 20, 1183–84.

Rossi, E. Thinking and intuition as opposites. Journal of Analytical Psychology, 1977, 22(1), 32–58.

Rothenberg, A. Creative contradictions. Psychology Today, June 1979, 55–62.

Russell, P. The brain book. New York: Hawthorn, 1979.

Sandner, D. F. Transformation in relationships. Inward Light, 1979, 42(93), 16–21.

Savage, R. D. Electro-cerebral activity, extraversion and neuroticism. British Journal of Psychiatry, 1964, 110, 98–100.

Schaefer, S. A study of sex and age differentials in typologies as derived from the test scores of 200 adults on the Jungian type survey and the Myers-Briggs Type Indicator. An unpublished paper, University of Minnesota, 1974 (copies not available).

Schlenker, B. R. and Miller, R. S. Egocentrism in groups: Self-serving biases or logical information processing? *Journal of Personality and Social Psychology*, 1977, *35*, 755–64.

Sears, R. Experimental studies of projection: I. Attribution of traits. *Journal of Social Psychology*, 1936, *7*, 151–63 (cited in D. S. Holmes, Dimensions of projection, 1968).

Shapiro, M. B. Experimental method in the psychological description of the individual psychiatric patient. In P. O. Davidson and C. G. Costello (eds.), *N = 1: Experimental studies of single cases.* New York: Van Nostrand Reinhold, 1969.

Shelburne, W. Synchronicity: A rational principle of explanation. *Anima: An Experiential Journal*, 1976, *3*(1), 58–66.

Sheppard, E. Systemic dream studies: Clinical judgment and objective measurements of ego strength. *Comprehensive Psychiatry*, 1963, *14*(4), 263–70.

Sheppard, E. and Saul, L. J. An approach to a systemic study of ego function. *Psychoanalytic Quarterly*, 1958, *27*, 237–45.

Shevrin, H. and Dickman, S. The psychological unconscious: A necessary assumption for all psychological theory? *American Psychologist*, May 1980, 421–33.

Shevrin, H. and Fritzler, D. Visual evoked response correlates of unconscious mental processes. *Science*, July 19, 1968, 295–98.

Shostrom, E. L. An inventory for the measurement of self-actualization. *Educational and Psychological Measurement*, 1964, *24*(2), 207–18.

Siegelman, M. College student personality correlates of early parent-child relationship. *Journal of Consulting Psychology*, 1965, *29*(6), 558–64.

Skinner, B. F. Behaviorism at fifty. In T. W. Wann (ed.), *Behaviorism and phenomenology.* Chicago: University of Chicago Press (Phoenix Books), 1964.

Spare, G. H. A study of the law of enantiadromia, as it relates to the attitudes of introversion-extraversion (Doctoral dissertation, Washington State University, 1968). *Dissertation Abstracts International*, *29*, 1850 (University Microfilms No. 68–15,799).

Spiegelman, M. Jungian theory and the analysis of thematic tests. *Journal of Projective Techniques*, 1955, *19*, 253–63.

Steele, R. S. and Kelly, T. J. Eysenck personality questionnaire and Jungian Myers-Briggs Type Indicator correlation of extraversion-introversion. *Journal of Consulting and Clinical Psychology*, 176, *44*(4), 690–91.

Stevens, H. A. and Reitz, W. E. An experimental investigation of projection as a defense mechanism. *Journal of Clinical Psychology,* 1970, *26*(2), 152–54.

Stevens, P. S. *Patterns in nature.* Boston: Little, Brown, 1974.

Stricker, J. L. and Ross, J. Some correlates of a Jungian personality inventory. *Psychological Reports,* 1964, *14*(2), 623–43.

Taylor, R. E. An investigation of the relationship between psychological types in the college classroom and the student perception of the teacher and preferred teaching practices (Doctoral dissertation, University of Maryland, 1968). *Dissertation Abstracts International, 29,* 2575A (University Microfilms No. 69–2235).

Thass-Thienemann, T. *The interpretation of language* (Vol. 1). New York: Jason Aronson, 1968.

Thigpen, A. and Cleckley, H. M. *Three Faces of Eve.* New York: McGraw-Hill, 1937.

Thomsen, A. Psychological projection and the election: A simple class experiment. *Journal of Psychology,* 1941, *11,* 115–17 (cited in D. S. Holmes, Dimensions of projection, 1968).

Thorne, F. C. Towards more realistic expectations of psychotherapists. *Journal of Clinical Psychology,* 1961, *17*(1), 101–102.

Tinbergen, N. On aims and methods of ethology. *Zeitschrift für Tierpsychologie,* 1963, *20*(4), 410–33.

Tranel, N. Effects of perceptual isolation on introverts and extroverts. *Psychiatric Research,* 1962, *1,* 185–92 (cited in Rossi and Solomon, Notes on reactions of extroverts and introverts to sensory deprivation, 1965).

Travers, R. M. W. A study in judging the opinions of groups. *Archives of Psychology,* 1941, No. 266 (cited in D. S. Holmes, Dimensions of projection, 1968).

Tuttle, M. C. An exploration of C. G. Jung's psychological types as predictors of creativity and self-actualization (Unpublished doctoral dissertation, University of California, Berkeley, 1973). *Dissertation Abstracts International, 35,* 4154B–4155B (University Microfilms No. 75–2212).

Tyler, L. *The psychology of human differences* (3rd ed.). New York: Appleton-Century-Crofts, 1965.

Ulanov, A. G. *The feminine in Jungian psychology and in Christian theology.* Evanston, IL: Northwestern University Press, 1971.

van der Post, L. *Jung and the story of our time.* New York: Pantheon, 1975.

Vincie, J. F. and Rathbauer-Vincie, M. *C. G. Jung and analytical psy-*

chology: A comprehensive bibliography. .New York: Garland, 1977.

von Franz, M.-L. The process of individuation. In C. G. Jung and M.-L. von Franz (eds.), Man and his symbols. Garden City, NY: Doubleday, 1964.

von Franz, M.-L. The problem of the puer aeternus. Santa Monica, CA: Sigo Press, 1980 (originally published, 1970).

von Franz, M.-L. Patterns of creativity mirrored in creation myths. Dallas, TX: Spring Publications, 1972. (a)

von Franz, M.-L. Problems of the feminine in fairy tales. Dallas, TX: Spring Publications, 1972. (b)

von Franz, M.-L. C. G. Jung: His myth in our time. New York: Putnam (for the C. G. Jung Foundation for Analytical Psychology), 1975.

von Franz, M.-L. and Hillman, J. Lectures on Jung's typology. Dallas, TX: Spring Publications, 1971.

Wallen, R. Individual estimates of group attitudes. Psychological Bulletin, 1941, 38, 539–40.

Wallen, R. Individuals' estimates of group opinion. Journal of Social Psychology, 1943, 17, 269–74.

Watson, J. D. The double helix. New York: Atheneum, 1968.

Wells, W. and Goldstein, R. Sears' study of projection: Replications and critique. Journal of Social Psychology, 1964, 64, 169–79 (cited in D. S. Holmes, Dimensions of projection, 1968).

Wheelwright, J. B. Reflections on marriage in the second half of life. Quadrant, 1970–71, (8 & 9), 26–31.

Wheelwright, J. B. Psychological types. San Francisco: C. G. Jung Institute of San Francisco, 1973.

Wheelwright, J. B. Personal communication, July 1980.

Whitmont, E. C. Analysis in a group setting. Quadrant, 1974, 16, 5–25.

Whyte, L. L. The unconscious before Freud. New York: Basic Books, 1960.

Wickes, F. The inner world of man. New York: Frederick Ungar, 1948.

Wickes, F. The inner world of childhood (rev. ed.). New York: Appleton-Century, 1966.

Williams, A. M. Personality typology as a factor in mate selection and marital adjustment (Unpublished master's thesis, University of Florida, 1971). Bulletin of Research in Psychological Type, 1977, 1(1), 47–48 (Abstract).

Winnicott, D. W. Review of "Memories, dreams and reflections" (by

C. G. Jung). *International Journal of Psychoanalysis*, 1964, 45, 450–55.

Witzig, J. S. Jung's typology and the classification of the psychotherapies. *Journal of Analytical Psychology*, 1978, 23(4), 315–31.

Wolff, T. *Structural forms of the feminine psyche* (P. Watzliwik, trans.). Zurich: Students' Association of the C. G. Jung Institute, 1956.

Wright, B. Altruism in children and the perceived conduct of others. *Journal of Abnormal and Social Psychology*, 1942, 37, 218–33 (cited in D. S. Holmes, Dimensions of projection, 1968).

Wylie, R. *The self concept: A critical survey of pertinent research literature.* Lincoln: University of Nebraska Press, 1961 (cited in D. S. Holmes, Dimensions of projection, 1968).

Zaidel, E. In *Brain/Mind Bulletin*, June 5, 1978, p. 1.

Index